green earth guide

traveling naturally in

SPAIN

green earth guide

traveling naturally in

SPAIN

Dorian Yates

North Atlantic Books
Berkeley, California

Published by
North Atlantic Books
P.O. Box 12327
Berkeley, California 94712

Cover photos of Antoni Gaudí works by Eduardo Leite/iStock
Cover photo of bougainvilla by Daniel Omar Cifani Conforti/iStock
Cover photo of olives by Diane Lundin/iStock
Interior photos by Dorian Yates
Cover and book design by Claudia Smelser

Printed in the United States of America

In keeping with the green approach to traveling naturally, this book was printed with soy inks and on recycled paper.

Green Earth Guide: Traveling Naturally in Spain is sponsored by the Society for the Study of Native Arts and Sciences, a nonprofit educational corporation whose goals are to develop an educational and cross-cultural perspective linking various scientific, social, and artistic fields; to nurture a holistic view of arts, sciences, humanities, and healing; and to publish and distribute literature on the relationship of mind, body, and nature.

North Atlantic Books' publications are available through most bookstores. For further information, visit our Web site at www.northatlanticbooks.com or call 800-733-3000.

LIBRARY OF CONGRESS CATALOGING-IN-PUBLICATION DATA

Yates, Dorian.
  Green Earth guide : traveling naturally in Spain / Dorian Yates. —1st ed.
    p. cm.
  978-1-55643-841-6
1. Spain—Guidebooks. 2. Environmental responsibility—Spain.
3. Green movement—Spain. 4. Sustainable living—Spain.
5. Ecotourism—Spain. I. Title.
  GE199.S7Y38 2010

  914.604'83—dc22   2009026137

1 2 3 4 5 6 7 8 9 United 14 13 12 11 10

To Kinder and Kerry and all that you inspire
To Margaret, Ariel incarnate
And to Auntie Pat, with love

Praise for *Green Earth Guide: Traveling Naturally in France*

"*Green Earth Guide* is the travel resource for all of us concerned about global warming and reducing our carbon footprints. It is an essential companion for every traveler wanting to make environmental choices on the road."

—ROBERT F. KENNEDY, JR, environmental lawyer and activist

"Filled with great information about where to find natural, organic foods and wines throughout France, *Green Earth Guide* is a must-have for food lovers and supporters of organic agriculture."

—NELL NEWMAN, President, Newman's Own Organics

"The first travel guidebook supporting a range of green economies from renewable energy and sustainable agriculture to natural health and public transportation, *Green Earth Guide* is full of invaluable resources about how to travel on any budget with an eco-conscience. Now you can make your individual journey a part of the Earth's journey toward healing."

—VAN JONES, author of *The Green Collar Economy*

"For those of you planning a trip to France, we highly recommend that book from Dorian Yates; much more than a travel book, the guide includes listings of health food stores and farmers' markets, public transit information, alternative health care facilities, green businesses, and yoga and spiritual centers."

—GREENTY, Green Travel Search Engine

"If you have an appetite for travel, a modest budget, and a carbon-conscious heart, look no further. *Green Earth Guide: Traveling Naturally in France* is your perfect travel companion."

—THE CARBON FUND

acknowledgments

The Green Earth Guides would not be what they are without the superb work of my editor, Elizabeth Kennedy, book designer Claudia Smelser, and all the wonderful folks at North Atlantic Books. As always, thanks to my beloved children and husband, who put up with endless detours to organic farms and health food stores. My deep appreciation and love go to my dear friends Carlta and Luis, Doina and Bill, who helped me in more ways than I could list, not the least of which were providing essential wifi and shelter in Madrid and Barcelona, offering moral support, and making me feel at home in Spain. Thanks to Jenny Ogston for being a delightful person and excellent Nerja guide, and to my whole Pueblo Inglés family for just being there. Thanks to Claudia Giménez Miralles for being so kind and welcoming in Valencia, and to Camilla Sharp for map support. Thanks would not be complete without mention of my core support: Leigh, Lis, Weezy, Gillis, Wende, and Mary. Thanks to Cliff and Collen for being so awesome. My back and hips thank Simon at Osprey Packs for making my traveling much more comfortable. My eternal gratitude to Olivier and Karin Raab for their beautiful *casa,* which made it possible for me to live with my family in a glorious Spanish setting. Much appreciation for my exceptional Spanish teachers *señoras* Grace Flemister and Emilia Bruce. And deep thanks to Jim Plummer and Jeb Buchwald, who by example taught me at a young age to think out of the box and live by the word.

contents

How to Use This Book   xiii

Traveling Naturally Whys and Wherefores   xvii

1 whole view   1

The Environmental Footprint of Our Lives   1

Carbon-Offset Programs   3

Global Warming and the Environment:
Information and Resources   4

2 go lightly

The Essence of Traveling Lightly   7

The Mind-Set of Traveling Naturally and Lightly   7

Before You Go   7
  Health   8
  Money   9
  Ecotravel Preparation   9
  Dry-Cleaning and Laundry   11

Europe-Wide Information and Resources   11
  Transportation   11
  Communication and Phone Calls   13
  Accommodations   14
  Eating   17
  Shopping   17
  Volunteer Tourism   18

United Nations World Heritage Sites   20
Sacred Sites   20

3 traveling naturally in Spain   21

Orientation, Arrival, and Getting Around   22
   Generally Green   23
   Communication   27
   Transportation   28

Accommodations   37
   Hostels   37
   Camping   38
   Guesthouses and Bed-and-Breakfasts
   Including Historical Inns and Rural Tourism   38
   Home Exchange and House-Sitting   42
   Eco-Accommodations   42

Eating and Food   48
   Vegetarian, Organic, and Gluten-Free Choices   48
   Health Food Stores   63
   Farm Stands, Markets, and Local Products   63
   Restaurants   74
   Special Diets   86

Recreation   89
   Hiking   89
   Biking   91
   Yoga   95
   Meditation   98
   Thermal Baths   99

Health   106
   Anthroposophical Medicine   107
   Massage   109
   Chiropractic   112
   Alexander Technique   112
   Naturopathy   113
   Homeopathy   114
   Ayurvedic Medicine   115
   Acupuncture and Traditional Chinese Medicine (TCM)   117
   Colon Hydrotherapy   120
   Biological Dentistry   120

    Herbs and Remedies   122
    Clinics and Spas   123

Shopping   126
    Natural, Untreated, and Organic Items   126
    Local Products   128
    Personal Care and Natural Cosmetics   130
    Fair Trade   131
    Thrift and Secondhand Stores   133
    Markets   133
    Bookstores   135

Ecobusinesses, Ecodestinations, and Places of Interest   138
    Organic Farms   138
    Organic Vineyards and Wines   140
    Biodynamic Wines   142
    Specialty Liquor   143
    Beer and Breweries   143
    Mineral Springs   145
    Wind and Sun Energy   145

UNESCO World Heritage Sites   147

Historical Sites and Other Sites of Interest   150

City and Regional Highlights   151
    Catalunya   152
    Barcelona-Specific   153
    Girona-Specific and the Costa Brava   156
    Valencia-Specific   159
    Madrid-Specific   162
    Bilbao and the Basque Region   163
    Navarra   170
    "The Green Coast": Cantabria and Asturias   171
    Salamanca Region   175
    Galicia   176
    Andalucía   178
    Jaén Province   186

Sacred Sites   186
    Black Madonnas   192

Color and Art   193

Wild and Natural Resources   194

Volunteer Tourism   200

4 resources   201

Language Resources   201

More Information about Traveling Naturally   202

Index   203

About the Author   211

how to use this book

The Green Earth Guides are designed to help travelers find ethical and green options easily. The goal is to make your traveling experience greener for you and the environment. This Green Earth Guide is divided into four chapters. The first is a general overview of why it is important to consider the environment in your consumer and travel choices. The second is about ecotravel in particular and covers Europe-wide green travel information. The third is the heart of the book and provides country-specific information, including listings of most things green and alternative in Spain. The final chapter is short, offering foreign words to help you travel naturally, as well as where to find updates and additional information about the Green Earth Guides and traveling naturally.

To get you in the groove of traveling naturally in Spain I have chosen to include Spanish terms in a number of the sections. This is what you will see when you are in Spain, so you can become familiar with the terms while you peruse this book. The Spanish word for organic is *biológico(a)* or *ecológico(a),* or *bio* and *eco* for short, so I have used *bio* (pronounced BEE-o) in many places throughout the book. *Bio* or *eco* combined with any word means it is organic, so *bio vino* is organic wine, *ecotienda* means organic store. The word *orgánica* usually refers to compost and you will find this on brown recycling bins in cities and villages.

Web sites are included so that you can have access to the maximum amount of information available. A number of the Web sites I have listed are for the respective tourist office. This is because the places either do not have Web sites of their own or do not have English versions. Some of the Web sites listed are only in Spanish. Where this is the case, I have tried to describe the easiest way to reach the pertinent information. Some Web sites are available in both Spanish and English. In these cases, often the English version is available by finding and clicking on a small British flag, usually in the upper right or upper left of the Web page (although it can be at the bottom as well), or by clicking on a scroll-down menu for "*idioma.*" See "Web Site Navigation Tips" for useful Spanish words.

Web Site Navigation Tips

Some helpful words to know while on a Spanish-only Web site:

Mercat or *Mercado* = market

Tienda = store

Ecotienda or *supermercado ecológico* = organic store

Encontrar nuestras tiendas = find our stores

Puntos de venta = points of sale, or retail outlets

Enlaces = links

Descubrir = discover

Espacio, acomodación = accommodation

Habitación = room (*individual* = single; *doble* = double)

Descargar = download

Página principal = home page

Alimentación = food

Alimentación ecológica = organic food

Productos = products

TIP Spanish Pronunciation Tips

V pronounced B	Y and I pronounced like hard E
C and Z pronounced TH	J pronounced H
LL pronounced YA	H is silent
Ñ pronounced ENYA	

The Fine Print

Great care and attention has gone into the preparation of this guidebook, but prices change, businesses move or close, schedules get revised. Please understand that these alterations are beyond our control, and that neither the author nor North Atlantic Books is liable for any loss, inconvenience, or injury. All health information and resources listed in the *Green Earth Guide* are for educational purposes only. Please use the information responsibly.

traveling naturally whys and wherefores

I believe my soft spot for Spain began when I was a mere eight years old and saw a summer-stock performance of *Man of La Mancha*. I was completely drawn in by Don Quixote and his compelling quest to fight unbeatable odds for what he believed to be right. That philosophy has guided me in much of my life and has informed my work and lifestyle choices. Although the environmental or green movement has sometimes been criticized as quixotic, in my view it is just that quixotism that makes things happen and moves us toward a more sustainable way of living. It seems most appropriate to offer a book about traveling with an environmental conscience through Spain.

The following explains the whys and wherefores of my choices for inclusion in the *Green Earth Guide: Traveling Naturally in Spain*. All the sites and businesses are listed at my discretion, based on my experience of more than thirty years working on environmental issues and with eco-conscious businesses, coupled with my personal passion for all things natural. In order to keep the *Green Earth Guide* light and small enough for handy traveling, I have chosen to concentrate on certain regions with details and provide Web-based search options for others to maximize the accessibility of useful information. Whatever your interests I hope the *Green Earth Guide* makes your travels healthier and greener.

Accommodation choices in the Green Earth Guides include hostels, guesthouses, home exchanges, and camping. These tend to be low-impact, small-scale, local enterprises with concern for the environment. Recycling systems are usually available, bedding is not changed every day, and small plastic bottles of synthetically perfumed toiletries are not available for you to use, take home, or throw away. These accommodation choices usually offer greater cultural experiences and are cozier and more interesting than chain hotels. Some of the supergreen eco-accommodations use solar or wind power and serve organic food (see "Green Earth Accommodations").

Food choices include large and small health food stores, organic and fair-trade labels, gluten-free brands, and local farm stands. By choosing organic and local foods you support a cleaner, more just, and sustainable environment. Organic food has been found to have higher nutrients than conventionally grown food, which means you will be taking better care of yourself, too.

Recreation information focuses on outdoor activities, especially hiking and biking, that have no or low environmental impact. Meditation and yoga facilities are included, as well as locations of hot mineral baths.

Due to their much smaller environmental footprint, complementary and alternative medicine choices are considered green options. Natural, plant-based remedies have been used for millennia without the environmental degradation being observed with pharmaceutical drugs. Researchers in Germany, Switzerland, Italy, Canada, the United States, and other countries have found dozens of drugs in our water and soil. Water contaminants include acetaminophen, caffeine, antiepileptics, antibiotics, antidepressants, beta-blockers and lipid regulators, chemotherapy drugs, and antimicrobials. The antidepressant Prozac has even been discovered in earthworms. Research results suggest that mixtures of drugs can affect human health at a cellular level and potentially affect the health of aquatic life. The global environmental consequences may include bacterial resistance to medications; endocrine (hormone) disruption in fish, humans, and other animals; and generally lower immune resistance and response in humans.

Alternative health care has a long history in Europe and is not considered "alternative" in many countries. Europe is replete with health practitioners, including massage therapists, natural doctors, and traditional Chinese medical doctors. Spas and clinics are plentiful, and natural remedies are often sold alongside pharmaceutical medicines in drugstores. There are many brands of high-quality personal care

The degree to which ecological principles are incorporated varies greatly among accommodations. Some will cover many or all of the criteria listed below; others will integrate only one or some of them.

- Serve organic and local food
- Situated on land managed by organic methods
- Employ renewable energy for electricity and/or heating
- Employ water and energy conservation methods and energy-efficient systems
- Use natural-fiber bedding and linens
- Use natural and renewable building materials in construction and furnishing
- Renovated an old building (as a form of recycling)
- Use environmentally friendly cleaning products
- Accessed by public transportation and/or near or on biking/hiking routes
- Use recycled products such as toilet paper
- Practice a towel and sheet laundry-reduction program
- Provide on-site recycling
- Maintain a no-smoking facility
- Low-impact—making use of an existing facility, such as a home or farm, as a bed-and-breakfast; and efficiently using space, such as multi-bed rooms in hostels

products such as shampoos, soaps, and cosmetics made with natural and organic ingredients.

Shopping information focuses on where to purchase natural, untreated, organic items, and includes secondhand stores, fair-trade products, and local specialties. Thrift or secondhand stores are wonderful places to shop. Full of clothes, books, art, furniture, kitchen gadgets, and more, they are a treasure trove for travelers interested in recycling and reusing items. These shopping choices are respectful of the environment, the artisans, the local economy, and in the case of secondhand goods, help to reduce the global load of consumer products.

Ecobusinesses and other places of interest are chosen based on their intrinsically natural and ecological characteristics, as well as their historical significance and natural beauty. Listings include organic farms and vineyards, wind farms, World Heritage environmental areas, bird and wildflower information, sacred and mystical sites, and ecotourism highlights.

I have included a small section on volunteer tourism because working with people in a foreign country toward a common goal is rewarding and greatly deepens your bond with the locale and its people.

one whole view

The *Green Earth Guide: Traveling Naturally in Spain* is designed for any and all travelers inclined to make green choices. It is not about choosing the most enticing ecotour. It is about extending your lifestyle choices and intentions to your world of travel. By choosing green options, you help support local economies, local ecology, and the greater environment, treading a little more lightly on the earth.

The Environmental Footprint of Our Lives

Whether we like it or not, we all add to the ever-increasing environmental degradation that plagues our planet. The choices and decisions we make, from crackers to car purchases, impact the degree of our contribution—the veritable size of our personal environmental footprint.

Global warming, caused by various chemical and environmental interactions that heat the atmosphere, is largely due to carbon dioxide emissions. For millennia, naturally occurring carbon has played a role in keeping the earth appropriately insulated from frigid outer space. In the last 150 years, humans have been releasing growing volumes of carbon into the atmosphere from coal, oil, and other sources, which disrupts the carbon balance, allowing the earth's atmosphere to become increasingly warmer.

Americans currently leave the largest environmental footprint, with average annual carbon dioxide emissions up to sixty thousand pounds per person. Europeans emit about half that amount per person, and the Japanese emit less than half—they are acknowledged as the most energy-efficient of all developed countries. By contrast, the annual carbon emissions of the average Bangladeshi are less than one percent (less than six hundred pounds) of the carbon emissions of the average American.

If you travel by air, you can quickly add to your carbon footprint. One round-trip flight between the United States and Europe can add between two and four tons of carbon emissions. Calculations depend on exact flight distance and class of travel. Economy seats, while uncomfortable, are calculated at a lower per-person emission—a small consolation for no leg room. One transatlantic flight generates more carbon than twenty Bangladeshi people will emit in a year.*

Everything we do, every choice we make has political and far-reaching effects whether we realize it or not. Many people understand this. That is why the green movement has been driven by consumer demand, not by corporate business interests. People want to do the right thing for themselves and the world. The more conscious and intentional we can be about how we live our lives, the greater the effect on the whole, and the smaller the footprint we leave.

Small footprints come in many sizes. We can make choices and decisions about little things and big things; we can follow one eco-option, or many. The more we do, the more we contribute to the ripple effect. As the ripple becomes a wave—a wave of increasingly environmentally sound ways to live and be on Earth—the smaller our footprints become.

As consumers, individual and collective purchasing power is enormous. Our footprints become smaller by supporting and frequenting businesses involved with organic and whole foods, efficient and renewable energy, recycling, natural and untreated products, natural health care, and local enterprises. This breeds diversity, healthy land, water, and air, and vital local economies—all healthier for you and the world.

While many of us may already make environmental consumer choices at home, it can be challenging when on the road, especially in places

*Flying Green: How to Protect the Climate and Travel Responsibly, Tufts Climate Initiative and Stockholm Environment Institute; www.tufts.edu/tie/carbonoffsets/TCI-offset-handout.htm.

where you do not speak the language well or at all. Your footprints can be small wherever you go, and traveling naturally helps you tread lightly by offering country-specific green information and resources.

It is critically important to offset the carbon footprints from air travel. The concept behind carbon-offset programs is to make reparations for emissions that we generate daily, as well as occasionally, like air travel. This usually involves paying for offsets, in the form of a donation or purchase, through various organizations.

Recently there has been an explosion of organizations and businesses that offer programs to offset carbon emissions. Some of these organizations invest in renewable energy and energy efficiency programs, some in reforestation initiatives. Whether or not you contribute to these efforts while at home, it can be beneficial to do so when you are traveling by plane since calculations show that one transatlantic round-trip flight generates at least one to four tons of carbon dioxide per person. You can donate to any of the organizations listed below or contribute to one of your favorite environmental groups.

Carbon-Offset Programs

Carbonfund.org puts donations toward efficiency and renewable energy, as well as reforestation programs. Carbonfund.org estimates that an individual generates about twenty-three tons of carbon per year, which they calculate as an annual donation for their offset programs of $99 for an individual or $326 for a family. The Carbonfund.org Web site offers details about offset programs, climate change, and more. For more information go to www.Carbonfund.org.

C~N~Do Scotland works with The National Trust for Scotland to offset carbon emissions by focusing on native peat restoration projects to conserve, restore, and expand peat moorlands, a primary "sink" for carbon. For more information go to www.cndoscotland.com/carbon-conservation.

Sustainable Travel International offers information for travelers about ecotravel tours and their carbon-offset program, which promotes renewable and energy-efficient technologies in developing countries. They calculate one round-trip flight from Boston to Zurich at 2.28 tons of carbon generated per person with an offset donation cost of

$34.77. For more information go to www.sustainabletravelinternational.org.

Conservation International works around the world conserving biodiversity through rainforest preservation, conservation, and reforestation programs. Their carbon calculator finds that an average individual generates twenty-four tons of carbon a year, and their annual donation suggestion to offset that quantity is $240. For an average American driver they suggest $50 annually to offset the emission effects. For more information go to www.conservation.org.

*Native*Energy is focused on developing and supporting renewable energy projects particularly on Native American land, which includes the first large-scale wind farm in South Dakota owned and operated by Native Americans, as well as three wind projects in Alaskan native villages where *Native*Energy is working to decrease the reliance on diesel-powered electricity. For more information go to www.nativeenergy.com.

Global Warming and the Environment: Information and Resources

In addition to carbon-offset programs, there are numerous organizations working on global warming and other environmental issues. The following groups offer educational and action resources.

The Natural Resources Defense Council (NRDC) works on a wide range of environmental issues from air and water quality, to wildlife protection, sustainable energy, and waste management. They are known for their staff of excellent consumer advocates and legal experts. NRDC's Global Warming information page can be found at www.nrdc.org/globalWarming/.

The Stop Global Warming Virtual March provides information about the dangers of global warming and tools to help you reduce your personal carbon emissions. Their Virtual March to stop global warming can be accessed at www.stopglobalwarming.org.

Personal carbon calculators can be found at EarthFuture, which offers a list of organizations and Web sites from around the world that provide calculation services. For more information go to www.earthfuture.com/climateenergy/calculators.asp.

Ben & Jerry's Ice Cream, the Dave Matthews Band, and SaveOur-Environment.org have joined forces for the Lick Global Warming campaign, which can be accessed by anyone but is geared toward children. Young and old can visit the site at www.lickglobalwarming.org/learn.cfm.

Background information on the movie *An Inconvenient Truth* is available at www.climatecrisis.net/thescience.

Climate Counts, a campaign organized by Stonyfield Farm, is focused on consumer and corporate responsibility. The site offers company scorecards so you can view what actions businesses are taking to reduce their environmental footprint, and a downloadable pocket shopping guide to help you make the best eco-choices. Visit Climate Counts at www.climatecounts.org.

The Intergovernmental Panel on Climate Change, established by the United Nations Environmental Programme and the World Meteorological Organization, can be found at www.ipcc.ch.

two go lightly

The Essence of Traveling Naturally

1. Be Where You Are: Stay connected to the local environment by taking the time to see, feel, and appreciate where you are.
2. Tread Lightly: Ecofriendly, low-impact choices are good for nature, good for you, good for the environment, and good for the world.

The Mind-Set of Traveling Naturally and Lightly

There is a state of mind that seeks out the other side of life—the vast network and virtual underground of organic and fresh foods, natural fibers, natural colors and scents, local farms and working land. This mind-set sees the beauty of humans working with the earth and with technologies that harness the bounty of the natural world, not trying to conquer, overpower, and destroy it. This mind-set notices gardens tucked into the crevices of life, between rail tracks and otherwise underutilized plots of land. This mind-set marvels at the beauty of a window box full of flowers, the colors of the buildings, the history and continuity of cultures. This mind-set honors our human differences and similarities.

Keep this viewpoint in mind as you make use of the information and resources included in this book, and as you make your own discoveries. Remember that cultural history often informs daily habits.

Most European countries, dealing with a lack of space and a history of war, have daily routines that many Americans consider trends or movements. For instance, a small country like Switzerland (twice the size of Massachusetts) has had no choice but to work with what they have, minimizing pollution and waste and maximizing beauty and cleanliness. For example, purchases like laundry detergent, rubbing alcohol, and hydrogen peroxide often come in refillable containers that you can replenish at the local drugstore or grocery store.

So, get into the groove! Bring your bags or baskets to the markets. Be ready to refill bottles, and to recycle when you can't refill. And get ready to enjoy the more inherently green infrastructure of many European destinations.

Before You Go
HEALTH

Travelers to Europe have many alternative remedies and treatments readily available. Some very helpful tips for general travel, and extensive homeopathic information for traveling where serious illness is more endemic, can be found in *The World Travellers' Manual of Homeopathy* by Dr. Colin B. Lessell.

For the traveler inclined to alternative and natural health care, it is a good idea to prepare your own travel health care kit. Essentials include lavender essential oil (for relaxation, to conceal bad smells, and as a mild antiseptic); Emergen-C vitamin C individual packets (for sickness prevention and for rehydration and energy during air travel); *Andrographis paniculata* tablets (for sickness prevention and shortening sickness duration); magnesium (for muscle cramps and to prevent traveler constipation); and arnica gel (for sore muscles—try *Traumeel,* made by the Heel company in Germany and sold worldwide).

Make sure any liquids and gels come in small container sizes (three ounces or less) if you are carrying them on the airplane.

If you are planning a trip involving spa or clinic reservations, make sure to schedule ahead, as many appointments are booked out for three months or longer.

If you are gluten sensitive or allergic, but do not have celiac disease, you may want to add Glutenzyme capsules to your natural health care travel kit. The enzymes can be helpful when traveling, especially when you find yourself surrounded by the plentiful wheat products often served as part of your inclusive accommodation breakfast and at numerous local bakeries. Pharmax makes a similar product for people who are lactose intolerant called Dairy-Ease. For more information go to Pharmax Nutriceutical and Biophysical Systems at www.pharmaxllc.com.

MONEY

Planning ahead can save you money when you travel. Check with your existing bank to see if the debit/credit card on your account charges foreign transaction fees (most do). If it does not, you are in luck! Use that card for all or most of your overseas expenses—both ATM withdrawals and credit transactions. You will save significant money this way. There are usually separate daily security limits for cash withdrawals and credit transactions. If your current card does charge a fee for each foreign transaction, shop around and see if any other local banks offer a card without those charges. Most major credit card companies do charge between one and nine percent on each transaction, and most banks charge between one and three percent on debit cards. You can find helpful card fee comparison charts using the "Resources" link at the Travel Finances Web site. For more information go to www.travelfinances.com.

ECOTRAVEL PREPARATION

Be prepared for your Green Earth travel. Pack a few lightweight but sturdy reusable shopping bags, as you will need these for shopping of any kind. You may want to practice the language of your destination. The BBC Languages Web site offers free courses in Spanish, French, Italian, German, and other languages. For more information go to www.bbc.co.uk/languages.

The Essentials List for the Green Earth Traveler

1. Medium-size, lightweight daypack

2. 2–4 canvas or other reusable shopping-size bags, not too heavy, with good handles

3. Extremely comfortable long-distance walking shoes and Smart-Wool™ socks

4. Natural health care kit (page 8 in the "Health" section)

5. Natural hand sanitizers with essential oils, like tea tree oil and lavender, rather than antibacterial chemicals. These come available as wipes in individual foil packs (Desert Essence brand), or in small bottles (EO Organic Lavender Hand Sanitizer). The wipes are great to carry on the airplane, as they meet the criteria for allowable items. You can pack the bottle in your checked luggage.

6. Reusable water bottle

7. A small language guide or dictionary

8. Appropriate electrical adapters

9. Mini reading light or flashlight

10. Hostel member card (if you are planning to stay at hostels)

For the ultimate green traveler, you can buy a backpack with solar panels that recharge your cell phone and digital audio player. Voltaic Systems solar bags come in five different sizes and four colors and are made from recycled soda bottles. Prices range from $199 to $249. The most expensive option is the Voltaic Generator at $499, and it produces enough power to charge a laptop. You can purchase the bags online or at one of their many stores around the world. For more information go to www.voltaicsystems.com.

At Earthtech Products you can find many solar bag choices, including Voltaic. Earthtech offers a solar camera bag, a solar bicycle trunk bag, and a solar tackle bag. Prices range from $113 to $249. For more information go to www.earthtechproducts.com/solar-back-packs.html.

Juice Bags, a solar bag from Reware, comes in several convenient, hip styles. PowerPockets, also available from Reware, are solar panel strips that can be used to charge your electronics. They fold up and are easy to carry in a bag or a large pocket. Prices range from $150 to $275 for the PowerPockets and from $200 to $350 for the Juice Bags. For more information go to www.rewarestore.com.

DRY-CLEANING AND LAUNDRY

Dry-cleaning involves a chemical called perchloroethylene, referred to as "perc," that has been found to adversely affect the nervous system, liver, and kidneys. It is considered a possible carcinogen. Perchloroethylene poses risks not only to human and animal health, but also to air and water quality. In 2007 California passed a law to phase out all perc-based dry-cleaning systems by 2023.

While there are some alternatives to traditional dry-cleaning that are being touted as green—wet-cleaning, and systems using silicone or carbon dioxide based solvents—all have questionable aspects to their processing. The ecotraveler is best advised to not pack dry-clean-only garments since ecological dry-cleaning options are not yet readily available.

Europe-Wide Information and Resources
TRANSPORTATION

Europe uses kilometers, not miles, to measure distance. One kilometer equals 0.62 mile. A few quick references are: 5 km = 3.11 miles; 7.5 km = 4.66 miles; 10 km = 6.21 miles; 50 km = 31.06 miles; 100 km = 62.14 miles.

Car Rentals
For environmental reasons this book is focused on public transportation, as well as travel by foot and by bicycle. For destinations or

schedules that require a car, take heart. Although currently there are no ecocar rentals in Europe, most cars are ecofriendly by default. In Europe, economy and standard class cars usually get 30 to 50 miles (48 to 80 km) to the gallon, often using no-fume diesel fuel and efficient engines. This is due not only to the long-standing higher fuel prices in Europe, but also to the fact that older, smaller roads, built long before cars were invented, require smaller cars. These efficient cars are available at global car rental companies, such as Avis, Hertz, and others, not just local companies.

Walking

The Web site Walk On Web—in English, Spanish, French, German, and Dutch—has digital sources of various hiking and walking routes through many European countries and includes a free walk planner. You can choose the length of walk, its intensity, its proximity to public transportation, and more. The site is still under development, so not all regions are represented, but it is very helpful for those that are. For more information go to www.walkonweb.org.

The European Ramblers' Association has a terrific Web site—in English, French, and German—and includes illustrations of the eleven long-distance walking paths that cross Europe. For more information, go to www.era-ewv-ferp.org/index.php?page_id=29.

At the *National Geographic* Web site go to the Places of a Lifetime section, click on any of the cities listed, and under "Multimedia" click on "Walking Tours" for maps and detailed descriptions of walking routes throughout each city; Web site: http://travel.nationalgeographic.com/places/places-of-a-lifetime.html. You can find podcast versions—National Geographic *Traveler* Magazine's 50 Walks of a Lifetime podcasts—at www.learnoutloud.com/Podcast-Directory/Travel/-/50-Walks-of-a-Lifetime-Podcast/19412.

Rail Travel

A word to the eco-wise: Traveling by train or bus generates three to seven times *fewer* emissions than plane travel.

See the Spanish rail services' Web sites listed in the "Public Transportation" section in Chapter Three for schedules, prices, itinerary planning, and in-country rail passes.

For multi-country rail passes it is best to comparison shop online at several European rail pass sites, although many of them really are selling the same passes at similar prices. For instance, the Eurail Global Pass is available only in first class, no matter which site you peruse, and the cost remains pretty consistent for a one-month pass: www.railpass.com ($1,200), www.raileurope.com ($1,194), www. eurail.com ($1,199). The Eurail site offers a special pass for travelers twenty-five years of age or younger. This is a second-class pass and costs $779. (Prices are accurate at the time of writing. Please check the Web sites for current pricing.)

Before you buy a rail pass, check out the differences between a rail pass and point-to-point fares at www.ricksteves.com/rail/comparetickets. htm. Rick Steves' site has lots of helpful information and reminds travelers that a rail pass is not always the most affordable solution for your travel plans. The site also offers a handy, printable worksheet to organize your travel plans and chart the best deals. It also includes a map with approximate fares between European cities.

Rick Steves' Guide to Eurail Passes, a PDF guide downloadable from www.ricksteves.com/rail/pdfs/09_RailGuide.pdf, is full of useful information to help you sort through the fine print. If you are purchasing a rail pass you should know that the Eurostar train between London and the continent does not honor the pass. However, if you book in advance there are sometimes a limited number of special reduced-fare seats for rail pass holders. For more information about Eurostar options, go to www.eurostar.com or www.raileurope.com.

For destinations not accessible by train, the Web site The Bus Station has links to bus Web sites all over the world and is searchable by continent and country. For more information go to www.busstation.net.

COMMUNICATION AND PHONE CALLS

In the burgeoning world of the Internet, printed phone books have become increasingly hard to find. If you need to look up a phone number of a business or friend you can try this link for a list of European countries and their respective yellow pages: www.superpages. com/global/europe.html.

Inexpensive calling cards usually can be purchased in most countries and are recommended. If you wish to purchase in advance, cards are available online. With any calling card, check not only the per-minute rate, but also look for the connection fee (does the card have a flat rate charge for connecting the call?), the billing increment (for example, are calls charged per minute, or per three minutes?), and if there is a pay phone surcharge fee. Knowing all the card fees will help you avoid any surprise charges. Also, find out if the card is "rechargeable" or if you need to purchase a new one each time you run out of minutes. For more information, go to www.callingcards.com.

Hostelling International (see contact information in the next section, "Accommodations") offers international calling cards as part of their membership benefits. Remember to compare all calling card fees and rates.

Voice over Internet Protocol (VoIP) programs are worth considering. Skype is a free download system that allows you to talk computer to computer. As with many cell phone plans, these calls are free if made from one Skype user to another Skype user. If you are calling a non-Skype user, however, there are charges. For Skype calls to work, your computer will need a microphone, speakers, and some sort of high-speed Internet access. If your computer has a camera, you can also enjoy video phone calls. This is a great option while traveling: You can see friends and family at home, and they get a chance to see you. For more information go to www.skype.com.

To locate wifi spots go to www.wifinder.com and search by country.

ACCOMMODATIONS

For hostel information, Hostelling International (HI) runs the most comprehensive Web site at www.hihostels.com. From there you can access worldwide hostel information. To become a member, visit the U.S. site, www.hiusa.org. You will need a membership to stay at many of the hostels. Annual membership is $28 and children under eighteen are free.

A good source for non-HI hostels and budget hotels can be found at www.hostelscentral.com and www.hostelworld.com. Look here for options in locations where Hostelling International does not have hostels.

When the weather is amenable, camping is an inexpensive and environmentally friendly option, but make sure you pitch your tent at a designated campground. Camping in unofficial campsites is prohibited in most European countries. See the country-specific information for campground listings.

Green Travel: The World's Best Eco-Lodges and Earth Friendly Hotels, a Fodor's travel guide, offers information on one hundred eco-accommodations around the world. *Green Places to Stay,* by Richard Hammond, part of the *Special Places to Stay* series, also lists eco-accommodations around the world. The eco-accommodations listed in these books tend to be high-end and spectacular.

Home Exchange

If you have a pleasant home in a desirable location you may consider a home exchange program. During a home exchange, you trade homes with someone—they stay in yours, you stay in theirs. The use of cars, bikes, and appliances can be included as part of the exchange, as well as cleaning responsibilities. Special preferences, like nonsmoking or pet-free homes, are usually part of the listing information.

As home exchange programs have grown, the exchange options have increased. In some instances, you no longer need to exchange homes at the same time. There are listings for second homes, and travel times are flexible. Some programs also offer rentals and house-sitting options. Some home exchange programs have a general focus, but others are limited to certain groups. For instance, there is a home exchange program for families whose children go to Waldorf schools, and there is another program for seniors.

Home exchanges: www.homeexchange.com ($99.95 annual listing and use fee), www.thevacationexchange.com (first year free; subsequent years $39.95 annual fee), Global Home Exchange: www.4homex.com ($39 annually).

Specialty exchanges: www.seniorshomeexchange.com (for seniors; $79 fee for three years or $100 lifetime fee); www.wheponline.com (Waldorf school affiliation; fee is $50 for one year). For home exchanges, house-sitting, and rentals, go to www.sabbaticalhomes.com (free to view; $55 to post a listing).

House-sitting is another accommodation option when traveling; however, it does usually require animal care—including cats, dogs, or farm animals—and/or plant care. This is a great, low-cost option if you like animals and want to be in one place for your stay. It is not the right choice if you plan to travel around. The Mind My House Web site offers an international search for house-sitters. For more information go to www.mindmyhouse.com. At Worldwide Housesitting, an Australian-based organization, homeowners list for free, and house-sitters sign up for $40/year. For more information go to www. housesitworld.com. At www.housecarers.com, another Australian-based organization, homeowners also list for free and house-sitters pay a $45/year membership. The Caretaker Gazette, at www.caretaker.org, is another resource for potential house-sitters.

For the adventurous and tight-budgeted, there is a fairly new non-profit organization called CouchSurfing. It includes a network of travelers and hosts, and you can bunk on a host's couch (or spare bed) for free. Go to www.couchsurfing.org for more information about safety issues and membership.

The main page at Craigslist provides links to just about any country or major city. Check the housing lists for great short- and long-term rentals or sublet options. For more information go to www.craigslist. org. Usually updated daily or weekly, Sublet.com also offers short-term housing options all over Europe. For more information go to www.sublet.com.

The European Centre for Ecological and Agricultural Tourism (ECEAT) focuses on farm stays and accommodations that are committed to the conservation of the environment, biodiversity, and supporting local and organic foods. ECEAT offers information on more than 1,300 small organic farms throughout Europe, which provide tenting or farmhouse rooms, plus hundreds of environmentally friendly bed-and-breakfasts, apartments, and guesthouses. Secretariat ECEAT - International, Radnicni 14, 16601 Tisnov, Czech Republic; Tel: +420 549 439 837; Fax: +420 541 235 080; e-mail: secretariat@eceat.org; Web site: www.eceat.org. You can search for listings online at www.eceat.travel.

EU Eco-label certifies some accommodations and campsites. For more information go to www.ecolabel-tourism.eu and www.eco-camping.net.

Green Earth Travel is a travel agency catering to vegetarians. They help with cruises, hotels, and tours geared toward vegetarians. For more information go to www.vegtravel.com.

For homestays, a grown-up version of the student exchange program, you can explore U.S. Servas. Servas started in 1948 as a worldwide cooperative exchange network of hosts and travelers working to foster peace and cultural understanding. There is domestic membership for a $50 annual fee, with an additional $15 fee for up to five "host lists" of potential hosts in different countries. International travel membership is $85 per year, with host lists available for an additional $25 fee. Stays are for three days and two nights unless the host invites you to stay longer. U.S. Servas, 1125 16th Street, Suite 201, Arcata, CA 95521-5585; Tel: 707-825-1714; Fax: 707-825-1762; e-mail: info@usservas.org; Web site: www.usservas.org.

Federation EIL, the worldwide network of the Experiment in International Living, runs a few different programs, including their Independent Homestay Program. Stays last from one to four weeks. Fees for a one-week stay are between $200 and $500. Federation EIL, 70 Landmark Hill, Suite 204, Brattleboro, VT 05301; Tel: 802-246-1154; e-mail: federation@experiment.org; Web site: www.experiment.org.

EATING

Slow Food International is a nonprofit organization promoting what they term "good, clean and fair" food. The Slow Food movement embraces healthy and local food, prepared with attention and consideration. The movement is growing worldwide, and many countries have their own Slow Food networks with Web sites. The international site can be found at www.slowfood.com.

The International Vegetarian Union (IVU) has a Web site with helpful but limited information about vegetarian restaurants and hotels in Europe. More information can be found at www.ivu.org. Happy-Cow also maintains an international database of vegetarian restaurants around the world. For more information go to www.happycow.net.

SHOPPING

Except in large cities (but sometimes there, too) stores generally close between noon and 2:00 p.m. The actual times vary per town and country. This is when the shopkeepers, and you, need a break. Get into the swing of it! It is refreshing and delightful to know that everyone has closed up shop and is relaxing and eating, walking, or playing.

Don't forget to bring your own bags. Many stores either do not have bags or charge for them, and often they are flimsy. Keep a stash of canvas or reusable bags rolled up in your daypack.

For recycled goods, you can try joining the local FreeCycle group. FreeCycle is an Internet bulletin board exchange where people offer things they no longer need or want. No money changes hands. At the Web site, you can access almost every state and many countries, including Spain and France. Joining the group makes sense only if you are going to be in one area for a decent length of time. More information can be found at www.freecycle.org.

VOLUNTEER TOURISM

Volunteers for Peace (VFP), founded in 1982, is a nonprofit organization specializing in short-term (two to three weeks) volunteer opportunities around the world for all ages. They have projects in more than one hundred countries. Basic registration is $300 per project, and there is a $30 annual membership fee. Other expenses include airfare to your destination and sometimes an additional fee for the project (depending on your destination). The types of projects vary, and there are options for all skill levels and interests. A full project directory and helpful travel links can be found at the VFP Web site. Volunteers for Peace, 1034 Tiffany Road, Belmont, VT 05730; Tel: 802-259-2759; e-mail: vfp@vfp.org; Web site: www.vfp.org.

Peaceful World Travel is a network of people and places all over the world that welcomes travelers and neighbors to participate in peace-building activities and to engage in conversations on matters of local and global peacemaking. Peaceful World Travel is working to create a global network of alternative travel resources, accessible to local and international travelers and hosts, with an emphasis on bed-and-breakfasts, cafés, hostels, and small hotels. Peaceful World Foundation, 1665 Haight Street, San Francisco, CA 94117; Tel: 415-864-1978; Fax: 415-863-3293; e-mail: comments@peacefulworldtravel.com; Web sites: www.redvic.com or www.peacefulworldtravel.com.

For organic farming opportunities explore WWOOF—World Wide Opportunities on Organic Farms—an international association with dozens of member countries plus hundreds of independent member farms. Each affiliated country has its own association, which requires membership. The fee is low, usually in the $25 range. Membership provides you access to the list of participating farms. You choose the farms where you would like to work, make contact with them, and make all of your arrangements. The association does not handle any of the arrangements but does offer tips on their Web sites for maximizing your contact and experience. These are not paid jobs, but rather organic farming work experiences. You and the host farm reach your own agreement about how many hours per day or week you will work in exchange for room, breakfast, and sometimes other meals. For more information go to www.wwoof.org.

Volunteers for International Partnership, part of the Experiment in International Living (see page 17), offers volunteer projects in nineteen countries. Fees depend on length of stay and location. For more information go to www.partnershipvolunteers.org.

Bill McMillon, Doug Cutchins, and Anne Geissinger, *Volunteer Vacations: Short Term Adventures That Will Benefit You and Others,* 10th ed. (Chicago: Chicago Review Press, 2009).

Charlotte Hindle et al., *Volunteer: A Traveler's Guide to Making a Difference Around the World* (Oakland, CA: Lonely Planet, 2007).

Paul Backhurst, *Alternatives to the Peace Corps: A Guide of Global Volunteer Opportunities,* 11th ed. (Oakland, CA: Food First, 2005).

UNITED NATIONS WORLD HERITAGE SITES

All the World Heritage Sites in the world, searchable by country and type, can be found at http://whc.unesco.org.

SACRED SITES

Extensive information and links to megalith sites can be found at www.stonepages.com.

The Megalithic Portal includes a searchable map of megalithic sites in Europe. For more information go to www.megalithic.co.uk.

The Sacred Destinations travel guide provides information about sacred sites and ancient wonders around the world at www.sacred-destinations.com.

three traveling naturally in Spain

Spain is a large country by European standards and has varied climates and terrain. I could fill Don Quixote–size volumes with all the wonders to see in Spain. Honestly, between rugged mountains, breathtaking, turquoise beach coasts, desert-like plains, lush farmland, magnificent rivers, bird sanctuaries, tropical flora, centuries-old stone villages, ruins, and a wide selection of fresh, local food hard to beat, Spain is a glory and bounty for anyone inclined to the natural. Spanish food delicacies include delicious, inexpensive wine, olives and olive oil, sheep and goat cheeses, seafood, and all manner of fruits, especially oranges, and vegetables.

The Spanish are decent and generous people. I have found this on all of my trips to Spain and was struck by how accurately George Orwell describes this in his *Homage to Catalonia* (see recommended books on page 136), "A Spaniard's generosity, in the ordinary sense of the word, is at times almost embarrassing. If you ask him for a cigarette he will force the whole packet upon you. And beyond this there is generosity in a deeper sense, a real largeness of spirit, which I have met with again and again in the most unpromising circumstances."

Spaniards also have a relaxed and happy quality to them, reflected in their schedule and pace of life. Most people must be at work by 9:00 a.m., but many have a generous lunch break or even a siesta-time in the afternoon. Dinner is served between 9:00 and 11:30 at night and then strolling, dancing, and hanging out in the plazas is common, especially in the warmer months. Stores and many museums are often closed all afternoon, so plan your shopping for the morning or late in the day, starting at about 5:00 p.m., depending on the store.

Public transportation is fairly extensive, and renewable energy is abundant—at just about every turn of your head you will see windmills. There are numerous rural guesthouses, many in restored, old stone buildings.

Since Spain was not part of World War II it escaped much of the serious bombing that destroyed many old structures in the rest of Europe, allowing buildings and whole villages that are hundreds of years old to survive, making Spain a visual orgy of historic sites, some dating from prehistory. Some areas did suffer aerial bombing from the Nazi and Italian Fascists who were collaborating with Franco's army, including the famous Guernica bombing in the Basque Country and numerous sites along the Mediterranean coast of the Valencia region.

Socially Spaniards tend to be very progressive and tolerant, a distinct reaction to the rigid thirty-six-year reign of the Franco dictatorship, which ended in 1975. Voter turnout is very high in elections in this country where many remember the decades without democracy and are happy to exercise their freedom and right to vote. Spain was the third country in the European Union to make same-sex marriage legal and has enacted other people-friendly reforms.

The Spanish live very much outside, in the fresh air. Most houses are designed with inner courtyards, open-air shafts, and terraces. Spaniards spend inordinate amounts of time outside sitting eating, drinking, and soaking up the action in the plazas, especially in the warmer months, as well as strolling, or hiking, through towns, parks, and the countryside. They get much more fresh air than Americans and lots of sunshine. This combined with copious amounts of olive oil, wine, and fresh food contribute to their health, vitality, and I would say, good cheer.

Spain is an easy country in which to travel naturally and lightly—enjoy everything it has to offer!

Orientation, Arrival, and Getting Around

The four largest cities in Spain in order are Madrid, Barcelona, Valencia, and Sevilla. Spain has seventeen communities or regions with fifty provinces spread among the regions. The regions are: Anda-

Regions of Spain

Seventeen regions total with fifteen on the mainland, two sets of islands, and two Spanish territories in Morocco

lucía, Murcia, Valencia, Castilla-La Mancha, Extremadura, Castilla y León, Madrid, Aragón, Cataluña (in English, Catalonia; in Catalan, Catalunya), Navarra, La Rioja, País Vasco (in English, Basque Country; in Basque, Euskadi), Cantabria, Asturias, Galicia, Baleares (the Balearic Islands—Mallorca, Ibiza, and Menorca), and Canarias (Canary Islands). See the Green Earth Map of Spain Regions above.

GENERALLY GREEN

There are a few Web sites in Spain that are focused on the environment and green living. You can explore these to get a taste of what is happening in Spain on these issues. The Terra Foundation provides two informative Web sites: www.terra.org and www.ecoterra.org; and their online store of environmental products is at http://biohabitat.terra.org.

Tidbits about Spain

Spain has a rich history of creative, brilliant, and progressive people, some of whom are well known, others who are not. A short list would have to include: Pablo Picasso (1881–1973), artist; Antoni Gaudí (1852–1926), architect; Joan Miró (1893–1983), artist; Francisco Goya (1746–1828), artist; Miguel Cervantes (1547–1616), writer; Federico García Lorca (1898–1936), writer; and Vicente Blasco Ibáñez (1867–1928), writer.

Spain has a number of newspapers and you may wonder what the differences are. In a nutshell, *ABC* tends to report more from the conservative-right perspective; *El País* is a center-left, socialist-leaning newspaper, likening itself to the *New York Times,* with inserts in the *International Herald Tribune; El Mundo* is more left leaning than *El País;* and *La Vanguardia* is a Spanish newspaper focused on the Catalonia region. In addition, each region usually has one or more local papers.

National holidays in Spain are similar to American holidays with two major exceptions. Much celebration takes place in Spain in commemoration of Columbus "discovering" the Americas on October 12, and Spain's Constitution Day is December 6, the day in 1978 when Spain officially became a democracy.

How to Read a Spanish Address

Name and/or name of business, C/ = Calle (or Carrer in Catalan) means Street + street name, + building number (or can read s/n, which means *sin número* (without a number), + sometimes an apartment number—for example, 7º, + postal code + City or Town, + often in parentheses, but not always and this can get confusing, the region. If the region name also happens to be a city name you can think that a business or hotel is in the city but it may actually be only in the region. Example: L'Hostal Blau, C/ del Forn, 2, 17113 Peratallada (Girona).

- Toilet paper is not always provided or available so having a pack of tissue in your bag can be helpful. In that same vein, don't be shocked if you find toilets without seats—many places leave them off.

- You will almost always need to show your passport when paying by credit card (a safety measure for you and the store), so make sure you have it safely with you.

- 1 euro coins are generally very useful as they are used for lockers, grocery carts, buses, newspapers, and lots more.

- When you are at a post office, or train station, look for the number machines. You will need to push a button and take the slip of paper with your number on it, then wait your turn, watching the signs for which teller to go to. Always be prepared to wait.

- At tourist offices you usually have to ask for maps, which tend to be behind the counter. At first I found this irritating, but then realized that it is their way of being able to ask you what country you are from for their statistics. Map = *mapa* or *plano*.

- July and August are the hottest months in Spain and are considered peak travel times. When making plans, take this into consideration. Places will not only be harder to book during this period but also much more crowded and substantially more expensive. Interestingly, certain places, like some markets, are closed during this period, especially in August, when Spaniards tend to go on holiday to beat the heat.

The *Revista Integral* magazine is sold in health food stores and is a natural health and lifestyle periodical with much of their information available online, in Spanish at www.larevistaintegral.com.

Greenpeace has a large presence in Spain. Greenpeace España, C/ San Bernardo, 107, 1°, 28015 Madrid; Tel: 914 441 400; e-mail: informacion@greenpeace.es; Web site: www.greenpeace.es. Their antinuclear campaign is called "I am antinuclear" with a Web site: https://colabora2.greenpeace.es/yosoyantinuclear/.

Cultura Natura is a Web library specializing in ecology; Web site: www.culturanatura.com.

Spaniards do not need much of an excuse to celebrate so you will find numerous festivals and fairs in every region. Many local food oriented festivals occur in the warmer months. Listed here are a sampling of some of the options.

FEBRUARY

Carnaval runs February 19–28 and different towns and cities choose which days they will celebrate. Carnaval originated from partying, feasting, and using up one's meat (*carne*), sweets, and fatty foods prior to the Catholic Lent.

MARCH

Las Fallas de Valencia runs from March 13 to 19 where papier mâché sculptures and models are made, processions are held, and then on March 19, St. Joseph's Day, all the sculptures are burned and there are fireworks. This is a very important festival in Valencia: often schools are closed, and sometimes shops as well, so take note if you are traveling to Valencia during this time.

Easter

Note that Semana Santa (Holy Week) between Palm Sunday and Easter Sunday is a major event in Spain, and many Spaniards take this as a holiday; therefore, hotels may be full during this time.

APRIL

In the middle of April the organic and health expo, Expo Eco-Salud, takes place in Barcelona—www.expoecosalud.es.

The last Sunday of April is the Fira de les Herbes (Herb Trade Fair) in Peratallada (in the Girona province of Catalonia).

MAY

In early May, Barcelona hosts BioCultura, an exposition of organic and fair-trade products— www.biocultura.org.

Note: July and August tend to be peak travel times.

JULY

On the first Sunday in July a large cherry fair is held in Paiosaco (A Laracha) in the region of Galicia. You can download the Festivals brochure for a full list of Galician Festivals at www.turismocostadamorte.com/en/upload/des/56-a-festas_ENG.pdf.

The first Saturday after August 2 is the Río Sella Canoe Festival, in Ribadesella and Arriondas in Asturias—an international canoeing event (called *Descenso Internacional del Sella* in Spanish). For full information see the English Web site at www.descensodelsella.com/eng/p_caract.asp.

The last Sunday in August in Arenas, in the region of Asturias, there is the Cheese Festival (Feria del Cabrales) with demonstrations, contests, and lots of the local Cabrales blue cheese. Web site: www.cabrales.org.

In late August the Natural Cider Festival—Fiesta de la Sidra Natural—is in Gijón, Asturias.

OCTOBER

At the end of October the Rosa del Azafrán (Saffron) Festival is held in Consuegra, in the Castilla-La Mancha region.

November: At the end of November Madrid hosts BioCultura, an exposition of organic and fair-trade products—www.biocultura.org.

DECEMBER

During the middle weekend in December in Girona there is the Eco-Sí Fair, an ecological products fair at a pavilion at the far end of the Parc La Devesa.

Numerous towns have Christmas markets throughout December.

COMMUNICATION

Four main languages are spoken in Spain—Castilian Spanish is the language spoken all over the country and is considered the official language. Galician (*Galego*) is spoken in the northwest and has similarities with Portuguese, Basque (*Euskara*) is spoken in the Basque region in northern Spain, and Catalan (*Català*) is spoken in Catalonia and on the Balearic Islands. Other regions have local dialects or languages but Spanish is the official language.

Online phone directories can be found at: www.paginas-amarillas. es, which provides yellow pages with a white pages (*páginas blancas*) link. These can be very helpful especially since printed phone books

Remember Spain is six hours ahead of U.S. Eastern Standard Time (EST). If you are calling using a calling card check the instructions, as you will have access numbers to enter.

Calling FROM Spain TO the U.S.
Direct call—00 + 1 + area code + 7 digit number

Calling TO Spain from the U.S.
Direct call—011 + 34 (Spain country code) + 2–3 digit city code + 6–7 digit number (total of 9 digits)

Example: calling one of the NaturaSí health food stores in Madrid: 011 + 34 + 91 (Madrid city code) + 5 445 663, so 011 34 915 445 663.

Calling WITHIN Spain
City code + number (total of 9 digits)

Example: calling one of the NaturaSí health food stores in Madrid: 91 + 5 445 663, so 915 445 663.

can be hard to find. Phone calling cards can be purchased with surprisingly inexpensive rates at local stores.

If you are using a cell phone, beware the roaming and international fees. Please check with your provider before leaving the United States to avoid bill-shock when you return home.

TRANSPORTATION

Car Rental
If you end up renting a car for any part of your travels in Spain, please be aware that rental cars are almost always standard shift in Europe. They do not ask your preference. So if you don't drive stick shift, it's best if you inquire about what options there are so you don't end up with a car you can't drive.

Public Transportation
Spain has more than forty airports—a lot to keep track of. The Web site for the Spanish airport authority is www.aena.es/csee/Satellite?pagename=Home&Language=EN_GB. Madrid has the largest and

busiest airport in Spain, with Barcelona a close second. The flight path between Madrid and Barcelona is said to be the busiest in the world. If you are coming into Spain from another European country and are flying the low-cost Ryanair into the Girona Airport (called Girona-Costa Brava or Barcelona-Girona Airport) there are fairly seamless bus connections to Barcelona city at the airport with schedules corresponding to incoming flights. You must buy your ticket at the counter in the Girona Airport, or at the Barcelona Estacio Nord bus station, not on the bus, and they do not take credit cards so be prepared with cash. See the Web site for Barcelona Bus for details: www.barcelonabus.com.

Madrid, Barcelona, Valencia, and Málaga airports all have train service. Madrid, the largest city, has six main train stations. Atocha and Chamartín stations are the two providing long-distance as well as commuter train service, Atocha servicing the high-speed AVE trains. The remaining stations—Príncipe Pío, Recoletos, Méndez Álvaro, and Nuevos Ministerios—all run commuter service. Metro tip: The Atocha Metro stop is not the connecting station for the Atocha train station—you want Atocha RENFE. All the other train stations are accessed by Metro stops with the same name as the train station with the exception of Recoletos, which is on Plaza de Colón so the Metro stop is Colón. Pay attention to your ticket as there may be trains arriving and/or leaving from Madrid at either Chamartín or Atocha stations and these are about a thirty-minute Metro ride, on the same line, from each other so you do not want any tight connections.

The Atocha train station in Madrid is huge and beautiful with a plant-filled atrium, cafés, and multiple security bag checks. Tired and hungry travelers will be happy to find a tiny health food store with gluten-free and other natural products in the Madrid Atocha train station in the AVE high-speed train arrival shopping concourse on the lower level. Auge 2000 Herbolario, Terminal AVE, Estación de Atocha, Madrid; Tel: 915 391 897.

The main railways in Spain are run by the government. The Red Nacional de los Ferrocarriles Españoles (RENFE) Spanish rail Web site is www.renfe.es. Here you can get schedules and fare information. The English version is available at www.renfe.es/horarios/English/index.html, although not all the options and information are available on the English page. This site will give information about the main stations. The local or suburban trains are called Cercanías and lists for them are available by clicking on "Stations" at the bottom right-hand corner of the English version Web site.

The big cities in Spain are well served by both trains and buses, but the outlying areas can be more difficult to reach—the transit system is not like Switzerland's where every hill and dale can be accessed by public transportation and/or a good walking stick.

While purchasing your ticket on the Internet can save time in theory, the Web site for RENFE is notoriously horrendous. The latest glitch is that you can purchase tickets on the RENFE site only if you have a Spanish credit card or American Express—no other cards will work, but you will not be told this—you will just suffer through countless unsuccessful attempts to purchase your ticket.

If you do have an American Express card, you are in luck. I suggest that you set up a user account so you only have to enter your pertinent information, including passport number, once on the RENFE site. If you do not have an American Express card (or by some other luck a Spanish credit card), then you are left with two options. Either go to a large train station (small stations usually sell tickets only for trains that stop at their station) and buy your ticket from a teller (be forewarned that only a few of the tellers speak English; most of them do not). If you know your train and time, it is best to write it out clearly for the teller before getting to the window. Remember to use the twenty-four-hour-clock system for your departure and arrival times.

On most trains, your ticket must be validated before boarding. Validate your tickets at the little, orange box-like machines usually at the end of the platforms or in the station. Also, confirm you are boarding the right train by matching the train number on your ticket to the number on the track sign.

Many tickets are for reserved seats. Your ticket will list the train number, coach number, and seat number. The following translations may help you make sense of your ticket:

Coche = coach/car	*Plaza* (place) or *asiento* = seat
Turista = second or tourist class	*Preferente* = first class
Corredor or *pasillo* = aisle	*Ventana* = window
Vía = track	*Ida* = one-way
Ida y vuelta = round-trip	

Option two is to find a travel agent near where you are staying. Travel agents can ticket for long-distance trains and while it will cost slightly more for your ticket (they charge a commission), the price is minuscule compared to the hours and days you might spend frustrated in front of your computer screen. A further note that is bizarre but true: if you try to purchase over the phone, the old-fashioned way, the RENFE reservation operators work the same way as the Web site and can take only American Express or Spanish issued cards. You can see why the travel agent option looks better by the minute.

Some regions have their own train services in addition to the RENFE trains serving the area. These are FEVE, for the northern Green Coast, Web site: www.feve.es; EuskoTren, for the Basque region, Web site: www.euskotren.es; the FGV for the Costa Blanca, Web site: www.fgv.es/page.php?idioma=_en; and the FGC for Catalonia, Web site: www.fgc.net/eng.

In general, trains in Spain are crowded. Routes between Madrid and Barcelona is some of the busiest in the world, so if you are hoping for a train ticket, book ahead; otherwise you may get caught with no available seats or having to travel first class to make a connection.

In Madrid, it is best to buy your tickets through the Internet and pick them up at one of the many handy machines in the station. Unfortunately, not all train stations in Spain have the machines to retrieve your Internet tickets. It is still usually quicker to purchase tickets over the Internet and pick them up at a special window than to purchase tickets at the train station, although this depends on the station—Madrid, Barcelona, and Valencia are especially busy. I have found easy, fast purchasing in Bilbao, Santiago, Sevilla, and other cities. There are usually special counters to pick up tickets purchased online. If you do not have Internet access, plan accordingly and be prepared for long waits—it can take up to an hour or longer to get your turn at a teller window. Note: There are machines where you get a number for your turn in line. Pay attention to your number and what line you are waiting in. There are different windows and tellers for short (*media distancia*) versus long (*larga distancia*) distances, AND different windows and tellers if you need to buy a ticket for a train leaving the same day as opposed to an advance purchase for a train leaving any day but the same day. Before your eyes glaze over, know that I have observed even the Spaniards getting confused by this system.

Note: Security for shorter-distance trains is often nonexistent unless your train is a high-speed AVE—these all require X-ray baggage checks like at airports. In Madrid, once you have gone through security you have some, but very limited, shopping options. In Barcelona you have zero. Also on the AVE your ticket is scanned after security but before you board the train.

Barcelona has two rail stations—Estació de França and Sants. Sants is the newer one and where the high-speed AVE departs from. The "left luggage" facility (*Consigna*) in Estació de Sants is open seven days a week from 5:30 a.m. to 11:00 p.m. and lockers cost 3 or 4.50 euros depending on size for up to twenty-four hours. Estació de França, the older station, tends to have the overnight European train departures. A word of warning: the left luggage facility at Estació de França is indefinitely closed, and—unrelated—the bathrooms have no toilet seats or toilet paper, so be prepared. Hold on to your ticket if you are entering Barcelona Sants via a local line—you need it to enter into the station once you have disembarked.

On trains and Metros most cars have either buttons or lift levers on or near the doors to open them. Don't be bashful: you need to push or lift to exit or enter the train or Metro car.

Horarios = times of trains

Precios = prices

Planos = maps/routes

Precio Internet = Internet price

Precio estación = price at the station

Prestaciones = services available

There are left luggage facilities in most of the major train stations except Estació de França in Barcelona.

For information about Spanish rail passes go to www.railpass.com/GContent/BRPE/Others-Browse_RailPass_Products#spain or www.eurorailways.com/products/trains_passes/single_country/spain.htm for travelers from the United States. For European travelers see: www.interrailnet.com/one_country_pass_spain. These sites are user-friendly with lots of helpful information. On the site for European travelers, the prices are quoted in euros. Note: Rail passes are not valid on the independent rail services such as FEVE along the northern coast (www.feve.es) and EuskoTren in the Basque region (www.euskotren.es).

The bus system is extensive, covers many towns not serviced by rail, and can be faster and cheaper than the train. Different independent companies run the buses, and depending upon your itinerary you could be taking buses operated by two or more different companies. At the Web site for Movelia, you can find many bus connections and book certain tickets; Web site: www.movelia.es. The Portillo bus company serves the Málaga area with buses to Ronda, Cádiz, and other towns in the area. Alsina Graells Sur serves Granada, Córdoba, and Sevilla. The largest bus company is ALSA with a Web site accessible in English and Castilian; Web site: www.alsa.es. PESA runs buses between Bilbao and San Sebastián; Web site: www.pesa.net.

For local transportation, cities have extensive Metro and bus systems and in most cases the best fares are to be had by purchasing a ten-ride ticket or series of tickets, or a multi-day tourist pass can be very helpful if you don't want to keep track of usage.

Madrid has a huge Metro subway system with information available at www.metromadrid.es/en/index.html. As in many cities, tickets can be purchased for certain zones or for the whole city, and can be purchased as single ride or with a good savings in a series of ten.

Barcelona's Metro and bus network is extensive (see "Barcelona Specific" later in this chapter). Valencia has a new tram and buses, but not as large a network as Barcelona or Madrid. The same is true for Sevilla and Bilbao. Most other cities have a bus network.

Bike Rentals
There are numerous commercial bike rental companies around Spain. The city of Barcelona has developed a system called Bicing similar to the Paris Vélib' program. There are currently one hundred stations around the city (they continually add new ones) where you can rent bikes for thirty-minute intervals. For 24 euros a year (about US$32) you can have access to the bright red and white bikes by swiping your card and entering your PIN. Sunday through Thursdays the bikes are available all day except from midnight until 5:00 a.m. On Fridays and Saturdays the bikes are available twenty-four hours a day.

You can also apply for a weekly card. As with the Parisian version, a 150 euro deposit is required. The office is located at Plaça Carles Pi I Sunyer, 8-10, Barcelona, Tel: 902 315 531; e-mail: atencioclient@bicing.com or info@bicing.com; Web site: www.bicing.com, available only in the two languages of the area, Spanish and Catalan; open 8:30 a.m. to 5:30 p.m.

Bicycling in Madrid is not so easy or cheap. There is no "Bicing," only private bike rental companies. Madrid is also not as bicycle friendly as Barcelona. Madrid is working on expanding its bike lanes and there are routes you can take to avoid the worst of the traffic. Although Madrid is not bicycle friendly for riding through the main streets, there is a 64 km bike path around Madrid and paths through the large park Casa de Campo (about four thousand acres), as well as the smaller Parque del Retiro (322 acres).

In Valencia, Do You Bike rents bikes for 10–15 euros/day and also by the hour. Weekend rates are 25 euros, one week is 40 euros, fifteen days is 55 euros, and a month will run you 75 euros. There are three locations of Do You Bike: Zona Puerto Aragón, Avda. Puerto, 143, Tel: 963 374 024, e-mail: puerto@doyoubike.com; Zona Universitaria P. Reig—B. Ibáñez, C. Puebla Larga, 13, Tel: 963 387 008, e-mail: benimaclet@doyoubike.com; and Zona Centro-Carmen, Plz. Horno de San Nicolas, Tel: 963 155 551, e-mail: info@doyoubike.com; Web site: www.doyoubike.com.

Sevici, like Bicing in Barcelona, is a program run by the Sevilla city government to encourage bicycle use throughout the city. There are 2,500 bicycles parked at stations around the city where for an unbelievably inexpensive rate you can pick up and drop off bicycles. You purchase a card over the Internet. For 5 euros you can buy a card for a seven-day period that gets you thirty minutes on any given bike for free; longer is charged at 1 euro per hour. A one-year card for 10 euros buys you the same but extra hours are charged at only 50 cents per hour. Like the Barcelona system, a one-time 150 euro deposit is charged to your credit card. Parking areas are supposedly no farther than about one-fifth of a mile, or one-third of a kilometer, from each other (about four city blocks). Sevici operates 24/7 every day of the year. Bikes have kickstands, three gears, a front basket for purchases, and adjustable seats. See the Web site for full information at http://en.sevici.es.

When you are standing at a red light waiting to cross the street, particularly in busy cities, you may wonder why most of the Spaniards waiting with you will stand there, not crossing, even though there is not a vehicle in sight. They know something you don't, trust me. I made the mistake of crossing on a red light in Barcelona, when there were no vehicles in sight, and next thing I knew I was being run over, literally, by a large motorcycle. Ambulances and police ensued. All involved were incredibly lovely and kind human beings, from the women who surrounded and protected me after the accident to all the professional personnel. However, since I crossed on the red, I was in the wrong, even though I was the one hurt. So I had to fork over 500 euros to the driver for the damage to his motorcycle, making the accident that much more excruciating for me. The moral: do *not* cross on a red light or outside of a crosswalk. Be patient, breathe through the red light, and trust its purpose.

In Córdoba you can rent bikes for 15 euros a day at Solo Bici, conveniently located a few blocks from the *mezquita-catedral*. Solo Bici, Ronda de Isasa, n° 10, 14003 Córdoba; Tel: 957 485 766 or 620 318 370; e-mail: info@solobici.net; Web site: www.solobici.net/IND_eng.htm.

In Santiago de Compostela they have a small version of Bicing called Combici with seven stations around Santiago. There is an office at the bus station open from 5:00 to 8:00 p.m. Combici, Tel: 981 587 589; e-mail: combici@tuimil.es; Web site: www.combici.com/ingles/index.html.

Other cities have bike rental companies as well for short- and long-term rental.

In Barcelona, Valencia, Sevilla, Bilbao, Ibiza, and Mallorca electric scooters can be rented starting at 25 euros/day at Cooltra Motos, Pg. Joan de Borbo, 80-84, 08039 Barcelona; Tel: 932 214 070; e-mail: info@cooltra.com; Web site: http://moto.cooltra.com with information in English. They also rent rollerblades.

Accommodations

The following accommodations meet at least one of the *Green Earth Guide* accommodations criteria (see "Green Earth Accommodations" on page 14). Lodging that is listed under the subheading "Eco-Accommodations" is distinguished as specifically and intentionally incorporating multiple ecological practices into their facilities. The conundrum of ecotravel is that many of the more eco-minded accommodations are rural, where access to public transportation can be more limited, and sometimes you really must have a car for logistical reasons.

At some hotels and *pensiónes* you pay when you check in, others when you check out (these tend to be smaller, more traditional establishments). *Pensiónes* are numerous and often have shared bathrooms. Some can be up more than one flight of stairs. If you think this might be an issue with your luggage, inquire when booking. A note about water faucets in Spain: The letter "C" does not mean cold, but rather stands for *caliente,* which means hot. The letter "F" is for *frío,* which means cold. Also note the tricky little lock mechanism on some older *pensión* doors. If you are having a difficult time opening or locking your door, look for a little push-button on the bolt mechanism, which should release the bolt for easy sliding.

HOSTELS

If you are traveling alone, or in a pair, hostels are one of the least expensive options since you are paying per bed, not per room. Hostels that are part of the Hostelling International network can be found at their Web site: www.hihostels.com. Spanish Youth Hostels lists more than two hundred hostels around Spain at www.reaj.com/index_en.html. There are also some independent hostels to be found on www.backpackers-planet.com, a Web site covering the world, but searchable by country under Europe, and at www.Hostelworld.com.

Remember that to have an enjoyable stay you should get into the hostel mind-set, which involves embracing noise, more of a social scene, and sharing space, including bathrooms. If you are in the mood, backpacking and staying at youth hostels are fun, cheap ways to travel. If you are not in the right frame of mind, they can seem nightmarish, and you are probably best advised to find an inexpensive *pensión* or *pensión*-style *hostal* to stay in where you can have your own room.

CAMPING

When the weather is amenable, camping is an inexpensive and environmental option. Spain has more than eight hundred camping areas so there are plenty of choices, but remember that the weather in northern Spain reaches freezing or below in the winter. The official guide to camping in Spain, *Guía Camping 2009: España, Portugal, Europa,* can be found at the Web site www.guiacampingfecc.com. The guide and Web site are in Spanish, but this is the best source of information and you can search for camping areas by province at the Web site.

For huts and refuges in the Pyrenees you can search alphabetically on the Web site www.pyrenees-refuges.com.

GUESTHOUSES AND BED-AND-BREAKFASTS INCLUDING HISTORICAL INNS AND RURAL TOURISM

On the high-priced, luxury end, the Spanish government runs a line of hotels called Paradores, and they are in renovated grand, historic buildings like castles, palaces, convents, monasteries, and in Santiago de Compostela, the old hospital for the poor right on the main plaza facing the *catedral.* See the Web site for all the locations and information: www.paradores-spain.com.

Lovely and reasonably priced guesthouses and bed-and-breakfasts are plentiful and these usually offer breakfast included with their nightly fee. Some can be found at the Web site www.bedandbreakfastinspain. com. Many you can find by strolling through your destination. Rural Houses of Catalonia (northeast Spain) lists rural guesthouses and hotels, many with very reasonable rates: www.casesrurals.com/angles. htm. An example of one of their listings is Sant Dionís, a renovated thirteenth-century stone farmhouse and farm, serving garden-fresh food, with rates from 46 euros/night for a single. Sant Dionís, 17457 Campllong (Girona); Tel: 902 109 124 or 932 008 183; Web site: www.candionis.com.

Pazos de Galicia has information about twenty-six rural guesthouses throughout Galicia in the northwest corner of Spain. The guesthouses are restored old buildings such as fifteenth-century stone manor houses. Prices range from 43 to 105 euros a night depending on season and accommodation. The Web site allows you to click on any of the guesthouse locations to access full information: www.pazosdegalicia.com.

Hotel Rural Doña Blanca is a seventeenth-century restored, six-room hotel with a small spa and local restaurant. Located in the northwest of Spain about one hour from Santiago, room prices start at 85 euros/night with breakfast included. Hotel Rural Doña Blanca, Plaza San Clodio s/n, San Clodio, Leiro, 32428 Orense (Galicia); Tel: 988 485 688; e-mail: reservas@casadedonablanca.com; Web site: www.casadedonablanca.com.

The Monasterio de Oseira has fourteen rooms for pilgrims or for those on religious retreat at 30 euros/night with a four-night minimum and includes three meals. Monasterio de Oseira north of Cea in Galicia; Tel: 988 282 004; e-mail: sp.cisterosera@planalfa.es.

Most of the eight rooms in Rectoral de Cobres, a renovated stone parsonage dating from 1729, have sea views through French doors. Rates range from 80 to 150 euros/night, depending on season and room. Rectoral de Cobres, San Adrian de Cobres, 36142 Vilaboa, Pontevedra (Galicia); Tel: 986 673 810; e-mail: info@rectoral.com; Web site: www.rectoral.com.

A restored sixteenth-century monastery and school now houses a luxury hotel, the Country Hotel or Hospedería Señorío de Casalarreina, located in the Rioja wine region of Spain. Rooms with breakfast included range from 110 euros a night for a single to between 140 and 155 euros for double rooms. The rural hotel is near nature reserves, dinosaur tracks, wineries, walking and biking trails including one of the routes to Santiago de Compostela. Hospedería Señorío de Casalarreina (also known as the Aranjuez of La Rioja), Plaza Sto. Domingo de Guzmán, 6, 26230 Casalarreina, La Rioja; Tel: 941 324 730; e-mail: info@alojamientosconencantodelarioja.com; Web site: www.alojamientosconencantodelarioja.com/hotel_rioja/hotel_casalarreina/spain_hotel/hotel_spain.htm.

At Mas Teixidor, northwest of Girona, restored Catalan stone farmhouses date as far back as the fourteenth century. These accommodations offer self-contained houses with two or more bedrooms, kitchen, living area, and bathrooms. Prices depend on size of the house and time of year, ranging from 310 to 540 euros for a weekend. Mas Teixidor, Km 56, Ctra. Besalú-Fig´eres, 17832 Veïnat de Pedrinyà, Crespià, Pla de l'Estany (Girona); Tel: 972 590 996; e-mail: info@elmasteixidor.com; Web site: www.elmasteixidor.com.

Part of the Turismo Rural Association and just over an hour north of Madrid, El Molino is a restored mill more than two hundred years old situated near castles, museums, and vineyards. Prices start at 48 euros per night per person. El Molino del Valcorba, Torrescárcela (Valladolid); Tel: 983 698 471; Web site: www.elmolinodelvalcorba.com.

Històric Hotel and Apartments has six double hotel rooms, plus five apartments with two double rooms, and two apartments with one double room. The apartments are less expensive at 90 euros/night. Hotel rooms range from 102 to 300 euros/night depending on the size of the room. The hotel has a restaurant serving local, fresh food. Històric Hotel and Apartments, C/ Bellmirall, 4A, 17004 Girona; Tel: 972 223 583; e-mail: info@hotelhistoric.com; Web site: www.hotelhistoric.com/eng.html.

Hotel Blau is in the ancient village of Peratallada near La Bisbal d'Empordà in the Girona province of Catalonia. Arriving by car, you must park in the lot at the village entrance (well marked). Hotel Blau, like all the other buildings in this eleventh–thirteenth-century village, is an old stone house complete with a medieval tower, situated behind the village castle. There are six beautiful rooms, two with terraces. Food is served from a local garden and bakery, and they make homemade jams. Rates range from 100 to 140 euros depending on the room. Breakfast is included, but not the seven percent value added tax (VAT). They are closed between 4:30 and 8:00 p.m. so arrive before or after, but no later than 10:00 p.m. L'Hostal Blau, C/ del Forn, 2, 17113 Peratallada (Girona); Tel: 972 634 185.

Can Carbó de les Olives is a high-end bed-and-breakfast in the countryside northeast of Figueres in Catalonia. The painstakingly restored fourteenth-century Catalan farm manor house sits among two and a half acres of woods and meadows. The old olive mill, wine press, dairy, and stables have been converted into suite-size luxury bedrooms. Breakfast of local goods is included in the rate. Can Carbó de les Olives, Ctra. De Peralada a Morassac, 17491 Peralada (Girona);

Tel: 972 538 623; e-mail: info@hotelcancarbo.com; Web site: www. hotelcancarbo.com.

The Empordà area of the Costa Brava has numerous restored *mas* or *masías* (farm and manor houses) that have been renovated and converted into beautiful accommodations. The *Empordà Guía*, a semi-annual guide to the area, lists numerous possibilities. The Web site also offers other very helpful information: www.empordaguia.com/indexing.php?lang=eng. For numerous rural tourism options in the Girona region of Catalonia, Turisme Rural Girona is an association listing almost three hundred rural guesthouses, many of which are in renovated old buildings. Turisme Rural Girona Web site: www.gironarural.org/?idm=3.

Casa de Verdes is a stone guesthouse in a rural setting near A Coruña in the Costa da Morte area of Galicia. There are seven double rooms and prices range from 36 to 50 euros a night depending on room and season. Casa de Verdes, Cundins (San Paio), 15149 Cabana de Bergantiños (A Coruña); Tel: 609 618 242 or 639 430 429; Fax: 981 748 622; e-mail: info@casadeverdes.com; Web site: www.casadeverdes.com/welcome.htm.

Casa Rural Ea-Asteí has beautiful stone, tile, and wood buildings and sits on a mountain overlooking the Bay of Biscay. Located 2 km from picturesque Elantxobe, 5 km from beaches, and 48 km from Bilbao, Casa Rural Ea-Astei offers two houses; one house can sleep two to six people, the other can sleep up to four. Casa Rural Ea-Asteí, Mertxe Beguiristain, Bº Olagorta s/n, 48287 EA (Bizkaia); Tel: 946 276 511; Mobile: 619 560 123; e-mail: info@astei.net; Web site: www.astei.net/Html/eng/Home_1_Frmst_eng.htm.

You can search easily at the Basque Country tourism Web site for "rural houses," which offers close to three hundred options for rural hotels, farms, homes, and apartments throughout the region; Web site: www.turismoa.euskadi.net/s11-18805/en/.

In the Basque area, 40 km from San Sebastián there is a rural house with nearby biking and hiking routes. Casa Rural Perugorria Berria, 31760 Etxalar (Navarra); Tel: 948 635 174; e-mail: nereaetxalar@msn.com; Web site: www.perugorriaberria.com.

Ahora Casa Rural of Repose and Center of Natural Therapies offers saunas, massage, Tai Chi, yoga, and other therapies. Ahora Casa Rural of Repose and Center of Natural Therapies, Finca la Vega, Cortes de la Front., Bda. El Colmenar (Est. de Gaucín), 29390 (Málaga); Tel: 952 153 046; Mobile: 696 720 889; e-mail: reservas@ahoraya. es; Web site: www.ahoraya.es.

Not a guesthouse, but a luxury hotel of note, the Hotel Marqués de Riscal, in the La Rioja wine region, was designed by architect Frank Gehry, who designed the Guggenheim Museum in Bilbao. The hotel design is inspired by the grapes and vineyards indigenous to the area, with purple and silver flowing roofs. The hotel features the Caudalié Vinothérapie Spa offering "wine therapy" massages and other treatments. Hotel Marqués de Riscal is 110 km (about 68 miles) from the city of Bilbao. Hotel Marqués de Riscal, C/ Torrea, 1, 01340 Elciego (La Rioja); Tel: 945 180 880; e-mail: marquesderiscal@luxurycollection.com; Web site: www.starwoodhotels.com/luxury/property/overview/index.html?propertyID=1539.

HOME EXCHANGE AND HOUSE-SITTING

For home exchange, house-sitting, and sublet possibilities see Chapter Two, "Europe-Wide Information and Resources". For spas and clinics, see the "Health" section later in this chapter.

Loquo is like a Spanish "Craigslist" Web classified with daily postings of room rentals for locals by locals in every major city, where you can sometimes find reasonable prices, especially under "rooms for rent / shared." You can choose Spanish cities from the left side of the home page. Loquo Web site: www.loquo.com/en_us.

ECO-ACCOMMODATIONS

Situated on an eighteen-acre organic farm, the Hotel Posada del Valle is in a restored stone and wood farmhouse near the Picos de Europa mountains in Asturias. Organic and local foods are served, and room prices range from 50 to 86 euros. Hotel Posada del Valle, Collia, Arriondas, 33549 Asturias; Tel: 985 841 157; e-mail: hotel@posadadelvalle.com; Web site: www.posadadelvalle.com.

Mas Fuselles is a family run, EU Eco-label accommodation with eight rooms surrounded by fruit trees, serving local food and wine. Mas Fuselles, s/n Pujals dels Pagesos, 17844 Cornellà del Terri (Girona); Mobile: 606 680 818; e-mail: ecoturisme@masfuselles.com; Web site: www.masfuselles.com/index.php?idm=3.

La Posada de Isar is an eight-room bed-and-breakfast about 90 km northwest of Madrid that serves local and organic foods, has wool and latex mattresses in their rooms, and is near the Peñalara Natural Park. They offer massage as well. Rooms start at 84 euros/night. La Posada de Isar, C/ Real, 18, 28749 Oteruelo del Valle, Rascafría; Tel: 918 691 515.

The Hoopoe Yurt Hotel in Cortes de la Frontera, Andalucía, sits among olive and cork trees. Each of the five yurts has its own acre of land, private bath, and hammocks. There is outdoor dining four nights a week with locally produced food. The hotel camp runs on solar power, uses ecological toilets, and has a chlorine-free swimming pool. Massages and yoga are also available. Trains do run to Cortes de la Frontera; otherwise you need a car. Nearby are the Cueva de la Pileta caves with paintings. The hotel is open from early May until mid-October with changeover days on Wednesdays and Saturdays, so bookings can be three, four, or seven days (or ten, eleven, or fourteen). A double yurt including breakfast for two is 130 euros/night. Ed and Henrietta Hunt, The Hoopoe Yurt Hotel, Apartado de Correos, 23, Cortes de la Frontera, 29380 Málaga; Tel: 951 168 040 (radio-phone with no answering machine; e-mail is the best way of contacting the hotel); Mobile: 696 668 388 or 660 668 241; e-mail: info@yurthotel.com; Web site: www.yurthotel.com.

On the island of Ibiza and open April to mid-October, Can Martí is a forty-acre organic farm and guesthouse with fans, but no air-conditioning; no pool or television, but land and activities. The four apartments have been renovated using eco materials—the walls have clay plaster and are painted with natural pigments and the wood has been treated with organic oil. Three of the apartments can accommodate two people each, while the fourth can hold four people. Rates range from 145 to 250 euros depending on the season and are per night per apartment and include linens, cleaning, bicycles, and taxes. The little store on the premises sells local produce, as well as organic and fair-trade products. Can Martí, Agroturismo ecológico, Venda de Ca's Ripolls, 29, 07810 San Juan de Labritja, Ibiza - Baleares; Tel: 971 333 500; e-mail: info@canmarti.com; Web site: www.canmarti.com/en/index.php.

Granja San Miguel is a rural "eco" guesthouse in the province of Valencia located on an old farm that has been restored with a restaurant serving local, seasonal food and a spa and wellness center complete with fitness room, Jacuzzi, steam bath, and massage services. Yoga, Pilates, and other classes are offered. Double rooms with breakfast range from 65 to 85 euros depending on the day of the week and length of stay. Granja San Miguel, C/ Benicadell, 10, 46843 Salem (Valencia, Vall d'Albaida); Tel: 962 883 515; Mobile: 663 081 221; e-mail: info@casasanmiguel.com; Web site: www.casasanmiguel.com.

L'ayalga Posada Ecológica, in northwest Spain, calls itself an "environmentally free guesthouse." Its five guest rooms are in an old farmhouse restored with environmental materials and it uses solar heat. The mattresses are natural latex and have down-filled comforters, and they provide 100% cotton towels. Rates run about 55 euros a night and include breakfast. Tai Chi and Chi Kung classes are offered. The guesthouse is part of the rural agricultural tourism system in Spain. L'ayalga Posada is east of Oviedo in a tiny village so it is best to have a car, but you can take the regional FEVE train to Infiesto, about 6 km away; if prearranged, the owners will pick you up. L'ayalga Posada Ecológica, La Pandiella; Tel: 616 897 638; e-mail: layalga@terrae.net; Web site: www.terrae.net/layalga/indexI.htm.

The Bio Aparthotel Venus Albir has twenty-four apartments distributed on the ground, first, and second floors. Each apartment has a double bedroom with two beds with natural latex mattresses, wooden slab mattress support, and 100% cotton sheets. Venus Albir has a restaurant serving organic food. There is a swimming pool, and massage therapy is available. Alicante is a beach city south of Valencia on the Costa Blanca. Bio Aparthotel Venus Albir, Plaza Venus, 7, 03581 Albir-Alfaz del Pi (Alicante); Tel: 966 864 820; e-mail: venusalbir@venusalbir.com; Web site: www.raycons.com/venusalbir/index.php?lang=en.

In the UNESCO recognized Terras Do Miño Biosphere in the northwestern Galician region of Spain, you will find A Fervenza, an eight-room hotel, in an old mill restored with stone, wood, and natural fibers surrounded by chestnut trees, situated in the almost nine-hundred-thousand-acre biosphere that contains the Río (River) Miño. Nearby there are ancient sites including the Muralla de Lugo and the village of Lucus Augusti, founded in AD 25, and an ongoing agricultural tradition. A Fervenza, Ctra. Lugo-Paramo, Km 11, 27163 O Corgo. (Lugo); Tel: 982 150 610; e-mail: info@fervenza.com; Web site: www.fervenza.com.

Eco Agro Turismo, part of the European Centre for Ecological and Agricultural Tourism (ECEAT), can be found at www.ecoagroturismo.es with information about rural farm visits and lodging focusing on accommodations that are committed to the conservation of the environment, biodiversity, and support of local and organic foods. For more information about ECEAT, see the "Europe-Wide Information and Resources" section in Chapter Two on page 16 and visit the Web site: www.eceat.travel/fx/en/accomodationlist/ac-/pc-/st-/acdst-spain/acstyle-/acuisine for organic farm accommodations throughout Spain.

Casa Gustavo is a renovated five-hundred-year-old farmhouse and farm off the beaten path with hiking trails, serving local and seasonal food. Casa Gustavo Guesthouse, Aliezo, Cillorigo de Liébana, 39584 Cantabria; Tel: 942 732 010; e-mail: stuartsinpicos@terra.es; Web site: www.picos-accommodation.co.uk.

Casa Manadero is a renovated stone house in the Sierra de Gata south of Salamanca. Rates range from 60 to 150 euros a night with a minimum two-night stay. The restaurant serves local and fresh food. Casa Manadero, C/ Manadero, 2, Robledillo de Gata, 10867 Cáceres; Tel: 927 671 118; e-mail: reservas@casamanadero.com; Web site: www.casamanadero.com/Ingles/Home.html.

The Sierra y Mar bed-and-breakfast, situated in one of the white villages in the Alpujarra and Sierra Nevada mountains, is in a series of houses connected by terraces and gardens. There are nine rooms with prices ranging from 42 to 84 euros per night. There is a three-hour-long bus ride from Granada to Ferreirola, with a connection in Pitres, if you are not driving. Sierra y Mar, C/ Albaycín, 3, 18414 Ferreirola (Granada); Tel: 958 766 171; e-mail: sierraymar@hotmail.com; Web site: www.sierraymar.com/en/hotel_alpujarra_ferreirola.php.

Casas Karen are a grouping of thatched cottages surrounded by natural parks and beaches on the Costa de la Luz in southwestern Spain. Available by the night or week, there are eleven Casas in total. Casas Karen, Camino del Monte, 6, Los Caños de Meca (between Vejer and Barbate) 11159 (Cádiz); Tel: 956 437 067; e-mail: info@casaskaren.com or casaskarencanos@yahoo.es; Web site: www.casaskaren.com.

La Casa del Alba calls itself a house of light, health, and relaxation serving ovo-lacto vegetarian food. They have sixteen rooms and offer health therapies. La Casa del Alba, Santiso, 13, 27579 Antas de Ulla (Lugo); Tel: 982 379 553; Mobile: 661 356 151; e-mail: info@lacasadelalba.org; Web site: www.lacasadelalba.org.

La Alquería de Morayma is a small rural hotel set on a one-hundred-acre organic farm where they grow organic almonds, olives, fruits, and wines near the Sierra Nevada mountains and the towns of Cádiar and Bérchules. They have a restaurant serving food typical of the region. There are twenty-three rooms with prices ranging from 65 to 110 euros. Organic wines produced on the farm are served. La Alquería de Morayma, Ctra A-348 (Km 50), Cádiar (Granada); Tel: 958 343 221 or 958 343 303; e-mail: alqueria@alqueriamorayma.com; Web site: www.alqueriamorayma.com/en/.

Los Castaños Casa Rural has rooms and bungalows, with a restaurant serving natural foods and day-spa services including massage, hydrotherapy, meditation, and yoga. Prices range from 35 to 75 euros a night. Los Castaños Casa Rural, C/ Emilio Serrano, 10, 28470 Cercedilla (Madrid); Tel: 918 521 798; e-mail: info@loscastanos.net; Web site: www.loscastanos.es.

La Casa Toya refers to itself as a house of relaxation, serving ovo-lacto vegetarian buffet meals, with rooms running between 30 and 42 euros a night. They have free wifi, and offer Reiki, polarity, and yoga. Located two hours from Madrid, one hour on the AVE high-speed train, in Sierra Vicor, in the Zaragoza area. La Casa Toya; Tel: 976 609 334; Web site: www.lacasatoya.com.

CEL: Centre Ecològic Llémena has an organic store, a restaurant serving organic and vegetarian meals, grounds using permaculture sustainable design, and a natural swimming pool. It is rural, in the country 25 km from the city of Girona. Situated in the Can Sala estate where there is a restored twelfth-century farmhouse, there are three double rooms, two suites, a room sleeping six people, and another sleeping eight in a hostel dormitory style. Prices range from

7.50 euros a night for camping to 95 euros for a suite-size double room. Organic meals cost an extra 10 to 13 euros. CEL: Centre Ecològic Llémena, Can Sala, Granollers de Rocacorba, 17153 Sant Martí de Llémena (Girona); Tel: 972 443 162; e-mail: camillocel@gmail.com; Web site: www.cel.org.es/index_en.html.

Mas de Noguera is a rural farm and guesthouse northwest of Valencia city serving local and organic foods. Prices range from 35 to 60 euros a night. Mas de Noguera, 12440 Caudiel (Castellón); Tel: 964 144 074; e-mail: masdenoguera@masdenoguera.coop; Web site: www.masdenoguera.coop.

L'Atelier is a vegetarian bed-and-breakfast in a beautiful white village in the Alpujarras serving organic, local foods. Room prices range from 35 to 50 euros. Walking trails surround the village. Vegetarian cooking courses are offered and the proprietor, Jean-Claude Juston, has written a book, *The New Spain: Vegan & Vegetarian Restaurants.* L'Atelier, C/ Alberca, nº 21, 18414 Mecina-Fondales (Granada); Tel: 958 857 501; e-mail: mecinilla@yahoo.com; Web site: www.ivu.org/atelier/index-eng.html.

Coses de La Vita is a rural hotel and restaurant in the northern region of Asturias along the "green" coast that offers in addition to their regular menu, pizzas and pastas made with gluten-free flour to accommodate guests with celiac disease or gluten sensitivity. Located in a small village, La Vita, around 4 km from Arriondas, room prices range from 50 to 80 euros per night. Coses de la Vita, La Vita, 25, 33549 Arriondas (Asturias); Tel: 689 176 796; e-mail: info@coses-delavita.com; Web site: www.cosesdelavita.com.

El Bosque is a hotel, spa, and restaurant north of Madrid city serving organic food with gluten- and lactose-free options. Prices in the restaurant range from 7 to 19 euros. El Bosque, Madrid Sierra, C/ Del Guerrero, 5, 28492 Mataelpino, Madrid; Tel: 918 573 149; e-mail: madridsierra@el-bosque.org; Web site: http://madrid-sierra.el-bosque.org.

At the Spanish Slow Food Web site, www.slowfood.es (see below), you can search by city and click on "Donde dormir" (where to sleep) on the left side of the page to find accommodations serving slow food and with environmental considerations around Spain.

Eating and Food

Fresh, delicious, locally produced food is plentiful and inexpensive in Spain. Weekly markets and produce stands fill every town, along with *carnicerías* (butcher shops) and local food stores. The Slow Food movement is big in Spain. See the Spanish Slow Food Web site, www.slowfood.es, or the international Slow Food Web site, www.slowfood.com, for more information. You can search for information about restaurants and hotels committed to the ideals of Slow Food at the Spanish site: Look for "Donde comer" (Where to eat) on the left side of the page when you click on a city.

VEGETARIAN, ORGANIC, AND GLUTEN-FREE CHOICES

Vegetarians beware, as the pig is big in Spain. Spaniards pride themselves on eating every part of the pig, from ears to hooves. Take heart—there is also an abundance of beautiful produce and Spain-grown rice, as well as local cheeses and other delicious food.

In Spain, organic agriculture is called *agricultura ecológica* or *biológica,* or *eco* or *bio* for short. Food grown organically is certified as *bio* by one of Spain's organic certification organizations, including: Asociación Comité Andaluz de Agricultura Ecológica (CAAE) (www.caae.es); Asociación Vida Sana (www.vidasana.org); and Sohiscert-Ecocert Spain (www.sohiscert.com). Fair trade in Spain is certified by the Asociación del Sello de Productos de Comercio Justo (ASPCJ)—look for the green and blue Fair Trade/Comercio Justo label. ASPCJ, C/ Gaztambide, 50, bajo, 28015 Madrid; Tel: 915 433 399; e-mail: info@sellocomerciojusto.org; Web site: www.sellocomerciojusto.org.

HEALTH FOOD STORES

There are many small and large health food stores throughout Spain. Many medium- to large-size chain health food stores are region-specific, not nationwide. While not at all a health food store, El Corte Inglés, the largest general chain store in Spain, does sell some natural and organic foods in their supermarket (*supermercado*) departments. In fact, often their health food section is larger than local *herbolarios.* The health food sections in El Corte Inglés usually have an extensive gluten-free section as well as local, regional items. For instance,

Organic agriculture involves farming by certain standards, which include and promote environmental sustainability, biodiversity, animal welfare, improving soil fertility, and producing high-quality food. Organic farming is implemented without the use of synthetic pesticides, herbicides, fungicides or fertilizers, genetically modified organism (GMO) seeds, antibiotics, hormones, or processing with irradiation.

Countries have their own organic certification agencies. In Europe, some countries have four agencies, while others have as many as thirty-six different certification organizations monitoring and certifying organic food and other products. The Organic Consumers Association (OCA) is a nonprofit organization in the United States working on many issues including organic food and sustainable farming. See the OCA for extensive information and resources at www.organicconsumers.org. The following book provides additional information about organic farming.

Anna Kruger, ed., *Rodale's Illustrated Encyclopedia of Organic Gardening* (New York: DK Publishing, 2005).

in Galicia you will find local seaweeds. For travelers arriving late into cities, El Corte Inglés tends to be conveniently open until 9:00 or 10:00 p.m. Health food stores are called *bio-supermercados* or *eco-tiendas*. Some of the health food stores around Spain are listed below. Unlike France, which has organized databases of health food stores, as well as national health food store chains, Spain has no centralized information source or national health food store chains—probably a holdover from their ideals of workers' co-ops and anarchy.

Herbolarios are abundant throughout Spain, with close to a hundred in Madrid. They are usually virtually microscopic stores that offer a variety of dry goods, often with fine gluten-free offerings and other special diet needs, supplements, herbs, and body care products. They also often have someone in the front (or back) who will do health consultations and administer herbal formulas for what ails you.

At larger supermarkets with shopping carts be prepared with 1 euro coins as you will need these to access the cart. You insert the coin into a slot on or near the cart handle to release the cart from the chain lock. When you return the cart after shopping, reattach it to the other carts, usually by chain, and you will get your coin back—an ingenious way to keep the carts out of the street and parking lot.

Barcelona

At the Traveling Naturally Web site you can find a map of health food stores in Barcelona: www.travelingnaturally.com/golightlyguide-bookmapofbarcelonahealthfo or at Google Maps search for Green Earth Guide: Traveling Naturally in Spain: Barcelona Health Food Stores.

Veritas is a grocery store chain selling organic and natural products. They have twelve stores in Barcelona, and one each in the suburbs of Sant Cugat, Castelldefels, Manresa, Granollers, and Sitges. Most of the stores are open Monday to Saturday 9:15 a.m. to 9:15 p.m. One store is a block or so from the Jaume I Metro station on the border of the old part of Barcelona. Veritas, Via Laietana, 28, Barcelona; Tel: 932 688 200. For the other store locations go to the Web site, www.veritas.es, click on "Supermercats Veritas," and choose a store to click on for store address, phone number, Metro, hours, and map.

Nutridiet has two locations, both with a small, but excellent selection of natural and gluten-free foods. One is by the FC Barcelona Camp Nou stadium, C/ Francesc Layret, 14, Barcelona; Tel: 934 493 431; and one is by the Sants train station, C/ Sant Medir, 28, Barcelona; Tel: 933 396 626.

The Forn Mistral has been a bakery since 1879 and they now make a line of organic breads from whole grains, including kamut and spelt. Forn Mistral, Ronda de Sant Antoni, 96, 08001 Barcelona; Tel: 933 018 037; e-mail: info@fornmistral.com; Web site: www.fornmistral.com; Metro: Universitat.

Marsan stores have been selling organic food, natural cosmetics, and nutritional supplements since 1974. There are close to thirty stores in Barcelona, seemingly in every neighborhood. One store is conveniently located just four short blocks from La Rambla in the old part. You can find the other store locations at the Web site. Marsan Raval, Pintor Fortuny, 33, 08001 Barcelona; Tel: 933 028 426; Web site: www.centresmarsan.com.

There are also a number of health food stores listed at the Sin Carne (Without Meat) Web site: www.sincarne.net/barcelona-health-food-shops.htm.

Madrid

Santiveri is a chain of small health food and supplement stores, as well as a brand of products; Web site: www.santiveri.es/santiveriuk/index.html. In Madrid, there are a few stores, including one on Plaza Mayor: Santiveri, Plaza Mayor, 24, 28012 Madrid; Tel: 915 482 330. An *herbolario* in Madrid's Atocha train station sells some Santiveri items as well as gluten-free products: Auge 2000 Herbolario, Terminal AVE, Estación Atocha, Madrid; Tel: 915 391 897. And another store at Centro Comercial Gran Vía de Hortaleza, Madrid; Tel: 913 819 547.

Eco Bar & Spa sells gourmet natural foods from Spain and around the world with a great selection of organic olive oils and other delights. They also have a full-service restaurant, bar, and spa (around the corner). Eco Bar & Spa, Paseo Pintor Rosales, 76, 28008 Madrid; Tel: 915 441 716; e-mail: infoecobarspa.com; Web site: www.ecobarspa.com; Metro: Moncloa.

The NaturaSì natural supermarkets are large by Spanish standards. Do not expect a Whole Foods store, as these are not even close by comparison. However, the stores have everything you could need with mostly Spanish organic and natural products from meats, dairy, produce, and wines to a full array of dry goods. There are two stores in Madrid: NaturaSì el supermercado natural, C/ Doctor Fleming, 1 (next to Estadio Bernabéu), Madrid; Tel: 914 583 254; Web site: www.naturasi.es; Metro: Bernabéu or Cuzco; open Monday to Saturday 10:00 a.m. to 9:00 p.m. NaturaSì el supermercado natural, C/ Guzmán El Bueno, 28 (on the corner of Meléndez Valdés), Madrid; Tel: 915 445 663; Web site: www.naturasi.es; Metro: Argüelles or Moncloa; open Monday to Saturday 10:00 a.m. to 8:30 p.m.

Similar to the NaturaSì stores, Origen is a large health food store by Spanish standards. It is a full-service store, slightly lacking in gluten-free options, but plentiful in everything else. Origen, C/ Doctor Gómez Ulla, 16, 28028 Madrid; Tel: 902 102 087; Web site: www.supermercadoecologico.com; Metro: Manuel Becerra; open Monday to Saturday 10:00 a.m. to 8:30 p.m.

El Vergel is a large-for-Spain natural foods store selling a full range of products with a vegetarian restaurant below. El Vergel, Paseo de la Florida, 53, 28008 Madrid; Tel: 915 471 952; Web site: www.el-vergel.com; Metro: Príncipe Pío.

La Biotika, open since 1979, is a small health food store with a vegetarian and macrobiotic restaurant in the back. Located in the middle of Madrid, between C/ Santa María and C/ de las Huertas, two blocks from the C/ de Atocha (a main street in Madrid) and the Metro stop. La Biotika, Amor de Dios, 3, 28014 Madrid; Tel: 914 290 780; Web site: www.labiotika.es; Metro: Antón Martín.

Ventas Ecológicas is a health food store selling produce, a large selection of oils, and meats, and it supplies their adjacent organic foods restaurant. Ventas Ecológicas, C/ Virgen de la Alegría, nº 10, 3ª planta, 28027 Madrid; Tel: 913 266 000; e-mail: ventas@ventasecologicas.com; Web site: www.ventasecologicas.com; Metro: Ventas or El Carmen; the store is open Monday to Friday 9:00 a.m. to 2:00 p.m./5:00 to 8:00 p.m., Saturday 9:00 a.m. to 6:30 p.m.

Ecocentro is an organic foods store with an adjacent restaurant, selling organic and natural foods, books, and herbs. Ecocentro, C/ Esquilache, 2, 4 y 6 (at Avda. Pablo Iglesias, 2), 28003 Madrid; Tel: 915 535 502; e-mail: eco@ecocentro.es; Web site: www.ecocentro.es; Metro: Ríos Rosas; open every day 10:00 a.m. to 10:00 p.m.

A Salto de Mata sells organic and fair-trade foods and is an organization promoting responsible consumer habits and lifestyles. A Salto de Mata, C/ Doctor Fourquet, 17, Lavapiés, Madrid; Tel: 915 304 428; e-mail: info@asaltodemata.org; Web site: www.asaltodemata.org.

Madrid is also full of independent *herbolarios* and you will undoubtedly walk past any number of these as you wander through the city since there are about a hundred in Madrid.

Valencia

There are health food stores throughout Valencia, although the mother lode is the J. Navarro Terra Verda store in the old part of the city not far from the train station. It is large and beautiful, the closest you will find to a Whole Foods type store in Spain, with a particularly large selection of gluten-free products. They have produce, beauty products, bulk foods, cold and frozen, an extensive cheese selection, basically anything you could want, as well as a little café and eatery where you can drink fresh-squeezed organic orange juice (*zumo*). J. Navarro Terra Verda, C/ Arzobispo Mayoral, 20, Valencia; e-mail: info@terraverda.com; open Monday to Friday 9:00 a.m. to 8:15 p.m., Saturday 9:30 a.m. to 8:15 p.m.

There are tiny health food stores sprinkled throughout the city. Another store with a good selection is out by the university, Ecorganic Ecomercat. This store is not huge but has a good selection and variety of food including gluten-free, goat and sheep cheese, yogurt, organic produce, a tiny bit of organic meat, plenty of dry goods, body care, and more. Ecorganic Ecomercat, Avda. Blasco Ibáñez, 66, Valencia; Tel: 963 892 003; Web site: www.ecorganicweb.com; open Monday to Saturday 9:30 a.m. to 8:30 p.m. The closest Metro is Aragón. Out of the Metro, walk up a few blocks and take a right onto Avenida Blasco Ibáñez.

Terra Verda natural foods stores have many locations in Valencia and they also have stores in Alicante, Castellón, and Mallorca. See www.terraverda.com/tiendas for a complete list of stores. ☛ green earth guide favorite.

Two other health food store options in Valencia are: Esencial, behind the Mercado Central; Esencial Centro de Salud y Herbodietetica, c/ Calabazas 21, Valencia; Tel: 963 940 741; open Monday to Friday 10:00 a.m. to 2:00 p.m. /5:00 to 8:00 p.m.; Saturday 10:00 am to 2:00 p.m. And, Herboristeria Russafa, not far from the train station. Herbosteria Russafa, Ruzafa 34, Valencia; Tel: 963 734 258.

La Morhada is the organic stall at the Mercado Central—see "Farm Stands, Markets, and Local Products" later in this chapter.

An eco-guide to Valencia is available online at www.revistaeina.net with an extensive directory and an "EcoMapa," accessible by clicking on the left-hand side of the Web page, with listings of health food stores, restaurants, exercise centers, and more. Other free, print eco-guides to look for while in Valencia are the *Guía Verde Valencia,* produced quarterly, and *Gamana,* a bimonthly guide and mini-magazine.

Girona

Santiveri is a chain of health food stores as well as a brand of natural foods; Web site: www.santiveri.es/santiveriuk/index.html. They have a convenient little store on the Plaça Catalunya, at the beginning of the old part of the city, where you can find gluten-free and other snacks. There is no produce. Santiveri, Pz. Catalunya, 6, 17004 Girona; Tel: 972 204 215.

Cenciana sells a small variety of natural foods including some gluten-free options, but mostly sells personal care, herbal remedies, homeo-pathics, and supplements and is located a few blocks from the train station. Cenciana, Ronde Pare Claret, 15, 17001 Girona; Tel: 972 208 787.

0% Gluten has a stall in the Mercat del Lleó (see "Farm Stands, Markets, and Local Products") and is open the hours of the market until 2:00 p.m. Monday to Saturday. They sell all manner of gluten-free foods including divine pastries (palmiers, croissants, wafer cookies, cakes, and more), breads (especially good baguettes), mini pizzas, and more. This is pure heaven for the gluten-free consumer. 0% Gluten, Plaça Mercat del Lleó, nº 200, 17002 Girona; Tel: 972 200 814; e-mail: girona@zeropercentgluten.com; Web site: www.zeropercent-gluten.com.

Ufana Ecomercats has stores in Girona, Figueres, Banyoles, and Olot. These stores are large by Spanish standards and lovely. They are stocked with everything you could want including organic produce. In Girona the Ufana store is a few blocks from the Mercat del Lleó and the old city, and about four blocks east of the RENFE train station. Ufana Ecomercats, Cr. de la Rutlla, 15-17, 17003 Girona; Tel: 972 206 056; Web site: www.ufana.com; open Monday to Saturday 9:30 a.m. to 1:30 p.m./4:30 to 8:00 p.m.

BioSpirit is a medium-size full-service health food and organic foods store with produce as well. Bright and light, it is south of the city center about four blocks from the Nana Bio store listed below and the

B-12 Cafè-Bar. Tienda BioSpirit, C/ Marquès de Caldes de Montbui, 114, 17003 Girona; Tel: 972 201 594; open Monday to Friday
10:00 a.m. to 2:30 p.m./4:30 to 8:30 p.m., Saturday 10:00 a.m. to
3:00 p.m.

The Nana Biosupermercats have six stores throughout the region.
They have an excellent selection of gluten-free, organic, and natural foods, as well as all manner of natural products from clothes and
books to personal care. The Nana stores are large by Spain standards,
and the one in Girona is south of the city center but is only about
a ten-minute walk from the train station. Nana Biosupermercat, C/
Migdia, 95 (corner of C/ Joan Regià), 17003 Girona; Tel 972 426
405; e-mail: info@nana.cat; Web site: www.nana.cat; open Monday
to Saturday 10:00 a.m. to 2:00 p.m./4:30 to 8:30 p.m.

Marsan Girona is a beautiful new store one block into the old city
from the main Rambla de la Libertat. You can learn more about the
Centres Marsan chain of health food stores at the Web site and find
other store locations. Marsan Girona, Mercaders, 6, Girona; Tel: 972
483 962; Web site: www.centresmarsan.com; open Monday to Friday 10:00 a.m. to 1:30 p.m./4:30 to 8:30 p.m., Saturday 10:00 a.m.
to 1:30 p.m.

Bonàpat is well south of the city center and while there may be a
bus that heads out that way, a car is the best bet to reach this medium-size store selling gourmet and natural foods, as well as prepared foods. Bonàpat, C/ de Barcelona, 215, 17003 Girona; Web
site: www.clubgurmetbonapat.cat; open Monday to Saturday 10:00
a.m. to 10:30 p.m., Sunday 11:00 a.m. to 4:00 p.m.

Costa Brava

L'Escala has two little health food stores around a block from each
other. The larger is lovely Espai Holistic, a long, bright *bio-botiga,*
selling foods, body care, household care and supplements. Espai Holistic, C/ Germans Masferrer, 41, 17130 L'Escala; Tel: 972 776 917;
e-mail: info@espaiholistic.com; Web site: www.espaiholistic.com;
open Tuesday to Saturday 10:00 a.m. to 1:00 p.m./4:00 to 7:30
p.m.

Saó Herbolari is fully around the block from Espai and is a smaller
store, but offers some organic produce and a greater selection of

herbs. They also sell organic wine. Saó Herbolari, C/ del Port, 36, 17170 L'Escala; Tel: 972 774 804; e-mail: sao@pangea.org; Web site: www.pangea.org/sao/ingles.html; open Tuesday to Friday 10:00 a.m. to 1:30 p.m./5:00 to 8:00 p.m., Monday and Saturday 10:00 a.m. to 1:30 p.m., closed Sunday.

Torroella de Montgrí has a serviceable market intertwined through the narrow streets of the old center on Monday mornings with vegetables in the plaza, and the rest is unexceptional clothing. On the street C/ Primitiu Artigas are two little food stores of note. One is Seli Carnisseria, a charcuterie with fresh meats, fish, and local and gourmet food items including local salt, sheep yogurt, and olive oil. The second is La Farigola Dietética, a small health food store with local, organic, and gluten-free goods including Spanish fruit jams with just fruit (no sugar), goat yogurt, teas, personal care items, but no produce. La Farigola Dietética, C/ Primitiu Artigas, 10, Torroella de Montgrí; Tel: 972 757 122. On the main avenue from which you enter in to the old city center, you can find Forn de Pa Artesa, a small bakery selling fresh breads, and a small selection of fair-trade (*comercio justo*) food items. A block down from that is Esnutrient: Salute es vida (Health is life) a tiny, almost microscopic health food store.

In Figueres there are two health food stores. Ufana Ecomercats is a lovely, bright health food store with a good range of organic options from produce to wines and liquor, to meats, and all manner of grains and other food. Ufana Ecomercats is located on the south end of Figueres as you enter from the C-31 road. Ufana Ecomercats, Cr. Nou, 173, 17600 Figueres; Tel: 972 672 969; Web site: www.ufana. com; open Monday to Friday 10:00 a.m. to 1:30 p.m./5:00 to 8:30 p.m., Saturday 10:00 a.m. to 1:30 p.m.

Les Bones Herbes, considered an *herboristería,* as well as a dietetic and health food store, has two locations in Figueres. One is a block away from La Rambla into the old town and the other is half a block down from La Rambla at the other end. The Caamaño store has a larger selection of food, including goat yogurt in glass jars and a large selection of gluten-free foods. Les Bones Herbes, C/ Besalú, 7 (in the old center a couple of blocks from the Museo Dalí), 17600 Figueres, Tel: 972 674 135; and C. Caamaño, 8, 17600 Figueres, Tel: 972 670 407; e-mail: info@bonesherbes.com; Web site: www.bonesherbes. com/ingles/index.html.

Look for the Nana Biosupermercats, a chain of six stores throughout the Costa Brava–Girona region. The Nana stores have an excellent selection of gluten-free, organic, and natural foods, as well as all manner of natural products from clothes and books to personal care. In Palamós, the store is the mother of health food stores in a large area stretching from L'Escala down to Palamós. This is where you can do some serious food shopping. In Palamós, Nana Biosupermercat, Av. Cataluyna, 5 (on the main avenue if you follow the signs for the city center and a few blocks from the old part), 17230 Palamós; Tel: 972 600 675; open Monday to Friday 9:00 a.m. to 1:30 p.m./4:30 to 8:00 p.m., Saturday 9:00 a.m. to 1:30 p.m./5:00 to 8:30 p.m., closed Sunday. In Platja d'Aro, Nana Biosupermercat, Av. Castell d'Aro, 62, 17250 Platja d'Aro; Tel: 972 825 085. See the "Girona" section above for information about the Girona store. In Olot, Nana Biosupermercat, C/ Pou de Glaç, 27, 17800 Olot; Tel: 972 273 952; Web site: www.nana.cat. ☛ green earth guide favorite.

Ufana Ecomercats has stores in Girona, Figueres, Banyoles, and Olot. These stores are not large, but lovely and larger than many of the other health food stores in the area. They are stocked with everything you could want including organic produce. See above for the Figueres and Girona locations. Ufana Ecomercats, Crta. Camós, 79, 17820 Banyoles; Tel: 972 582 907. Ufana Ecomercats, Cr. Pare Roca, 8, 17800 Olot; Tel: 972 272 103; Web site: www.ufana.com.

In La Bisbal d'Empordà, there are two health food options, as well as the organic produce stand at the Friday market. Bisbal Natura, a medium-size, full-service health food store, is found easily just across the street behind the Castell Palau and the Plaça del Castell. Bisbal Natura, C/ Cavallers, 36, 17100 La Bisbal d'Empordà; Tel: 972 645 042; open Monday to Saturday 9:00 a.m. to 1:00 p.m./5:00 to 8:30 p.m., Saturday 9:00 a.m. to 1:00 p.m.

Eduard Casas is the lovely and friendly proprietor of Can Temporada, a store filled with organic and local specialty items including octopus and other local fish delicacies prepared without additives and chemicals. Can Temporada, C/ de la Rierra (off the Plaça Major), 12, 17100 La Bisbal d'Empordà; Tel: 972 640 796; e-mail: eduard.cypsela@microdatta.com; Web site: www.totbisbal.com/pg/detallsPg.php?pIdEmpresa=243; open Monday to Saturday 10:00 a.m. to 1:30 p.m./5:00 to 8:30 p.m.

Basque Country
Bilbao

Bio-Bio is a lovely full-service health food store with produce, refrigerated items, dry goods, body care, and some natural house products including Livos natural paints, conveniently located within walking distance of the RENFE train station and the city center. Bio-Bio, Elcano, 25, 48008 Bilbao; Tel: 944 210 362; open Monday to Friday 10:00 a.m. to 8:00 p.m., Saturday 10:00 a.m. to 2:00 p.m.

EquiNatur is a small but not tiny health food store selling organic food and offering some health services including massage. EquiNatur, General Eguía, 1, 48010 Bilbao; Tel: 944 447 624; open Monday to Friday 9:00 a.m. to 1:30 p.m./4:30 to 8:00 p.m., Saturday 9:00 a.m. to 1:30 p.m.

Ekodenda: Ekologikoak ("organic food" in Basque) feels like a mini co-op and sells produce, dry goods, body care, but no gluten-free items. You have to find those around the corner at the Centro Internacional de Dietética y Nutrición Herboristería (see next entry). Ekodenda, C/ Carmelo Gil, nº 3, Ametzola, Bilbao; Tel: 944 434 362; open Monday to Friday 10:00 a.m. to 1:30 p.m./5:00 to 7:45 p.m.

This jam-packed store has a good gluten-free section and lots of supplements. Centro Internacional de Dietética y Nutrición Herboristería, Av. Autonomía, Bilbao; open Monday to Friday 10:00 a.m. to 2:00 p.m./5:00 to 8:00 p.m., Saturday 10:00 a.m. to 1:30 p.m.

The Ceres Herbolario is pretty tiny, bordering on microscopic, but packed with items. Ceres Herbolario, Pablo Alzola, 2, 48012 Bilbao; Tel: 944 270 693; open Monday to Saturday 10:00 a.m. to 1:30 p.m./4:30 to 8:00 p.m., Tuesday 5:00 to 8:00 p.m., closed Saturday.

Located in the old part of Bilbao (Casco Viejo) is Ekologistak Martxan, an organic and natural foods store. Ekologistak Martxan Ekodenda, C/ Pelota, Nº 5, 48005 Bilbao; Tel: 944 790 119; e-mail: bizkaia@ekologistakmartxan.org; Web site: www.ekologistakmartxan.org/45.html; open Monday to Friday 9:30 a.m. to 1:30 p.m./5:30 to 9:30 p.m.

San Sebastián (Donostia)

In the old part of San Sebastián, across the street from the Mercado de la Bretxa is Gastronomía Aitor Lasa, a store full of products from the local area including all manner of cheese including the local specialty, Idiazábal sheep cheese, shellfish (frozen), cider, fresh apples, and jars of delicacies. Gastronomía Aitor Lasa, C/ Aldamar, 12, 20005 Donostia; Tel: 943 430 354; open Monday to Friday 8:30 a.m. to 2:00 p.m./5:15 to 8:00 p.m., Saturdays 8:30 a.m. to 2:30 p.m.

Galparsoro, a bakery since 1933, sells *artesanal* and organic baked goods in the old part of the city. A small modern store, it mixes the old with the new, storing the bread in large, old baskets. A sign in the window proudly displays Nekazaritza Ekologikoa, Basque for *agricultura ecológica* or organic agriculture. Galparsoro Okindegia, Nagusia, 6, Donostia/San Sebastián; Tel: 943 421 074; open Monday to Friday 8:00 a.m. to 2:00 p.m./4:30 to 8:00 p.m.

Forua is a decent-size health food store in the Egia neighborhood by the park and RENFE train station. Forua Alimentación Biológica-Dietética-Belardenda, Egia, 9, 20012 San Sebastián; Tel: 943 292 186.

Galicia
Bio Centro Eira is in the old part of Santiago just minutes from the cathedral and is a medium-size health food store selling a good assortment of natural and local foods. Bio Centro Eira, Rúa Nova, 5, bajo, Santiago de Compostela; Tel: 981 573 971; open Monday to Friday 10:00 a.m. to 2:00 p.m./4:30 to 8:30 p.m., Saturday 10:00 a.m. to 2:00 p.m.

Herbonature sells a variety of cosmetics, perfumes, *herbolario,* and *dietética* foods including gluten-free, and natural foods. The store is across from the Cee covered market and is about 10 km from Fisterra and minutes from Corcubión. Herbonature, C/ Estatuto de Autonomía de Galicia (across from the new mercado), 3, 15270 Cee; Tel: 981 706 019; open Monday to Friday 10:00 a.m. to 1:00 p.m./4:30 to 8:00 p.m.

Andalucía
Granada
Down the lane from the Oasis Backpackers' Hostel in the old part of Granada on the very Kasbah-like old street of Calderería Nueva there is the Eco Tienda el Panadero Lico, a small health food store selling

dry goods and fresh baked treats. Eco Tienda el Panadero Lico, Calderería Nueva, 14, 18010 Granada; Tel: 958 229 279; open Monday to Friday 10:00 a.m. to 2:00 p.m./5:30 to 8:30 p.m., Saturday 10:00 a.m. to 2:00 p.m.

La Charca is a small but well-stocked store in the tiny Placeta de la Charca, in the old Albayzín district of Granada, that sells some local products from the Alpujarra mountain towns. Lovely Hatha (pronounced Hata) is the proprietor. There is a weekday morning market down the street in the Plaza Larga. La Charca, C/ Horno de San Agustín, Granada; Tel: 958 289 797; open Monday to Friday 10:00 a.m. to 2:00 p.m./5:00 to 8:30 p.m., Saturday 10:00 a.m. to 2:00 p.m.

For a range of local, Spanish food items including cheeses there are various *charcuterías* including Jamones Casa Diego, C/ Santa Escolástica, 13, Granada; Tel: 958 227 091; e-mail: info@jamonescasadiego.com; Web site: www.jamonescasadiego.com.

Córdoba

Almocafre feels like the mother of health food stores even though it is not that large. It is a cooperative market and has beautiful produce, goat and cow dairy, fresh baked breads, and every kind of food, mostly organic from Spain. It is easy to get to from the *mezquita* area. Walk to the Puerta Sevilla, cross the major Avenida Conde Vallellano, walk down Custódios for two blocks, and Almocafre is set back on the right. Almocafre, Avda. de los Custodios, nº 5, 14004 Córdoba; Tel: 957 414 050; e-mail: almocafre@almocafre.com; Web site: www.almocafre.com; open Monday to Friday 10:00 a.m. to 1:30 p.m./6:00 to 8:00 p.m., Saturday 10:00 a.m. to 1:30 p.m.
☛ green earth guide favorite.

Ecotienda Planeta Azul is combination health food store, esoteric bookstore, and alternative health center. Food items are organic and natural. There is no produce and only a minute amount of refrigerated items so there are mostly dry goods, natural body products, books, and an array of natural therapies offered including various massage modalities and yoga. If you are in the old city, make your way to the Puerta de Almodóvar on the west edge of the Judería (Jewish quarter), cross the mildly harrowing traffic circle—you must go to one end of it or the other—and a few blocks down is Alcalde

Velasco Navarro. Ecotienda Planeta Azul, C/ Alcalde Velasco Navarro, 1, 1º C, 14004 Ciudad Jardín neighborhood of Córdoba; Tel: 957 468 057; e-mail: ecotiendaplanetazul@hotmail.com; Web site: www.ecotiendaplanetaazul.com.

Two Comercio Justo (Fair Trade) stores provide a supplement to the natural foods options. El Reposo de Bagdad-Comercio Justo is a tiny store selling fair-trade goods with a small selection of foods including refreshing orange-mango juice in the old city near the Puerta de Almodóvar. El Reposo de Bagdad-Comercio Justo, C/ Fernández Ruano, 21, 14003 Córdoba; Tel: 957 294 793.

The other store is much larger and is on a main street across from the Roman columns: Comercio Justo, C/ Claudio Marcelo, Córdoba; open Monday to Friday 10:00 a.m. to 2:00 p.m./5:00 to 8:30 p.m., Saturday 10:30 a.m. to 2:30 p.m./5:00 to 8:30 p.m.

El Edén is a sister store to La Gloria in Málaga selling a small variety of supplements, foods including gluten-free, and body care products. El Edén, C/ Escritor Gonzalo Serrano, 3, 14006 Córdoba in the Santa Rosa neighborhood; Tel: 957 272 484.

Sevilla
La Ortiga Cooperativa is a consumer cooperative for ecological products, but anyone can shop at the store. It is a great store offering a full range of natural and organic products from produce and dry goods, to frozen and refrigerated items, Spanish organic wines, olive oils, and body care. It is a little off the beaten track but does not take long to walk there from the old center near Plaza Encarnación. La Ortiga Cooperativa, C/ Cristo del Buen Fin, nº 4, 41002 Sevilla; Tel: 954 906 306; e-mail: correo@laortiga.com; Web site: www.laortiga.com; open Monday to Friday 10:30 a.m. to 2:00 p.m./6:00 to 9:00 p.m., Saturday 10:30 a.m. to 2:00 p.m.

Biotienda is a small store selling books, body care, natural remedies, esoterica, and organic and natural foods. It is located down the block from a post office and one block from the Bus 32 bus stop heading from the Sevilla RENFE train station toward Plaza Encarnación. Biotienda, C/ Lope de Vega, 15, 41003 Sevilla; Tel: 954 534 048; a second location at Pamplona, 56, 41014 Sevilla; Tel: 954 693 973; open Monday, Tuesday, Wednesday, and Friday 9:45 a.m. to 1:30

p.m./5:30 to 8:30 p.m., Thursday 10:00 a.m. to 2:00 p.m./4:00 to 9:00 p.m., and Saturday 9:30 a.m. to 2:00 p.m.

The Gaia health food store is partnered with the Gaia Eco Bar listed under "Restaurants." It is a medium-size health food store on a main street in Sevilla. It has a limited selection of gluten-free products, but you will find enough to get by. It has some produce as well as a small refrigerated section with organic Manchego cheese made from sheep milk. Centro Gaia Tienda Ecológica, C/ Arjona, 5, Sevilla; Tel: 954 561 831; Web site: www.gaiaecosalud.com; open Monday to Friday 10:00 a.m. to 2:00 p.m./5:30 to 8:30 p.m., Saturday 10:00 a.m. to 2:00 p.m.

La Casa de la Salud (house of health) has a small selection of food items, body care, and quite a few herbs. A sweet Spanish woman runs it who speaks no English—be prepared with your phrase book. La Casa de la Salud, Lda. Rosa Ma Gallardo, 4, Sevilla, just below Plaza Encarnación toward Plaza Salvador in the old part.

The Sattva Herbolario is a small store with mostly dry goods and supplements. They have a good variety of gluten-free products and some fresh-baked gluten-free bread. They are conveniently located a couple of blocks from the large Plaza Nueva. Sattva Herbolario, C/ Zaragoza, 18 (just west of Plaza Nueva), Sevilla; open Monday to Friday 9:30 a.m. to 1:30 p.m./5:00 to 8:30 p.m., and Saturday 9:30 a.m. to 1:30 p.m.

La Carmella Fresca Frutas, directly across the street from the indoor, covered market, Mercado del Arenal, sells fresh produce and has a tienda ecológica (organic store) section. They also make fresh juice (*zumo*). La Carmella, C/ Pastor y Landero, 23-25, Sevilla; Tel: 954 220 330.

Málaga
La Gloria is a medium-size store a block from the main boulevard. La Gloria, C/ Panaderos, 10, 29005 Málaga; Tel: 952 608 537; open in winter Monday to Friday 9:00 a.m. to 8:30 p.m., Saturday 9:30 a.m. to 2:30 p.m., and in the summer Monday to Friday 9:00 a.m. to 9:00 p.m., Saturday 9:30 a.m. to 2:30 p.m.

Cuídate is a tiny store, conveniently located a block from the Plaza del Mercado, with a limited selection of goods and limited hours.

Cuídate, C/ Victoria, 10 (just off Plaza del Mercado), Málaga; Tel: 952 225 003; e-mail: cuidate@cuidate.com; Web site: www.cuidate.com; open noon to 2:00 p.m./6:00 to 8:00 p.m.

BioNatura has been in the nearby towns of Marbella and Fuengirola for twelve years selling organic produce and other natural foods. Bio-Natura, Avda. Los Boliches, 112, Los Boliches-Fuengirola; Tel: 952 660 757; e-mail: info@bionatura.es; Web site: www.bionatura.es.

BioNatura, C/ Félix Rodríguez de la Fuente, s/n, Edif. Berrocal, 29600 Marbella; Tel: 952 900 401; e-mail: info@bionatura.es; Web site: www.bionatura.es.

Eco Tienda Pura Vida in Gaucín sells breakfast and organic food and drink from 9:00 a.m. to 3:00 p.m., open Monday to Saturday 10:00 a.m. to 3:00 p.m.; in summer Tuesday to Friday 6:00 to 9:00 p.m. Eco Tienda Pura Vida, C/ Convento, 166, Gaucín, 29480 Málaga; Tel: 952 151 369.

Other Regions

For other health food stores and groceries around Spain by region check out www.celiacos.org (see below in "Special Diets"); www.Holistika.net is a comprehensive guide to eco and organic services. Point your cursor at "Nutrición" in the upper center bar for the drop-down menu and choose "Alimentos ecológicos," where you will find healthy food around Spain listed by province. You can also click on "Guías" at the far right and choose "Ecotiendas."

FARM STANDS, MARKETS, AND LOCAL PRODUCTS

Most towns and cities around Spain have markets. Check at the tourist office in the city or town where you are staying for the days, times, and locations of the local markets. Also look under the "Organic Farms" section for farm stands, and under "Markets" and "City and Regional Highlights" for other market listings.

In Barcelona, La Boqueria is one of the largest covered markets in Europe with fresh food galore. The Web site provides a color-coded map of the market by type of food and product. The site also offers a history of this vibrant market from its origins in 1200 until the present day. Mondays are not known for the freshest goods but every other day is full of fresh fish and a bounty of other foods—every part of every kind of animal from hoof to tongue, as well as fruits and vegetables from floor to ceiling. La Boqueria is like a living museum—not to be missed. La Boqueria, Plaça de la Boqueria, off of La Rambla, 08001 Barcelona; Tel: 933 182 584; Web site: www.boqueria.info/Eng/index.php; Metro: Liceu; open Monday to Saturday 8:00 a.m. to 8:00 p.m. (20:00), closed Sunday.

Markets in the Girona Region of Catalunya

Mondays: Cadaqués, Colera, Blanes, Olot, Santa Coloma de Farners, Osor, Riudellots de la Selva, Montellà i Martinet, and Torroella de Montgri.

Tuesdays: Besalú, Caldes de Malavella, Girona, Hostalric, Lloret de Mar, Palamós, Pals, Castello d'Empúries, Figueres, Campdevànol, Sant Joan les Fonts, Bordils, Becanó, and Verges.

In the city of Girona there are two markets. In the winter months from September to June the Mercat de les Ribes del Ter is held on the banks of the Ter River at the northwest side of the Parc de la Devesa. In the summer months from June to September the market is along the south end of the Parc de la Devesa. Winter and summer the market is open Tuesday and Saturday mornings until 1:30 p.m. The Mercat de les Ribes del Ter is a large market full of clothes, household items, and food, but no used items.

Girona city's permanent covered food market, Mercat del Lleó, is open Monday to Friday 5:30 a.m. to 1:30 p.m., and Saturday 5:00 a.m. to 2:00 p.m. Fruit and vegetable stalls line outside of the covered Mercat del Lleó on Tuesday and Saturday mornings.

Wednesdays: Amer, Begur, Banyoles, Sarrià de Ter, Sant Antoni de Calonge, Sant Pere Pescador, Maçanet de Cabrenys, Maçanet de la Selva, Flaçà, Salt, Sarrià de Ter, Cervià de Ter, Cassà de la Selva, and Llanç.

Thursdays: Alp, Beliver de Cerdanya, L'Estartit, Calonge, Figueres, Vidreres, Riudarenes, La Cellera de Ter, Llagostera, Sant Julià del Llor i Bonmatí, Llívia, Sant Pau de Segúries, and Tossa de Mar.

Fridays: La Bisbal d'Empordà, Sils, Castell-Platja d'Aro, Porqueres, Celrà, Salt, Les Planes d'Hostoles, Platja d'Aro, Molló, El Port de la Selva, and Portbou.

La Bisbal d'Empordà is a great, large market. The highlight is the organic farm stand with a large selection of truly delicious and beautiful fruits and vegetables, organic olive oil, and organic wine, the best bottle of which will set you back 6 euros.

Saturdays: Empuriabrava, Figueres, Vilafant, Girona, Cassà de la Selva, Llívia, Ribes de Freser, Ripoll, Santa Cristina d'Aro, Riells i Viabrea, Santa Coloma de Farners, Castellfollit de la Roca, La Canya, Sant Jaume de Llierca, and Sant Feliu de Pallerols.

A market dedicated to organic products of all kinds is the Mercat Ecològic held in Sant Martí Vell, near Flaçá, starting at about 9:30 a.m. on the second Saturday of the month, with organic food, divine honey, fruits and vegetables, wines, oils, oysters, meat, breads, and other goods including the Valle de Brezos eco-honey (see the Palafrugell market below) in the Plaça de l'Església (Plaza of the Church). Park on the hill where you will see other cars and walk into the village, moving toward the church, which looms above everything else. Sant Martí Vell is northeast of Girona city. EcoVilosa is the Agrobotiga that has the organic produce stall at the La Bisbal market and is based in Sant Martí Vell. EcoVilosa, Francesc Planellas Moradell, Sant Martí Vell; Tel: 908 835 591; e-mail: ecovilos@intercom.es.

Sundays: Arbúcies, Anglès, Breda, Camprodon, Palafrugell, Puigcerdà, Roses, Bàscara, L'Escala, La Jonquera, Sant Feliu de Guíxols, Sant Gregori, Fornells de la Selva, Sant Hilari Sacalm, and Sant Joan de les Abadesses.

The L'Escala market is small with very limited food and not so worth the trip, but it does have a few fun, inexpensive clothes and household items. The other extreme is the Sunday market in Palafrugell, which is enormous and crammed with people even in the winter months. Within the Sunday outdoor market, the small, daily covered market for meat, Mercat de Carne, adjacent to an open-air, covered vegetable and fruit market connected to the fresh fish covered market are open Sunday mornings to greet the crowds of people who come to Palafrugell for the Sunday street market lining the sidewalks of the old town off the Plaça Nova. In the *bio* realm, there is a man who collects honey from hives in the natural park, which is unsprayed and *ecológico*. He has around ten varieties of honey, but the primo one is his *miel de brezos* (honey from heather). He claims it has the most nutrients. I can attest to its having the most incredible rich flavor, as if a chef had prepared some wonderful confection, which those bees certainly did. He also sells homemade pizza with vegetables, mushrooms, and olives. The dark-chocolate-covered pine nut balls he makes are delicious. Look for his stand with honey, pizza, and chocolate balls. His honey is labeled Valle de Brezos—ecoflor (Valley of Heather—wild flowers). Valle de Brezos honey is also sold at the Sant Martí Vell Organic Market listed above. A variety of organic honeys can be purchased online from ecoflor at www.ecoflores. com. ☛ green earth guide favorite.

On a street on the other side of the Plaça you can find a small booth selling organic chocolates and teas, but no sign of the delightful organic fruit and vegetable vendor from the La Bisbal d'Empordà market on Friday (see above). However, in the covered Carne (meat) Mercat there is a health food stall, BioHera, unfortunately not open on Sundays. Although I am sure that Palafrugell gets its fair share of tourists in the warmer months, it is clearly a "real" people's town. The streets are full of Spaniards and the stores cater to Spaniards doing their weekly shopping.

Andalucía Region

On any day of the week there are markets going on in some neighborhood (*barrio*) of Málaga. The same holds true for towns surrounding Málaga. A sampling of the markets in the area include Mondays in Marbella; Tuesdays in Nerja and Fuengirola; Thursdays in Torre del Mar; Saturdays in Marbella and Fuengirola again; and Sundays in Ronda, Nerja, Antequera, Fuengirola, and Málaga.

In Córdoba the Mercado de la Corredera is open every morning except Monday, from 8:30 a.m. to 2:00 p.m. Ignore the enticing stall named Consumo Ecológico, since it is permanently closed, but you can happily find all they had offered and a lot more at the above-listed Almocafre store. For fresh fruit and vegetables, flowers, and other items at reasonable prices, go to the Sunday street market at El Arenal.

Basque Region

In Bilbao the massive covered Mercado de la Ribera, located in the old part of town (Casco Viejo), has an organic vegetable stand by the main door. The Ribera stop on the tram is right across the street from the market. In the winter from September 16 to June 14 the market is open Monday to Thursday 8:00 a.m. to 2:00 p.m./4:30 to 7:00 p.m., Friday until 7:30 p.m., Saturday 8:00 a.m. to 2:30 p.m. Summer hours are slightly different. Web site: www.mercadodelaribera.com.

Monday morning is the big market day in Gernika for Basque local products sold with the Eusko label of origin. The market is a few blocks from the Peace Museum and train station. Look for cheese, cider, honey, beans, kiwis, peppers, and *txakoli,* a Basque white wine.

South of San Sebastián in the Basque Country on the edge of the Sierra de Aralar, the town of Ordizia holds a large market filled with Basque products every Wednesday in a large square.

The market in Vitoria is on Thursdays in Plaza de Abastos.

Navarra Region
In Pamplona the Mercado de Santo Domingo is the oldest of Pamplona's markets, held behind the city hall in Plaza de Santiago.

Galicia Region
Weekly market days in Fisterra are Tuesday and Friday; in Laxe every Friday; in Malpica every Saturday; in Cee every Sunday; in Carnota every Sunday; other Costa da Morte towns have markets less regularly.

In Santiago de Compostela the Mercado de Abastos de Santiago is held in the Praza de Abastos in the old town. Open Monday to Saturday 8:30 a.m. to 2:00 p.m. Mercado de Abastos de Santiago, Web site: www.mercadodeabastosdesantiago.com.

Valencia Region
There are twenty-four municipal markets throughout the city, the largest of which is the Mercado Central, a beautiful, enormous, covered market with seemingly hundreds of stalls. Open Monday to Saturday 7:30 a.m. to 2:30 p.m. Web site: www.mercadocentralvalencia.es. Look for the organic stall, La Morhada, at stall number 225-227 with good organic produce and a small variety of dry goods and refrigerated items. La Morhada is open Monday to Saturday from 8:00 a.m. to 2:30 p.m.; Web site: www.lamorhada.com. There are also outdoor street markets throughout the region and the city in dif-

ferent neighborhoods (*barrios*) every day of the week, including the Mercado de la Plaza Redonda on Sundays all year long.

Asturias Region

In the capital, Oviedo, the market, Mercado del Fontán, known as La Plaza, is held every Thursday and Saturday at the La Plaza del Fontán.

Local Specialties

In addition to plentiful markets, Spain has numerous stores selling a variety of local specialties. One such business is Morera Agrocomerç, comprising nine stores in the Catalunya region selling local and organic products. Visit the Web site for a full listing of store locations. Morera Agrocomerç, C/ Verge del Carme, 1, Olot; Tel: 972 261 587; and Ctra. Palafrugell, 10, Girona; Tel: 972 218 791; e-mail morera@ morera.net; Web site: www.morera.net.

In Barcelona countless stores exist selling regional specialties. One such store, a block behind La Rambla, Granja Viader is a nonsmoking café, as well as a gourmet and local foods store. Granja M. Viader, C/ Xucla, 6, Barcelona; open Tuesday to Saturday 9:00 a.m. to 1:45 p.m./5:00 to 8:45 p.m., Monday 5:00 to 8:00 p.m., closed Sundays, holidays, and Monday mornings.

Local produce and products are quite abundant and easy to find in Spain. Look for the delicious Manchego sheep cheese from the Castilla-La Mancha region; Idiazábal, a smoked sheep cheese from the Basque Country; and olives, a Spanish bounty. Like *mâche* in France, *escarola* is a common, bountiful, and cheap green that makes wonderful salads—a 16-inch-diameter head costs only 1 euro!

Pata negra, literally "black hoof/leg," is a Spanish delicacy. The black pigs are native, descended from wild boars that roamed Spain's peninsula. Officially called Iberian jamón bellota (*bellota* means acorn), these free-range black pigs live on acorns from cork trees and other wild plants. *Pata negra* has no resemblance to American ham; rather, it is leaner, denser, and has a rich, distinct taste. Be prepared for sticker shock as prices range from $100 to $170/pound depending on whether it is boneless or not. If someone offers you some, don't pass up the chance to taste it!

Although not usually associated with Spain, there are numerous truf-

Biológico(a) or *ecológico(a)* = organic

Leche = milk

Huevo = egg

Pan = bread

Pollo de corral = free-range chicken

Queso = cheese; *queso de cabra* = goat cheese; *queso de oveja* = sheep cheese

Miel = honey

Aceite de oliva = olive oil

Sal = salt

Vino = wine—red wine is *vino tinto;* white is *vino blanco*

Aceite esencial = essential oil

Hecho en España = Made in Spain

Azafrán = saffron

Pimientos = peppers

Naranja = orange

Herbs: thyme = *tomillo* (in Catalan, farigola); rosemary = *romero* (in Catalan, romaní); basil = *albahaca* (in Catalan, alfàbrega); oregano = *orégano* (in Catalan, *orenga*); sage = *salvia* (same in Catalan); mint = *menta* (same in Catalan)

Ajo = garlic

Higos = figs

Tés = teas: *menta* = mint, *tila* = lime blossom, *manzanilla* = chamomile

fle plantations in Spain. The largest truffle plantation in the world is in Navaleno, a village in the Abejar area near Soria, north of Madrid, where there are almost 1,500 acres of holm oaks that produce black truffles, called *trufa negra de Soria.* Truffles grown in Spain include the *Tuber melanosporum* and the *Tuber brumale,* both harvested between December and March, and the *Tuber aestivum,* harvested from May to December. Truffles are sold in markets and specialty stores in the region and in Catalunya, including La Boqueria in Barcelona, but be prepared for sticker shock as the going price is around 850 euros per kilogram, or about $425/pound.

For more information about the delights of truffles, including recipes, see the book *Truffles* by Elizabeth Luard (London: Frances Lincoln, 2006).

The León region is known for its abundant mushrooms of all kinds. See "City and Regional Highlights" for information about León's mushroom picking routes.

Galicia is known for its fish and seafood. One specialty is octopus, commonly prepared by boiling or grilling, served with olive oil and paprika (made from red bell or chili peppers), called *pulpo a la Gallega*. Another Galician delicacy is small pancakes filled with apple cream and sorbet made from *orujo* (grape skin liqueur) called *filloas rellenas de crema y manzana con sorbete de orujo*.

L'Escala, on the eastern Costa Brava, is considered the anchovy capital, and the anchovies packed in olive oil and salt are the best I have ever tasted—especially divine on toasted bread with garlic and tomato rubbed on the bread and then an anchovy on top, a local specialty often served as an appetizer. Anxoves de L'Escala can be found at www.anxovesdelescala.es.

Embotits La Gleva makes organic sausage called *secallona*. Embotits La Gleva, C/ Marqués de Palmerola, 29, 08508 La Gleva-Vic (Barcelona); Tel: 938 570 138; e-mail: embotits@lagleva.com; Web site: www.lagleva.com/lagleva/eindex.htm.

Saffron, *azafrán* in Spanish, has been grown in Spain for centuries and is a delicacy worldwide. One source of organic saffron, certified organic by CCPAE, is grown for Safinter SA, C/ Teodoro Roviralta, 21-23, 08022 Barcelona; Tel: 932 120 422; e-mail: info@safinter.com; Web site: www.safinter.com.

Look for *pimentón* peppers that seem to be at every market and local foods store. The smoked paprika comes in three types—dulce is sweet, agridulce is bittersweet, and picante is hot.

Cava is a Spanish, sparkling white wine made the same way as French champagne. *Cava* is available all over Spain, but most of the producers are in the eastern, Catalunya region of Spain. Look for the four-pointed star at the base of the cork, which denotes true *cava*.

Varieties range from sweet (*dulce*) to very dry (*extra brut*). See "Organic Vineyards and Wines" for more information.

Olive oil in Spain is abundant, varied, delicious, and generally quite inexpensive. In the nineteenth and early twentieth centuries, Spaniards used olive oil in lamps. Every area produces olive oil and many Spaniards have a variety in their cupboard. It is worth sampling oils from many different areas and producers to witness how each has its own distinct taste. Nonorganic olive oil is really dirt-cheap—bottles can be had for 1–2 euros. Organic olive oil is more, but still substantially cheaper than what you pay in the United States—about one-third to one-half the price—so a 750 ml bottle of organic olive oil in Spain runs about the equivalent of $10, while a 500 ml bottle is about $6.

Full of olive oils from all over Spain with at least nine organic oils, the Patrimonio Comunal Olivarero looks like it would be high priced, but it is not; rather, it is truly a cooperative organization to promote olive oils. A must stop for any olive oil lover or connoisseur. Patrimonio Comunal Olivarero, C/ Mejía Lequerica, 1, 28004 Madrid; Tel: 913 080 505; e-mail: tienda@pco.es; Web site: www.pco.es; Metro: Alonso Martínez (exit Pl. Santa Bárbara and walk down the street to the end of the Plaza—Olivarero is on the corner).

In Barcelona a store called Oro Líquido sells olive oils from all over Spain as well as the Mediterranean. Oro Líquido, C/ de la Palla, 8, 08002 Barcelona; Tel: 933 022 980; Web site: www.oroliquido.es; Metro: Liceu or Jaume I; open Tuesday to Saturday 10:30 a.m. to 8:30 p.m., Sunday 11:00 a.m. to 3:00 p.m., closed Monday.

Some producers of organic olive oil in Spain include:

Olivar de la Luna is an organic olive oil made by a family company in the Córdoba province in the Sierra de los Pedroches. Olivar de la Luna, C/ Ancha, 5, 14400 Pozoblanco (Córdoba); Tel: 957 771 208; e-mail: info@olivardelaluna.es; Web site: www.olivardelaluna. es/en/.

Rincón del Segura sells organic grains, breads, and olive oil, all certified organic. Panadería Rincón del Segura, Camino Viejo de Férez, s/n (Villares), 02439 Elche de la Sierra (Albacete); Tel; 967 410 462; e-mail: rincondelsegura@artesaniadelasierra.com; Web site: www. artesaniadelasierra.com/rincondelsegura.

Alcubilla produces Luque organic olive oil from Castro del Río, between Córdoba and Granada in Andalucía. Alcubilla 2000, CN 432, Km 315.8, Castro del Rio (Córdoba); Tel: 957 374 005; e-mail: luque@alcubilla2000.com; Web site: www.alcubilla2000.com. ☛ green earth guide favorite.

Eco Vizcántar olive oil comes from Andalucía between Granada and Córdoba. Eco Vizcántar, Ctra. de Zagrilla, s/n, 14800 Priego de Córdoba (Córdoba); Tel: 957 540 266; e-mail: vizcantar@aceitesvizcantar.com; Web site: www.aceitesvizcantar.com/index.php?idm=ing.

Oleum Viride olive oil comes from the mountains in the Cádiz area. Oleum Viride, C/ Alta, 10, Zahara de la Sierra (Cádiz); Tel: 956 139 006; e-mail: info@oleumviride.com; Web site: www.oleumviride.com.

Ecojaén, a CAAE-certified organic olive oil from the Jaén region, is sold, among other places, at the café-bar in the Barcelona Estació de França rail station. Ecojaén, Ctra. de la Higuera, s/n, Santiago de Calatrava, Jaén (Andalucía); Tel: 953 528 270; e-mail: info@ecojaen.net; Web site: www.ecojaen.net/ing/E_empresa.htm.

Isul and Graccurris extra virgin organic and unfiltered olive oils are produced in the La Rioja region. Almazara Ecológica de La Rioja, S.L., C/ Muro Alto, 9, 26540 Alfaro (La Rioja); Tel: 941 181 512 / 600 871 792; e-mail: almazara@fer.es; Web site: www.isul.es.

Fruit Nature Olive Oil is from the Ebro River area in Tarragona. Fruit Nature Olive Oil, Joseph Manel Ambrós Ortiz, C/ Sant Antoni, 8, 43790 Riba-Roja d'Ebre (Tarragona); Tel: 977 416 078; e-mail: info@fruitnature.com; Web site: www.fruitnature.com.

For organic olive oil, as well as organic olives, from the Sevilla area: Chambergo Cia. de Exportación S.L., Aptdo. Correos / P.O. Box 99, 41400 Écija (Sevilla); Tel: 954 832 709; e-mail: info@biochambergo.com; Web site: www.biochambergo.com.

Casa Pareja makes certified organic olive oil from the sun-soaked region of Murcia. Casa Pareja, Ctra. Jumilla-Venta del Olivo, Km 9.3, Aptdo. 178-30, 30520 Jumilla (Murcia); Tel: 968 780 281; Web site: www.casapareja.es.

Olivar de Segura is an olive cooperative with an organic and award-winning olive oil called Oro de Génave. Olivar de Segura, Second

Degree Andalusian Cooperative, Ctra. Córdoba—Valencia, s/n, 23350 Puente de Génave (Jaén); Tel: 953 435 400; e-mail: pedidos@olivardesegura.es; Web sites: www.olivardesegura.es, www.sierradegenave.com.

Ecoato is a delicious olive oil made from olives grown in the sunsoaked region of Murcia. Ecoato, Cooperativa Coato, Ctra. de Mazarron, s/n, 30850 Totana (Murcia); Tel: 968 424 621; Web site: www.coato.com/ingles/aceite.asp. ☛ green earth guide favorite.

Northwest of Barcelona in the Sierra de Guara Natural Park, Ecostean makes a variety of organic olive oils. Hacienda Agrícola Ecostean, Plaza Portal, 11, 22312 Costean; Tel: 974 308 495; e-mail: info@ecostean.com; Web site: www.ecostean.com/eng/index.html.

La Casona makes certified organic olive oil from the Jaén region, which has more than sixty million olive trees. La Casona; Tel: 953 241 335; e-mail: info@aceiterajaenera.es/en-index.html; Web site: www.aceiterajaenera.es/en-index.html.

Ecolive is organic olive oil from the La Rioja region. Ecolive Rioja, Crta. Grávalos, Km 2, 26540 Álfaro (La Rioja); Tel: 620 907 129; e-mail: ecolive@ecoliverioja.com; Web site: www.ecoliverioja.com.

Can Solivera makes olive oil, soap, and perfume from their own organic Arbequina olives. Botiga d'oli Can Solivera, Camí de Fitor, 1, Vullpellac; Tel: 972 634 096; e-mail: info@solivera.com; Web site: http://en.solivera.com; open Saturday 11:00 a.m. to 2:00 p.m./5:00 to 8:00 p.m., Sunday 11:00 a.m. to 2:00 p.m.

Spain is not the first country to come to mind when one thinks of chocolate, but Spaniards love chocolate and Spain produces plenty of delicious chocolate. Some organic Spanish chocolate brands include:

Chocolate Solé makes a range of chocolates including an unusual flavor—chocolate with walnuts (*nueces/nuez*). Chocolates Solé, C/ Edison, 7-9, 08210 Barbera del Vallès (Barcelona); Tel: 937 290 018.

Chocolates Oliva are handmade by artisan José Oliva Ortega using organic chocolate and sold in some health food stores. José Luis Oliva Ortega, Mas Prim del Bosc, s/n, 17832 Crespià (Girona); Tel: 972 193 030; e-mail: xocooliva@yahoo.es.

Santiveri is a brand of health food products and has a line of health food stores. They make organic chocolate products available in their own stores and other health food stores as well as the health food section of the El Corte Inglés supermarkets.

Lluch Bio Chocolates are certified organic by CCPAE. Saudom, Camí Vell de Tàrrega, 17-19, 25310 Agramunt; Tel: 973 390 030; Web site: www.alluch.es.

Biogra Bio Chocolates are certified organic by CCPAE. Sorribas, C/ Santiago Rusiñol, 19, 08213 Polinyà (Barcelona); Tel: 937 132 324; e-mail: Correo@sorribas.com; Web site: www.sorribas.com.

Balleros is a store in Barcelona dedicated to organic chocolates; these are from Austria, not Spain. Balleros Chocolates Biológicos, Arimon, 29, Barcelona; Tel: 932 113 921; Metro: Lesseps or Vallcarca; open Monday to Friday 10:00 a.m. to 2:00 p.m./5:00 to 8:00 p.m.

RESTAURANTS

For a country that prides itself on eating every part of a pig, and where many people do not understand the meaning of vegetarian, Spain's large cities have a good selection of vegetarian and natural foods restaurants. Following are some natural foods, vegetarian, and organic restaurant options as well as others for special diet needs like gluten-free. Spaniards eat dinner late so don't be surprised by the hours of many restaurants, which don't open or start serving dinner until 8:00 or 10:00 p.m.! Helpful words to know include: *la cuenta* = the bill/check; *estaba buenísimo* = that was delicious. To order mint tea: *infusión de menta poleo;* you can usually just ask for *poleo.*

Jean-Claude Juston runs a vegetarian bed-and-breakfast in the Alpujarra mountains (see L'Atelier under "Eco-Accommodations") and has written a book covering what he considers to be the one hundred best vegetarian restaurants in Spain, *The New Spain: Vegan & Vegetarian Restaurants;* Web site: www.ivu.org/atelier/index-eng.html.

Note: Don't be surprised if while you are sitting enjoying your meal you see peddlers coming into restaurants selling flowers, handmade ashtrays out of soda cans (recycling at its ultimate), and other items. Whereas in the United States these people would be shooed out, in Spain they are often (but not always) tolerated by the establishment as well as by the customers.

The no-smoking laws in Spain are a little ambiguous. Smoking is allowed in the open air, and in bars and restaurants smaller than a hundred square meters. Larger bars and restaurants can designate a smoking section as large as about a third of their establishment. In many cases the laws are not enforced. Many natural foods restaurants are nonsmoking. The following two links allow you to search all of Spain or by region for nonsmoking restaurants. (*Local totalmente libre de humo* means totally free of smoke—i.e., nonsmoking.)

www.nofumadores.org/ociosinhumos/buscador.asp

www.20minutos.es/locales-sin-humo/

Barcelona

You can search Google Maps for the Green Earth Guide: Traveling Naturally in Spain: Barcelona Vegetarian Restaurants for a visual of all these restaurants in the city.

If you are on or near the busy La Rambla there are a number of organic and vegetarian eating options. If you want an outdoor café, one of the organic restaurants has outdoor seating one to two blocks from La Boqueria in the little Plaza Sant Agusti. Otherwise, the less touristy outdoor cafés can be found one block west of La Rambla.

Hàbaluc is a lovely restaurant a few blocks over from the Passeig de Gràcia avenue and Metro stop, between Valencia and Mallorca streets. Hàbaluc serves organic and natural foods including organic meats. Prices range from 10 to 18 euros. At the Web site, click on the colored boxes for the page links. Hàbaluc, C/ d'Enric Granados, 41, L'Eixample, 08008 Barcelona; Tel: 934 522 928; Web site: www.habaluc.net; Metro: Passeig de Gràcia; open every day 8:00 a.m. to 1:00 a.m.

Juicy Jones is a funky, bar-like restaurant serving fresh juices, salads, soups, and sandwiches in the heart of the old part of Barcelona just steps from the Plaza de Pi and La Rambla with meal prices in the 8 to 10 euro range. Juicy Jones, C/ Cardenal Casañas, 7, Ciutat Vella,

08002 Barcelona; Tel: 933 024 330; Metro: Liceu; open every day 10:00 a.m. to midnight.

La Flauta Mágica is a natural and organic foods restaurant with vegetarian options and free-range meat dishes. Rock record album covers decorate the menus. La Flauta Mágica, C/ dels Banys Vells, 18, Barcelona; Tel: 932 684 694; Metro: Jaume I; open only at night from 9:00 p.m. to midnight, closed Tuesday.

At Amaltea, a vegetarian and natural foods restaurant, lunch and dinner are served for reasonable prices (10 euros for lunch *menú del día;* 14.50 euros nights and weekends), with a small buffet salad bar as one of the first course options, as well as soups, and entrée dishes. Amaltea, C/ de la Diputación, 164, Eixample, 08015 Barcelona; Tel: 934 548 613; Web site: www.amalteaygovinda.com/; Metro: Urgell; open Monday to Saturday for lunch 1:00 to 4:00 p.m. For dinner the hours are Monday to Thursday 8:00 to 11:00 p.m., Friday and Saturday 8:00 to 11:45 p.m., closed Sunday.

Unicornius serves organic food for lunch Monday to Saturday, and supper every Thursday, Friday, and Saturday. Unicornius vegetarian restaurant, C/ Jovellanos, 2 (between Pelai and Tallers, near the north end of La Rambla), 08001 Barcelona; Tel: 933 171 829; Web site: www.restaurantunicornius.com; open for lunch 1:00 to 4:30 p.m. and supper 8:30 to 11:00 p.m., with prices ranging from 8.50 to 16.20 euros.

Vegetalia Natural Restaurant, near La Rambla, is an outgrowth of Vegetalia, a natural and organic foods producer and distributor (www.vegetalia.com). Vegetalia Natural Restaurant, C/ Escudellers, 54, 08002 Barcelona; Tel: 933 173 331; Web site: www.vegetalia.es/eng_restaurant.htm; Metro: Drassanes; open 10:00 a.m. to midnight, with prices from 9 to 11 euros.

Arco Iris is a vegetarian restaurant serving lunch in a darling two-story, tiled bistro-style restaurant with a *menú del día* for 9 euros. Arco Iris, C/ Roger de Flor, 216 (at Avda. Diagonal), Eixample, 08013 Barcelona; Tel: 934 582 283; Metro: Verdaguer; open 12:45 to 4:00 p.m., closed Sunday.

Govinda is a Hindu Indian vegetarian restaurant with a salad bar and three-course fixed-price menus, running about 10 euros for lunch on weekdays. Govinda, Plaza Villa de Madrid, 4-5, 08002 Barcelona;

Tel: 933 187 729; Web site: www.amalteaygovinda.com; Metro: Catalunya; open Monday to Thursday 1:00 to 4:00 p.m./8:00 to 11:00 p.m., Friday and Saturday until midnight, Sunday open only for lunch 1:00 to 4:00 p.m.

Acai is a natural and organic foods restaurant including organic wines with prices in the 40–50 euro range for a three-course meal. Acai, C/ Elkano, 69, Barcelona; Tel: 936 007 839; open Tuesday to Saturday 9:00 to 11:30 p.m.

BioCenter is an organic and vegetarian restaurant three blocks from La Rambla serving organic wines and meals with a *menú del día.* For dinner the *menú de noche* is 15 euros. The portions are ample and tasty. BioCenter, C/ del Pintor Fortuny, 25, 08001 Barcelona; Tel: 933 014 583 (day) or 667 042 313 (evening); Web site: www.restaurantebiocenter.es; Metro: Liceu; open Monday to Saturday 1:00 to 11:30 p.m., and Sunday 1:00 to 4:30 p.m.

Sésamo is an organic and vegetarian restaurant and bar serving lunch and dinner with à la carte and fixed menus. From Monday to Saturday the *menú del día* is three courses for 9 euros, and evening à la carte options will run between 5 and 12 euros. Sésamo, C/ Sant Antoni Abat, 52, 08001 Barcelona; Tel: 934 416 411; e-mail: sesamo@sesamo-bcn.com; Web site: www.sesamo-bcn.com/i_home. htm; Metro: Sant Antoni; open Monday, Wednesday through Saturday 1:00 to 5:00 p.m./8:00 p.m. to 1:00 a.m., Sunday 8:00 p.m. to 1:00 a.m., closed Tuesday.

Organic, a vegetarian and organic foods restaurant serving regional dishes, fresh squeezed juices, salads, and more, has two locations a few blocks from La Rambla, with prices starting at about 8 euros. Organic is more in the style of a cafeteria and take-out, than a restaurant. They have a lunch counter at the back of La Boqueria market serving up their organic foods, where their slogan is "Organic is Orgasmic." See "Farm Stands, Markets, and Local Products" above for La Boqueria location. The C/ de la Junta de Comerç location has outdoor seating in the small Plaza Sant Agusti. Organic Restaurant, C/ de la Junta de Comerç, 11, Barcelona; second location a few blocks away at Xucla, 15; Tel: 933 010 902; e-mail: organicrestaurant@gmail.com; Web site: www.antoniaorganickitchen.com; Metro: Liceu; open every day 12:30 p.m. to midnight.

La Rita is not a health food or vegetarian restaurant but serves good local food at an amazing prix fixe during the week of 8.50 euros per person for a three-course lunch. The black rice, made with squid ink, is not to be missed. Be prepared to wait in line for a table as it is a popular spot. La Rita, C/ Arago, 279, 08007 Barcelona; Tel: 934 872 376.

For anyone craving Nepalese food, the Kathmandû Restaurant serves up lunch and dinner with many vegetable dishes. Kathmandû Bar Restaurant Nepali, C/ Corsega, 421, 08037 Barcelona; Tel: 934 593 769; e-mail: kathmandubcn@gmail.com; Web site: www.kathmandurestaurant.com; Metro: Verdaguer; open Monday to Saturday noon to 4:00 p.m./8:00 p.m. to midnight, Sundays 1:00 to 4:00 p.m.

The Sin Carne Web site offers lists of vegetarian restaurants in Barcelona: www.sincarne.net/barcelona-vegetarian-restaurants.htm.

Girona

B-12 is a pleasant little café serving organic wines, beers, coffee, and vegetarian pastries, tapas, and other vegetarian and organic options, with free wifi (you have to ask for the password). B-12 is south of the city center, near the Nana Bio health food store. From the train station, walk a few blocks east to Migdia street, then head south for about nine blocks and you will come to the Nana Bio health food store on the corner; go left and a block and a half down you will come to Rutlla street—B-12 is across from the little playground. B-12 Cafe Bar Vegà, Rutlla, 147-155, 17003 Girona; Tel: 972 911 333; e-mail: cafebar-b12@riseup.net; open Monday to Thursday 8:00 a.m. to 9:00 p.m., Friday 8:00 a.m. to 10:30 p.m.

Valencia

At Espai Visor the restaurant part is small—about five or six tables—but the menu is fabulous. The gallery space, exhibiting works by local and international photographers, is small, but lovely. The three-course dinner is a prix fixe of 18 euros. Espai Visor Café and Gallery, Corretgería, 40, bajo izq. 2, 46001 Valencia; Tel: 963 922 399; e-mail: info@espaivisor.com; Web site: www.espaivisor.com; the café and gallery are open Tuesday to Saturday 5:00 to 9:00 p.m., the restaurant is open 9:00 to 11:30 p.m.

La Tastaolletes is a small restaurant serving up delicious natural foods dishes—the unusual seaweed salad is recommended. Tapas prices range from 4.50 to 9 euros, salads 8 to 9.50 euros, and entrées 10 to 11 euros. La Tastaolletes, C/ Salvador Giner, 6, Barrio de Carmen, 46003 Valencia; Tel: 963 921 862; open Tuesday to Saturday for lunch 2:00 to 4:00 p.m. and Monday to Saturday for dinner 9:00 p.m. to midnight, closed all day Sunday, and closed Monday until dinner.

Les Maduixes is a natural foods restaurant serving lunch and dinner, with lunch menus around 12 euros. Les Madiuxes, C/ Daoíz y Velarde, 4, Valencia; Tel: 963 694 596; open 1:30 to 4:00 p.m. for lunch and 9:00 p.m. to midnight for dinner, closed Sunday.

Kimpira is a beautiful restaurant designed with feng shui principles in the old part of the city a few blocks from the Plaza de la Virgen and the cathedral. It serves truly divine tasting food with an emphasis on vegan, macrobiotic, and organic foods, all with gourmet flair both in taste and presentation. Kimpira, C/ Juristas, 12, 46001 Valencia; Tel: 963 923 422; e-mail: movimientoalimento@hotmail.com; Web site: www.patriciarestrepo.org; open for lunch Monday to Sunday 1:30 to 4:00 p.m., Thursday to Saturday also for dinner 8:30 p.m. to midnight. ☛ green earth guide favorite.

Miobio serves natural foods for breakfast and lunch with specialty menus without gluten, lactose, or sugar. Miobio, Universidad Politécnica, Av. Del Tarongers, s/n, Edificio (building) Galileo Galilei, 46022 Valencia; Tel: 963 387 998; e-mail: info@miobio.es; Web site: www.miobio.es; open Monday to Friday 9:00 a.m. to 4:30 p.m.

Ana Eva serves vegetarian and natural foods in the old part of the city, around the block from the University Botanical Garden, not too far from the Turia Metro stop. Their lunch *menú del día* price is 12 euros. Ana Eva, C/ Túria, 49, Valencia; Tel: 963 915 369; open Thursday to Sunday for lunch 1:30 to 4:00 p.m., and for dinner 9:00 to 11:00 p.m.

La Lluna is a vegetarian and natural foods restaurant serving lunch and dinner Mondays to Saturdays, closed Sunday. Near C/ Corona in the old part of the city by the Torres de Quart, La Lluna is a small restaurant tucked into an old building lined with beautiful tiles. Their *menú del día* runs 13 euros and you can also order à la carte. La Lluna, C/ San Ramón, 23, Valencia; Tel: 963 922 146.

Madrid

Eco Bar & Spa is a fancy-end, organic and natural foods restaurant with a connected spa and health food store. Eco Bar & Spa, Paseo Pintor Rosales, 76, 28008 Madrid; Tel: 915 441 716; e-mail: info@ ecobarspa.com; Web site: www.ecobarspa.com.

Yerba Buena is an orange and green brightly painted small restaurant with soups, salads, and full vegetarian entrées near Plaza Mayor and Puerta del Sol. Yerba Buena, C/ Bordadores, 3, 28013 Madrid; Tel: 915 480 811; Web site: www.yerbabuena.ws; open Monday to Friday 1:30 to 4:00 p.m./8:00 p.m. to midnight; Saturday and Sunday 8:00 p.m. to midnight.

Vegetarian Art is a vegetarian restaurant serving lunch and dinner with prices starting at 10 euros. Vegetarian Art, C/ Fernán González, 77, 28009 Madrid; Tel: 914 097 722; e-mail: info@vegetarianart. com; Web site: www.vegetarianart.com/EN/indexen.htm; open Tuesday to Friday 1:00 to 4:30 p.m./9:00 to 11:30 p.m., Friday and Saturday until midnight, closed Sunday nights and all day Monday.

El Vergel is a large vegetarian and natural foods restaurant set downstairs from their large-for-Spain natural foods store above. El Vergel, Paseo de la Florida, 53, 28008 Madrid; Tel: 915 471 952; Web site: www.el-vergel.com; Metro: Príncipe Pío.

La Biotika, open since 1979, is a vegetarian and macrobiotic restaurant in the middle of Madrid, between C/ Santa María and C/ de las Huertas, two blocks from the C/ de Atocha (a main street in Madrid) and the Metro stop. La Biotika daily menus run between 10 and 12 euros. There is a small health food store as you enter, with the restaurant in the back. La Biotika, Amor de Dios, 3, 28014 Madrid; Tel: 914 290 780; Web site: www.labiotika.es; Metro: Antón Martín; open 1:00 to 4:30 p.m./8:00 to 11:30 p.m., closed Sunday nights.

Vegaviana is a vegetarian, natural and organic foods restaurant in the heart of Madrid in what is considered the gentrified gay neighborhood of Chueca. Their daily menu is about 10 euros. Vegaviana, C/ Pelayo, 35, 28004 Madrid; Tel: 913 080 381; Metro: Chueca; open Tuesday to Sunday 1:30 to 4:00 p.m., Tuesday to Saturday also 9:00 p.m. to midnight.

Artemisa is a whole foods restaurant serving beautiful salads and full entrées—portions are generous so I would recommend sharing unless you are a big eater or starving. Their tiramisú dessert is divine but could feed a small army. Artemisa, Ventura de la Vega, 4, Madrid; Tel: 914 295 092; Metro: Sevilla. Second location: Tres Cruces, 4 (near Plaza del Carmen), 28014 Madrid; Tel: 915 218 721; Metro: Gran Vía; open daily from 1:30 to 4:00 p.m. /9:00 p.m. to midnight.

El Estragón is a vegetarian and natural foods restaurant a few blocks from the Plaza Mayor. El Estragón Vegetariano, Plaza de la Paja, 10, 28005 Madrid; Tel: 913 658 982; e-mail: elestragonvegetariano@ hotmail.com; Web site: www.guiadelocio.com/estragonvegetariano; Metro: La Latina; open every day.

Maoz, meaning falafel, is a fast food style vegetarian food bar with two locations in busy areas—good for quick, inexpensive re-fortification. Prices are between 4 and 7 euros. Maoz Vegetarian, C/ Mayor, 4 (right off the Puerta del Sol), Madrid; Metro: Sol; open all week 11:00 a.m. to 2:00 a.m. Also at C/ Hortaleza, 7, Madrid; Web site: www. maozusa.com; Metro: Gran Vía; open all week noon to 2:00 a.m.

La Galette is a sweet, small vegetarian and natural foods restaurant near the Retiro park. La Galette, Conde de Aranda, 11, 28001 Madrid; Tel: 915 760 641; Metro: Retiro (just two blocks from the Metro); closed Sunday nights. Their second location is La Galette II, Bárbara de Braganza, 10, 28004 Madrid; Tel: 913 193 148; Metro: Colón; closed Sunday nights.

La Isla del Tesoro is a vegetarian and natural foods restaurant with great atmosphere, located in the heart of the city about four blocks from a Metro stop. La Isla del Tesoro, Manuela Malasaña, 3, Madrid; Tel: 915 931 440; Metro: Bilbao; open every day.

Al Natural is a vegetarian and natural foods restaurant in the center of Madrid just behind the Palacio del Congreso de los Diputados. Their *menú del día* is around 12 euros. Al Natural Restaurante Vegetariano, C/ Zorrilla, 11, 28014 Madrid; Tel: 913 694 709; e-mail: acero@alnatural.biz; Web site: www.alnatural.biz/en/index.html; Metro: Banco de España; open 1:00 to 4:00 p.m./8:30 to 11:30 p.m., closed Sunday nights.

La Mazorca is an ovo-lacto vegetarian restaurant serving organic beers, wines, soups, salads, and tapas up the avenue from the Atocha RENFE train station. La Mazorca, Paseo de la Infanta Isabel, 21,

Madrid; Tel: 915 017 013; Metro: Atocha Renfe; open 1:30 to 4:00 p.m./9:00 to 11:30 p.m., closed Sunday and Monday nights.

El Vegetariano de Teresa is a vegetarian and natural foods tapas bar and restaurant with prices starting from 7 to 10 euros. El Vegetariano de Teresa, C/ Hermosilla, 157, 28028 Madrid; Tel: 913 553 653; Mobile: 607 325 099; e-mail: contacto@elvegetarianodeteresa.com; Web site: www.elvegetarianodeteresa.com; open Monday to Sunday 1:30 to 4:30 p.m., Thursday, Friday, and Saturday 9:00 to 11:30 p.m.

El Restaurante Vegetariano is a bustling vegetarian and natural foods restaurant down the block from the No Solo Pasta gluten-free restaurant (see entry under "Special Diets") between the Royal Palace and Plaza Mayor. El Restaurante Vegetariano, C/ Santiago, 9, Madrid; open Tuesday to Saturday 1:00 to 4:00 p.m./8:30 to 11:30 p.m., Sunday 1:00 to 4:00 p.m.

Ventas Ecológicas is a health food store and organic foods restaurant. Ventas Ecológicas, C/ Virgen de la Alegría, 10, 3ª planta, 28027 Madrid; Tel: 913 266 000; e-mail: ventas@ventasecologicas.com; Web site: www.ventasecologicas.com; Metro: Ventas or El Carmen; the restaurant is open Monday to Friday 9:00 a.m. to 4:15 p.m., Saturday 9:00 a.m. to 6:30 p.m.

Ecocentro is an organic foods restaurant serving lunch and dinner offering organic wines and entrées for between 12 and 15 euros. Ecocentro, C/ Esquilache, 2 al 12 (at Avda. Pablo Iglesias, 2), 28003 Madrid; Tel: 915 535 502; e-mail: eco@ecocentro.es; Web site: www.ecocentro.es; Metro: Ríos Rosas; open every day 1:00 to 5:00 p.m./9:00 p.m. to midnight.

Many Cacao Sampaka stores sell only their unusual line of chocolates. The store on Orellana street not only has their regular chocolate offerings, but also a café in the rear serving coffee, teas, chocolate drinks, pastries, salads, and lunch items. Cacao Sampaka, C/ Orellana, 4, 28004 Madrid; Tel: 913 195 840; e-mail: madrid-centro@cacaosampaka.com; Web site: www.cacaosampaka.com; Metro: Alonso Martínez; open Monday to Friday 10:00 a.m. to 9:00 p.m.—full restaurant fare of salads and sandwiches from 10:30 a.m. to 4:00 p.m., Saturday and Sunday 10:00 a.m. to 2:00 p.m./3:30 to 9:00 p.m. They have a second store at Paseo de la Habana, 28, 28036 Madrid;

Tel: 915 633 138; e-mail: madrid-chamartin@cacaosampaka.com; Web site: www.cacaosampaka.com.

See the "Special Diets" section below for more restaurants in Madrid.

Andalucía

Málaga

Cañadú has been cooking vegetarian and organic meals for ten years. Cañadú Restaurante Vegetariano, C/ Plaza del Mercado 21, Málaga; Tel: 952 602 719; e-mail: info@canadu.es; Web site: www.canadu. es; open every day 1:30 to 4:00 p.m./8:00 to 11:00 p.m., Friday and Saturday 8:30 p.m. to midnight.

La Tetería is a tea shop as well as a restaurant serving crepes, teas, fresh juices, and more. The *sorbete de fruta natural* is some divine fresh fruit drink they make. I had the *piña* (pineapple), which was unbelievably delicious. La Tetería, C/ San Agustín, 9, Málaga; Tel: 650 656 560; e-mail: lateteria@la-teteria.com; Web site: www.la-teteria.com; open noon to 10:00 p.m. ☛ green earth guide favorite.

Situated across from the cinema and near the Roman theater, El Vegetariano de la Alcazabilla has indoor and outdoor seating and a fun and funky atmosphere. El Vegetariano de la Alcazabilla, C/ Pozo del Rey, 5, Málaga; Tel: 952 214 858; open 1:30 p.m. until late. ☛ green earth guide favorite.

El Huerto is a vegetarian restaurant serving soups, salads, and more either à la carte or by the *menú del día,* with free wifi for an hour. El Huerto de los Apañaos, C/ Dos Aceras, 18-20, Málaga; Tel: 952 212 868; e-mail: restaurante_elhuerto@hotmail.com.

Granada

Up a cobblestoned street from the major *calle* (street) Reyes Católicos, Canela y Clavo is a lovely, inexpensive, and excellent restaurant with high-quality clean, fresh food, with both meat and vegetable options. Canela y Clavo also has gluten-free dishes with rice and polenta although they are not billed as such. They also serve delicious olives. They charge extra for bread so if you don't want it, tell them before they bring it. Canela y Clavo, Placeta Sillería, 7, 18010 Granada; Tel: 958 229 706. ☛ green earth guide favorite.

Hicuri is in the hip Realejo section of Granada and it has great hours, good natural foods, and a light atmosphere. Hicuri café bar restaurante, C/ Santa Escolástica, 18009 Granada; Tel: 958 221 282; open Monday to Friday 8:00 a.m. to 11:00 p.m., Saturday 10:00 a.m. to 4:30 p.m./8:00 p.m. to midnight, Sunday 1:30 to 4:30 p.m.

Córdoba

Amaltea, brightly painted with rich, lively colors, serves vegetarian as well as meat and fish dishes. Conveniently located near the *mezquita,* Roman bridge, and other attractions in the old city. Amaltea, Ronda de Isasa, 10 (a few blocks from the Roman bridge and Porta Triunfa), Córdoba; Tel: 957 491 968; open for lunch and dinner.

Restaurante Tetería Hammam is adjacent to the Hammam baths in the old city a few blocks from the *mezquita.* The Tetería serves a variety of herbal and caffeinated teas. The restaurant serves a full menu of Middle Eastern and Spanish foods including a variety of salads. The Tetería also has wifi if you eat or drink there. Restaurante Tetería Hammam, C/ Corregidor Luís de la Cerda, 51, 14003 Córdoba; Tel: 957 482 891; e-mail: info@restaurantehammam.es; Web site: www.restaurantehammam.es; restaurant open Monday to Friday noon to midnight, Saturday and Sunday noon to 2:00 a.m.; Tetería open Monday to Saturday 3:00 p.m. to midnight.

Museo de la Tapa y el Vino offers indoor and outdoor seating just below the small Plaza del Potro, known for an old inn where Miguel Cervantes lived for a while, and where the current Museum of Fine Arts is located. Museo de la Tapa specializes in tapas made from local foods and wines. Extremely reasonably priced with different-size portions available—tapas, half ration, and (full) ration. I had fantastic olives (*aceitunas*), tuna and red peppers, and fried lettuce and garlic—all delicious, all tapas size, plus a cup of tea for a total of 5.70 euros—hard to beat. Not organic at all, but local, good food and easy for vegetarians to find options. Museo de la Tapa y el Vino, C/ Enrique Romero de Torres, 3, at Plaza del Potro, 14002 Córdoba; Tel: 957 480 877.

Sevilla

The Kiwi fresh juice bar is tucked into part of the old city. It is a tiny bar serving pastries, coffee, teas, and really delicious fresh squeezed juices—try the *Aborigen* with apple, pineapple, and kiwi—it is so refreshing. Kiwi Juice Bar, C/ Candilejo, 4A, 41004 Sevilla; e-mail: zumos@kiwijuicebar.com; Web site: www.kiwijuicebar.com; open Monday to Thursday 9:30 a.m. to 8:30 p.m., Friday to Sunday 10:00 a.m. to 9:00 p.m.

Bliss makes fresh fruit juices, smoothies, and they have a daily soup at two locations: C/ Jimios, 25, and C/ San Pablo, 16, Sevilla; Tel: 954 216 841; Web site: www.blissjuicebar.com/English/Contacts.html.

The Gaia Eco Bar is a wonderful natural and organic vegetarian restaurant serving some vegan options. The creamed vegetable soup (made without milk) is delicious. They serve local organic wines, and many other beverages, as well as a full menu. Nearby there is an affiliated health food store and natural health therapies center. Centro Gaia, Restaurante Ecológico, C/ Luis de Vargas, 4, Sevilla; Tel: 954 211 934; Web site: www.gaiaecosalud.com; open Monday to Sunday 1:30 to 4:00 p.m., also Monday to Thursday 8:00 to 11:00 p.m. and Friday and Saturday 8:00 to 11:45 p.m.

La Habanita offers vegetarian foods as well as meat and fish. La Habanita, C/ Golfo, 3, (Alfalfa) Sevilla; Tel: 606 716 456; open 12:30 to 4:30 p.m./8:00 p.m. to midnight.

Bilbao

Restaurante Vegetariano serves a lunch *menú del día* for 12 euros with three courses plus dessert and tea. There is no à la carte. Conveniently located within walking distance of the RENFE train station. Restaurante Vegetariano, Alameda de Urquijo, 33, 48008 Bilbao; Tel: 944 445 598; open for lunch Monday to Saturday 1:00 to 4:00 p.m.

Garibolo is a fairly large natural foods restaurant serving lunch with their *menú del día* for 12 euros on weekdays, 15 euros on Saturday, or you can mix and match options such as juice, soup, and salad for 5 euros. Garibolo, C/ Fernández del Campo, 7, 48010 Bilbao; Tel: 944 223 255; open for lunch Monday to Saturday 1:00 to 4:00 p.m.

For restaurants around Spain serving gluten-free and natural foods check out www.celiacos.org (see below in "Special Diets"). For other organic and vegetarian restaurants around Spain by region check out www.Holistika.net, a comprehensive guide to eco and or-

Cortado = small strong coffee with a little milk

Tortilla = not what a Mexican tortilla is—in Spain it is an omelet with potatoes, eggs, and onions

Tapas = variety of appetizer foods/bar snacks—common and usually inexpensive, sometimes free with drinks

ganic services. Under "Guías" at the far right, choose "Restaurantes Vegetarianos."

SPECIAL DIETS

Gluten-free (*sin gluten* in Spanish) foods are plentiful and easily available in Spain at health food stores, and also a range of gluten-free products can be bought in the following supermarkets: Alcampo, Carrefour, El Corte Inglés, Hipercor, Mercadona, Sabeco, and Bon Preu.

The Spanish Federation of Celiacs—Federación de Asociaciones de Celíacos de España—offers a list of restaurants and health food stores that serve and sell gluten-free food at www.celiacos.org. They publish an annual guidebook listing products by category with brand names and specific items, color coded, with an index. Online, you can click on the "Dieta Sin Gluten" and then "Puntos de Venta" (points of sale or retail outlets), where you can click on a map and access a list of stores and restaurants with contact information.

At the site www.celiacosmadrid.org click on the Mapa Web at the upper left, and on the page that appears click on "Herbolarios" for lists of health food stores around Spain. You can also find regional celiac associations at this site as well.

There is a Spanish magazine dedicated to food allergies, especially gluten allergies, called *Vivir sin gluten y alergias;* Web site: www.glutenyalergias.com.

A pizzeria that makes gluten-free pizzas! Also serving appetizers and salads for delivery or to eat there. Pizza Sana (behind Pizzeria Nicanora), Avda. Machupichu, 16, 28043 Madrid, Tel: 913 004 252; e-mail: pizzasana@pizzasana.es; Web site: www.pizzasananicanora.es; open every day 1:30 to 4:15 p.m./8:00 to 11:45 p.m.

No Solo Pasta restaurants in Madrid and Tres Cantos offer gluten-free pizzas as well as other gluten-free foods. In Madrid, C/ Santiago, 3 (between Plaza Mayor and the Palacio Real), 28013 Madrid; Tel: 915 474 203; Metro: Sol. In Tres Cantos, Avda. de Viñuelas, 45, 28760 Tres Cantos; Tel: 918 038 717; information for both including menus can be found at the Web site: www.nosolopasta.com.

In Madrid, Artediet makes traditional pastries without gluten (bless their hearts), including to-die-for chocolate croissants, tiramisu, and many other delights. Artediet, C/ Villardondiego, 22, 28032 Madrid; Tel: 913 719 525; Web site: www.artediet.es; Metro: Vicálvaro; open Monday to Friday 9:00 a.m. to noon/5:00 to 8:00 p.m., Saturday and Sunday 9:00 a.m. to noon.

Like Mana from heaven, this store is for everyone needing gluten-free products. They have dry goods to fridge and frozen as well as gluten-free beers. Maná, C/ Lanuza, 19, 28028 Madrid; Tel: 917 255 661; e-mail: mana@jhernando.com; Web site: www.manaproductossingluten.com; open Monday to Friday 9:30 a.m. to 1:30 p.m./5:00 to 8:00 p.m., Saturday 9:30 a.m. to 1:30 p.m. With a second location at C/ Manuel Fernández Caballero, 1, 28019 Madrid; Tel: 914 604 712.

Sense Gluten makes gluten-free mini-pizzas, breads, rolls, and "barra mediana," a delicious baguette style bread. Sense Gluten, Forn Ricardera, C/ De la Damunt, 4 bx, 08519 Folgueroles (Barcelona); Web site: www.fornricardera.com.

In the Girona covered market (see "Farm Stands, Markets, and Local Products") there is a stall called 0% Gluten. They sell Sense Gluten and Artediet products (see above) as well as many others. A true haven for people needing gluten-free food. 0% Gluten, Plaça Mercat del Lleó, nº 200, 17002 Girona; Tel: 972 200 814; e-mail: girona@zeropercentgluten.com; Web site: www.zeropercentgluten.com; open Monday to Saturday until 2:00 p.m.

Coses de La Vita is a rural hotel and restaurant in the northern region of Asturias along the "green" coast that offers in addition to their regular menu, pizzas and pastas made with gluten-free flour to accommodate guests with celiac disease or gluten sensitivity. Located in a small village, La Vita, around 4 km from Arriondas, room prices range from 50 to 80 euros per night. Coses de la Vita, La Vita, 25, 33549 Arriondas (Asturias); Tel: 689 176 796; e-mail: info@coses-delavita.com; Web site: www.cosesdelavita.com.

El Bosque is a hotel, spa and restaurant north of Madrid city serving organic food with gluten- and lactose-free options. Prices in the restaurant range from 7 to 19 euros. El Bosque, Madrid Sierra, C/ Del Guerrero, 5, 28492 Mataelpino, Madrid; Tel: 918 573 149; e-mail: madridsierra@el-bosque.org; Web site: http://madrid-sierra.el-bosque.org.

Restaurante Marymar is a restaurant specializing in fried fish dishes using gluten-free breading. Restaurante Marymar, Paseo Marítimo, Sabinillas (Málaga); Tel: 952 890 271; Web site: www.restaurantemarymar.com/in/index.html.

The maker of the Spanish beer Estrella Damm produces a gluten-free version of their beer, with the same name but with "Apta para Celíacos" on the label, sold in gluten-free stores and in some supermarkets including the Mercadona and Bon Preu chains.

To find more restaurants serving gluten-free options go to www.celiacosmadrid.org, click on "Direcciones," and then choose "Hoteles y restaurantes" in the drop-down menu.

Gluten-free brands to look for when shopping include: Gerblé, Schar, Proceli (www.proceli.com), Sense Gluten, Artediet, and El Horno de Leña (makers of whole grain and gluten-free products in Fuenlabrada (Madrid); Web site: www.elhornodelena.com). You must read the label carefully on the El Horno products since some are with gluten and some are without. At the Terra Verda stores you can find the delicious None Glu brand. Look for a Spanish favorite—"digestive" cookies with chocolate. While these are usually made with wheat flour, you can find the Virginias in many conventional supermarkets that are made without gluten and lactose—www.virginias.es. Adpan Europa makes *medias noches* buns, with a corn-flour base, free from gluten, lactose, and eggs. Adpan Europa, Avda de Langreo, 7B, XiXún, El Berrón, Siero, 33186 Asturias; Tel: 985 743 627; Web site: www.adpancel.com.

For people with bovine/cow-dairy allergies, Spain has a bounty of goat (*cabra*) and sheep (*oveja*) milk products, often (though not always) tolerated by those who cannot consume cow-dairy. Some of the most amazing cheeses are made with goat or sheep milk, the most famous being Manchego, a hard cheese from the La Mancha region of Spain. If you cannot consume bovine/cow-dairy products, read labels carefully as sometimes cheeses are made with a combination of milks—*vaca* means cow in Spanish so if it says it contains *leche de vaca,* avoid it.

Recreation
HIKING

There are endless possibilities for walking and hiking in Spain. Every village has walking routes, and there are countless parks, coastal areas, and mountain areas with hiking paths. Cities have parks and promenades almost always filled with people. Some of the options for longer routes are listed here.

As in France the long-distance trails in Spain are marked with red GR signs (Gran Recorrido). The GR trails are longer than 50 km. The yellow PR (Pequeño Recorrido) signs are for short trails that are 10 to 50 km long. Green markers are for local paths up to 10 km long called Senderos Locales (SLs).

There are three European trails (marked with E) that cross Spain into the rest of Europe. E3 enters Spain and crosses along the north to Santiago de Compostela (see "UNESCO World Heritage Sites" and "Sacred Sites"). The Spanish portion of E3 is 700 km long. E4 is the European long-distance trail crossing diagonally across Spain from southwest to northeast continuing into France, Switzerland, Germany, Austria, Hungary, and Bulgaria. The Spanish portion is 2,300 km long. E7 runs west to east across the middle of Spain (actually starting in Portugal), going from Villel to Catalunya and into Andorra with a length in Spain of 1,500 km. More information can be accessed at the European Ramblers' Association Web site: www.era-ewv-ferp.org. In Spain the responsible trail organization is FEDME—the Federation of Mountain and Climbing Sports; Web site: www.fedme.es.

Walking paths along the length of the Costa Brava coast from Blanes in the south to Llançà in the north, almost at the French border, were originally used to spot pirates and other invaders. At the Costa Brava tourism page, click on "Sports," then on "Walking and hiking," and you can access a long list of GR, PR, SL, and coastal hiking routes; Web site: http://en.costabrava.org/main/home.aspx.

In the Basque region there are almost 130 km of greenway trails, as well as thirteen GR long-distance paths. GR11 runs the length of the Pyrenees.

The Centro Nacional de Información Geográfica (CNIG) publishes detailed maps of areas in Spain. Click on "Welcome" in English for the English site at www.cnig.es.

Under *Senderismo* (hiking) on the FAM Web site you can access general maps of the hiking trails through the Andalucía region. Under *Enlaces* (links) you can access other regional hiking federations. Federación Andaluza de Montañismo (FAM), Footpaths Commission, Camino de Ronda, 101, 18003 Granada; Tel: 958 291 340; Web site: www.fedamon.com.

The Greenways, known as Vías Verdes, are reclaimed old railway routes, converted into walking and biking trails (no motorized vehicles allowed) that cover 1,500 km in Spain. To find routes and information go to www.viasverdes.com/GreenWays. See the map of approximate greenway routes on page 91.

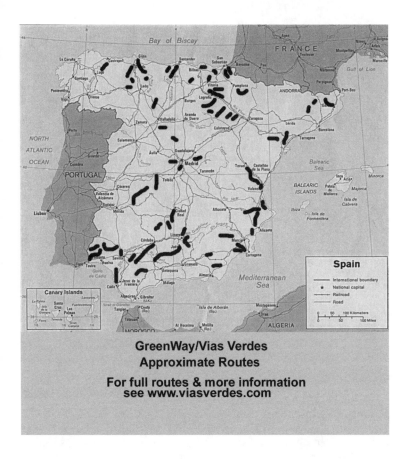

GreenWay/Vias Verdes
Approximate Routes

For full routes & more information
see www.viasverdes.com

There are a number of routes to Santiago de Compostela, Spain. See the "Sacred Sites" section for more information. There are also numerous other hiking possibilities listed in the "City and Regional Highlights" and "Wild and Natural Resources" sections. See the *Green Earth Guide* Map of Gran Recorrido Walking Trails in Spain on page 92.

BIKING

Biking (*ciclismo* in Spanish) is a wonderful recreational activity, and many people enjoy the multiple bike routes that run through Spain. Like hiking, biking can also be a practical transportation choice (see "Bike Rentals" in "Orientation, Arrival, and Getting Around" and see additional biking information in the "City and Regional Highlights" section). For long- and short-distance biking routes through Spain, explore the site for the European Cyclists' Federation (ECF),

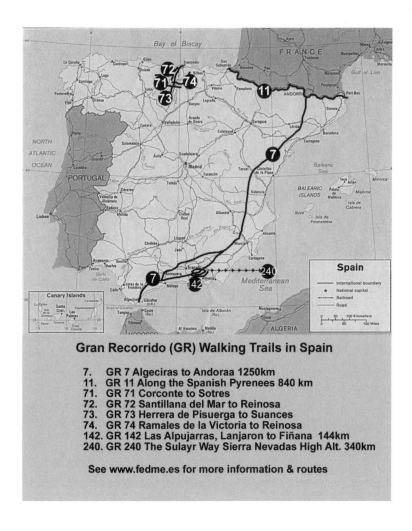

Gran Recorrido (GR) Walking Trails in Spain

7.   GR 7 Algeciras to Andoraa 1250km
11.   GR 11 Along the Spanish Pyrenees 840 km
71.   GR 71 Corconte to Sotres
72.   GR 72 Santillana del Mar to Reinosa
73.   GR 73 Herrera de Pisuerga to Suances
74.   GR 74 Ramales de la Victoria to Reinosa
142. GR 142 Las Alpujarras, Lanjaron to Fiñana 144km
240. GR 240 The Sulayr Way Sierra Nevadas High Alt. 340km

See www.fedme.es for more information & routes

which lists routes all over Europe on the European cycle route network or EuroVelo; ECF Web site: www.ecf.com. The Spanish Federation of Cycling (Federación Española de Ciclismo) can be found at www.rfec.com.

The Greenways, known as Vías Verdes, are reclaimed old railway routes, converted into walking and biking trails (no motorized vehicles allowed) that cover 1,500 km throughout Spain. To find routes and information go to www.viasverdes.com/GreenWays. In the Basque region there are almost 130 km of greenways. In the Girona region you can bike part or all of the Vías Verdes from Sant Feliu de Guíxols on the Costa Brava coast north of Tossa de Mar through Girona to Olot through to Ripoll almost 135 km if you go the whole way. See the map of approximate greenway routes on page 92.

The Girona region in northeastern Spain, about one hour north of Barcelona, is known as the base training home for Tour de France contenders. At the Costa Brava tourism page you will have access to pages of biking routes for the area. You can travel over the same routes Lance Armstrong and others have used to train for the Tour de France. There are posted trails and "greenway" trails built over old railroad tracks. The same Web site also offers twelve places to rent bicycles in the area (go to the "Maps and transports" section of the Web site, then to "Motorbikes and bicycles rental"). Costa Brava Web site: en.costabrava.org/main/home.aspx, click on "Sports," then on "Cycling and mountain biking," then on "See all" for biking routes.

In Llançà at the north end of the Costa Brava coast, the tourism office provides free guided tours on bike and on foot. Their Web page provides the routes, and if you don't have a bike, the tourist office rents them. Llançà Tourist Office, C/ Camprodon, 16-18, 17490 Llançà; Tel: 972 380 855; e-mail: turisme@llanca.cat; Web site: www.llanca.cat.

In the Andalucía region of southern Spain, the city of Málaga makes a good base for exploring by bicycle because it is surrounded by beaches and natural parks. While Málaga does not have a citywide bike program as in Sevilla and Barcelona, there are a number of bike rental and bike touring options. Málaga Bike Tours and Rentals have reasonable rentals for 10 euros a day. They also offer guided bike tours of the city and the surrounding area. Málaga Bike Tours, Pasaje la Trini, 6, 29012 Málaga; Tel: 606 978 513; e-mail: info@malaga-biketours.eu; Web site: www.malagabiketours.eu.

Bike2malaga is located at C/ Victoria, 15 (close to Plaza del Mercado), Málaga; Tel: 650 677 063; e-mail: info@bike2malaga.com; Web site: www.bike2malaga.com.

Another bike rental company in Málaga is Málaga By Bike, offering three businesses—Málaga By Bike, Cyclo Point, and Málaga By GPS; Web site: www.malagabybike.com. Cyclo Point rents bikes with a lock and helmet starting at 12 euros a day for the mountain-bike style, and 10 euros a day for city-style bikes. Refundable bike deposits are 50 euros for a city bike and 100 euros for a mountain

BIKING

Approximate EuroVelo Routes in Spain

1. EuroVelo Route 1 "Atlantic Coast Route"

3. EuroVelo Route 3 "Pilgrimage Route"

8. EuroVelo Route 8 "Mediterranean Route"

See www.ecf.com for more route information

bike. Málaga By Bike, Avda. Juan Sebastián Elcano, 50, 29017 Málaga; Tel: 952 297 324; Web site: www.cyclo-point.com; open Tuesday to Saturday 10:00 a.m. to 9:00 p.m. Take bus #11 from the city center to the shop.

Málaga By GPS rents GPS machines for use on bikes or on foot for 16 euros a day, and 10 euros for every subsequent day. Málaga By GPS, Avda. Juan Sebastián Elcano, 50, 29017 Málaga; Tel: 952 297 324; Web site: www.malagabygps.com.

There are numerous other biking possibilities. See the "City and Regional Highlights" and "Wild and Natural Resources" sections. See the *Green Earth Guide* Map of Euro Velo Biking Routes above.

YOGA

Yoga means "union"—the integration of body, mind, and spirit. It involves both gentle and strenuous stretching exercises, meditation, and breathing techniques to help calm the mind and strengthen the body. There are more than forty different types of yoga, some of the most common being Iyengar, a gentle, classic style using props; Ashtanga, also called power yoga, which moves more quickly from pose to pose; Bikram, or hot yoga, which is done in a heated room around 100°F, and makes for an intense workout; and Hatha yoga, a gentle, relaxing, and meditative form. Kripalu, Kundalini, and Sivananda are other common yoga types.

A sampling of yoga centers around Spain is listed below. Three online directories allow you to search for and locate yoga classes all over Spain. At the Web site for the Spanish Kundalini Yoga Association click on "Centros y Socios" and then when the map appears, click on an area to access the list of yoga centers; Web site: www.aeky.es. The Spanish Iyengar Yoga Association allows you to click on "Lista de profesores" for lists of yoga centers by region; Web site: www.aeyi. org. The International Yoga Centers Directory also lets you search Spain for yoga centers by region; Web site: www.yoga-centers-directory.net/spain.htm.

Barcelona

In Barcelona there are two Arcadia Yoga Centers: Baixada de Sant Miquel, 2, 2º 2ª, Barcelona; Tel: 670 593 565; e-mail: info@arcadiayoga.com; and C/ Ortigosa, 14-16, 2º, porta 11; Barcelona; Tel: 617 075 677; e-mail: info@arcadian.es; Web site: www.arcadiayoga.com.

The Anahata Center for Yoga and Holistic Therapies offers classes in yoga, massage, Reiki, classes, and retreats. Anahata Center, C/ D'Aribau, 61, Barcelona; Tel: 605 656 738; e-mail: yoga@anahata-bcn.com; Web site: www.anahata-bcn.com/html/en/home.html.

Mandiram, conveniently located near Plaça Catalunya, offers classes in Hatha, Vinyasa, and Ashtanga yoga. Mandiram Yoga Dinámico, C/ Pelayo, 52, 2º1A, Plaça Catalunya, 08001 Barcelona; Tel: 933 010 204; e-mail: info@yoga-dinamico.com; Web site: www.yoga-dinamico.com/index.php?lang=en; Metro: Universitat.

Essence offers yoga and Pilates classes, plus massage therapies. Essence, C/ Caballero, 87, Barcelona; Tel: 933 638 358; e-mail: info@

essence-barcelona.com; Web site: www.essence-barcelona.com/essence_eng/index_eng.htm.

Hot yoga, also called Bikram, is done in a room that is heated over 100ºF. Bikram Yoga, Pau Claris, 97 (between Diputación and Gran Vía), 08009 Barcelona; Tel: 933 025 130; e-mail: info@bikramyoga.es; Web site: www.bikramyoga.es.

Sisecel offers Naam yoga (using sacred sound), Ayurvedic massage, reflexology, and other body treatments. Sisecel, C/ Muntaner, 157, Ático, Barcelona; Tel: 933 215 062; Web site: www.sisecel.com.

Be Yoga, C/ Buenos Aires, 52, entlo 3º, Barcelona; Tel: 687 549 612; e-mail: info@beyogabcn.com; Web site: www.beyogabcn.com.

Valencia

Yoga Valencia is in a building on the beautiful Plaza del Patriarca in the center of the city. Yoga classes are held throughout the day on Monday through Friday for 14 euros for one class or 60 euros for an unlimited monthly pass. Yoga Valencia, Plaza del Patriarca, 4, pta. 4, 46002 Valencia; Tel: 687 423 076; e-mail: info@yoga-valencia.es; Web site: www.yoga-valencia.es.

Pranapana offers yoga classes for children and adults. Pranapana, C/ Quevedo, 5, 1º 1ª, 46001 Valencia; Tel: 667 739 866; e-mail: info@pranapana.com; Web site: www.pranapana.com.

Patricia Restrepo teaches yoga, and her Web site includes information about her Zen and Ashtanga yoga classes, as well as for the lovely Kimpira restaurant, shiatsu treatments, and more. Patricia Restrepo Yoga, C/ San Vicente Mártir, 71, puerta 5-12, 46007 Valencia; Tel: 963 524 675; e-mail: movimientoalimento@hotmail.com; Web site: www.patriciarestrepo.org.

Madrid

Mangalam offers yoga and meditation. Mangalam Yoga, C/ Camino de los Vinateros, 47, 28030 Madrid; Tel: 914 308 296; e-mail: info@mangalam.es; Web site: www.mangalam.es; Metro: Vinateros.

City Yoga offers daily classes in yoga, Pilates, plus massages. City Yoga, C/ Artistas, 43, 28020 Madrid; Tel: 915 534 751; Web site: www.city-yoga.com; Metro: Cuatro Caminos or Nuevos Ministerios.

Avagar offers Kundalini yoga. Avagar Centro de Yoga y Salud, C/ Bravo Murillo, 243, 1ºD, 28020 Madrid; Tel: 915 797 282; e-mail: info@avagar.es; Web site: www.avagar.com; Metro: Tetuán.

Ecocentro is a health center offering Reiki, yoga, and other modalities. It has an adjacent organic foods store and restaurant. Ecocentro Salud, C/ Esquilache, 2 al 12 (junto Avda. Pablo Iglesias, 2), 28003 Madrid; Tel: 915 531 299; e-mail: info@ecocentrosalud.es; Web site: www.ecocentrosalud.es; Metro: Ríos Rosas or Cuatro Caminos; open Monday to Thursday 11:00 a.m. to 3:30 p.m./5:00 to 9:30 p.m.

The Sivananda Yoga Center offers classes all week from 10:30 a.m. to 8:30 p.m. depending upon level. Centro de Yoga Sivananda Madrid, C/ Eraso, 4, bajo, 28028 Madrid; Tel: 913 615 150; e-mail: madrid@sivananda.net; Web site: www.sivananda.org/madrid; Metro: Diego de León.

Hatha and Iyengar yoga and Pilates classes are offered at Centro Dharana. Centro Dharana Yoga, C/ Hermosilla, 102, bajo D, Madrid; Tel: 913 093 607; e-mail: dharana_yoga@yahoo.es; Web site: www.dharanayoga.com; Metro: Goya.

Arteduna offers classes in Hatha yoga, pranayama, Tai Chi, and Chi Kung, and art therapy. Arteduna, C/ Campomanes 6, 5º derecha, Madrid; Tel: 915 413 237; Web site: www.centroarteduna.com; Metro: Ópera.

Ashtanga offers classes daily from Monday to Saturday. Ashtanga Yoga, C/ Juanelo, 12 Ent. B, Madrid; Tel: 913 690 033; Mobile: 667 652 600; e-mail: info@ashtangayogamadrid.com; Web site: www.ashtangayogamadrid.com/english.html; Metro: Tirso de Molina.

The teachers at Centro Mandala have thirty years' experience teaching Hatha yoga and classes in Tai Chi. Centro Mandala, C/ Cabeza, 15, 2ºD, Madrid; Tel: 915 399 860; Metro: Tirso de Molina; open Tuesday and Thursday 10:00 to 11:30 a.m./2:30 to 4:00 p.m./8:30 to 10:00 p.m.

Gimnasio Arian has classes in aerobics, Pilates, yoga, Tai Chi, karate, and more. Gimnasio Arian, C/ Flora, 3, 28002 Madrid; Tel: 915 590 514; Web site: www.gimnasioarian.com; Metro: Ópera.

A few other great yoga places can be found at these Web sites: www.ayusyoga.com; www.narayaniyoga.com; www.despacioyoga.com.

Sevilla

As in Madrid, there are copious yoga classes in Sevilla. Listed here are just a few of the possibilities: Centro Integral de Yoga, Web site: www.centrointegraldeyoga.com; Lãshala, Web site: www.lashala.com; Sadhana, www.sadhanasevilla.com; TerraYoga Sevilla, www.terrayogasevilla.com; and Diksha traditional integral yoga, C/ Relator, 15 (enter at Feria y Alameda), Sevilla; Tel: 954 378 623; e-mail: yoga-shakti@hotmail.com; Web site: www.diksha.vpweb.es/.

MEDITATION

There are numerous opportunities for meditation practice in Spain. The following are only a few of the many options. Some of the centers listed under "Yoga" also offer meditation. Siestas are popular especially in summertime. See health centers in the "Massage" section that offer relaxing locations for twenty- to thirty-minute refreshing siestas and some that offer combination siesta with massage packages.

For Vipassana meditation explore the Vipassana Meditation Centre: Dhamma Neru is located about 56 km northwest of Barcelona city. Dhamma Neru, Apartado Postal 29, Santa María de Palautordera, 08460 Barcelona; Tel: 938 482 695; e-mail: info@es.dhamma.org; Web site: www.neru.dhamma.org/index.php?id=966_L=0.

The Center for Tibetan Buddhism (Centro Budista Tibetano) is 85 km northwest of Barcelona in the Montseny Natural Park. Centro Budista Tibetano Tushita, Mas Casanova d'en Crous, Apartado de correos nº 69, 17401 Arbúcies (Girona); Tel: 972 178 262; e-mail: tushitaes@interausa.com; Web site: www.budismotibetano.net/tushita.

At the Web site www.budismotibetano.net in the right column click on Centros Budistas for a list of the Buddhist Centers in Spain. You can also find information at the House of Tibet in Barcelona, C/ Rosselló, 181, 08036 Barcelona; Tel: 932 075 966; e-mail: info@casadeltibetbcn.org; Web site: www.casadeltibetbcn.org.

Madrid

The Centro Budista Vajrayana provides a list of meditation places (*Clases de Meditación*) in Madrid at their Web site: www.MeditaEnMadrid.org.

Valencia

Nagarjuna Valencia is a Tibetan Buddhist center offering meditation and other activities. Nagarjuna Valencia, C/ General Urrutia, 43, pta. 2, 46006 Valencia; Tel: 963 951 008; e-mail: nagarjunavalencia@ono.com; Web site: www.nagarjunavalencia.com.

Meditation is offered on Thursdays at 8:30 p.m. at Yoga Valencia in the center of the city. Yoga Valencia, Plaza del Patriarca, 4, pta. 4, 46002 Valencia; Tel: 687 423 076; e-mail: info@yoga-valencia.es; Web site: www.yoga-valencia.es.

Sevilla

The Kadampa Buddhist Center in Sevilla offers various meditation times: check the Web site. Centro Budista Kadampa Mahamudra, C/ Yuste, 9, Sevilla; Tel: 954 901 270; e-mail: epc.sevillamahamudra@gmail.com; Web site: www.sevilla.kadampa.es.

Meditation is also available at these two lovely centers: www.seikyuji.org and www.zensevilla.org.

THERMAL BATHS

Called *baños* or *balnearios* in Spanish, thermal baths have been popular for centuries. Some of these listed are actually naturally occurring thermal hot springs, but some are heated baths in the Arab style. All the baths and spas listed require swimsuits. If you do not want to spend hours bathing suit shopping, a number of the Arab baths sell basic navy blue one-piece suits for 12 euros. The National Association of Balnearios in Spain has a Web site where you can locate balnearios all over Spain; Web site: www.balnearios.org. Look at the "Clinics and Spas" listings for other spa facilities.

Spain's only thermal spring–fed lake is in the northeastern part of the country in Alhama de Aragón, 204 km from Madrid. The lake sits among almost seventeen acres of parks and gardens. The water is so warm—at 32°C/90°F—you can swim in it comfortably all year long. The thermal complex offers full spa services as well as traditional thermal bath therapies. Termas Pallares Spa, Autovía Madrid-Zaragoza Km 204, 50230 Alhama de Aragón; Tel: 976 840 011; e-mail: balneario@termaspallares.com; Web site: www.termaspallares.com/en/?lang=en.

Andalucía
Granada

You need to make reservations for the Hammam Baños Árabes in Granada, an authentic Arab-style bath experience. The baths are housed in an eleventh-century building, renovated into the baths almost thirteen years ago. This is not a big thermal bath facility, but a small, atmospheric Arab bath, with separate changing rooms for men and women. Note: traditional baths do not allow men and women to bathe on the same days. While fashioned after traditional baths, Hammam Baños Árabes is designed for tourists and locals alike. Men and women can bathe together (and many couples do). There is a cold pool, a hot pool, and the largest pool is medium temperature. You can pay extra for a fifteen-minute massage done in open cubicles in an area beyond the pools. Open 10:00 a.m. to 10:00 p.m. with appointments every two hours. Bath only is 19 euros, and 28 euros for bath and massage. Suits are required, towels provided. The Hammam sells suits for 12 euros. Conveniently located just past the tourist office off of Plaza Nueva in the shadows of the Alhambra. Hammam Baños Árabes, C/ Santa Ana, 16, 18009 Granada; Tel: 902 333 334; e-mail: reservasgranada@hammamspain.com; Web site: www.granada.hammamspain.com.

At the Aljibe, there are seven pools with different temperatures. Partaking of just the baths costs 17 euros; with a fifteen-minute massage the total is 26 to 28 euros. Aljibe is about eight blocks south of the cathedral toward the Federico García Lorca Park. Aljibe Baños Árabes, C/ San Miguel Alta, 41 (on the corner of C/ Obispo Hurtado), 18002 Granada; Tel: 958 522 867; e-mail: reservas@aljibesanmiguel.es; Web site: www.aljibesanmiguel.es; open every day 10:00 a.m. to 10:00 p.m. with appointments every two hours.

For the Elvira Spa baths, offering a variety of massages, you must enter through the Hostal Arteaga located west of the cathedral between Gran Vía and Elvira streets. Baños de Elvira Spa, C/ Arteaga, 3, 18010 Granada; Tel: 958 208 841; e-mail: hostalarteaga@hostalarteaga.com; www.banosdeelvira.com.

Lanjarón, off the A-44 highway between Granada and the coast, is known for its spa and medicinal waters. Open from February to December, the balneario makes use of the six different natural springs. Balneario de Lanjarón, Avda. de la Constitución, s/n, 18420 Lanjarón (Granada); Tel: 958 770 137; e-mail: informacion@balneariodelanjaron.com; Web site: www.balneariodelanjaron.com/index.php?id=276.

Córdoba

The Hammams de Al Andalus, housed in an old, restored Córdoban building near the mosque (*mezquita* in Spanish), has traditional baths with pools of different temperatures—a cold room, temperate, and a hot room, plus a Turkish steam bath. The baths cost only 24 euros; with a fifteen-minute massage the total is 32 euros. Swimsuit required. Hammams de Al Andalus, C/ Corregidor Luís de la Cerda, 51, 14003 Córdoba; Tel: reception: 957 484 746; reservations 902 333 334; e-mail: cordobareservas@hammams.es; Web site: www.hammamspain.com/cordoba/; open 10:00 a.m. until midnight with appointments every two hours.

Sevilla

The Aire de Sevilla Baños Árabes (Arab Baths) have a small cold pool, a small to medium-size hot pool that is not that hot, and a large warm pool. In addition it has a warm Jacuzzi, a Turkish bath (steam bath), which was dripping burning hot water and not steaming when I went, and a relaxation room. The tea room and relaxation rooms are beautiful, but the rest of the baths are not nearly as nice as the ones in Córdoba and Granada. One and a half hours in the baths costs 20 euros, plus additional massages start at 31 euros and go up to 85 depending upon time and treatments. Aire de Sevilla, Baños Arabes (Arab Baths), C/ Aire, 15, 41004 Sevilla; Tel: 955 010 024/25/26; e-mail: recepcion@airedesevilla.com; Web site: www.airedesevilla.com/eng/gallery.html. The baths are open 10:00 a.m. to 2:00 a.m., and body treatments are available until midnight. The Tea

Room (Tetería) is open Sunday to Thursday 3:30 to 10:30 p.m., Friday and Saturday 3:30 p.m. to 2:00 a.m.

Málaga

The El Hammam Baños Árabes is five years old and offers traditional Arab baths and massages. You can walk in for the baths, but if you want a massage you should book ahead. Currently the streets around the baths are under construction making it all look a little sketchy—day and night. The best way to find it is off of C/ Granada by the Cacao Sampaka. Prices range from 24 euros for just the baths, with optional massages for fifteen, thirty, or sixty minutes costing about 1 euro a minute. Baños Árabes, C/ Tomás de Cózar, 13, 29001 Málaga; Tel: 952 212 327; e-mail: info@elhammam.com; Web site: www.elhammam.com; open seven days a week from 10:30 a.m. until 10:00 p.m.

Catalunya

In the Girona Pyrenees and Costa Brava in the northeast corner of Spain you can find thermal baths at the following locations:

Centre Lúdic Termal (Thermal Leisure Center) de Catalunya is a huge thermal bath and day-spa complex near Girona. Basic thermal bath prices start at 25 euros and go up from there. Spa treatments are also available. Open every day 11:00 a.m. to 10:00 p.m. on weekdays and until 11:00 p.m. on weekends. Centre Lúdic Termal Magma, Veïnat de Vall, s/n, 17430 Santa Coloma de Farners (Girona); Tel: 972 843 535; e-mail: info@magma-cat.com; Web site: www.magma-cat.com/eng/index.html. Two hotels are affiliated with the thermal baths: Balneari Termes Orión, Veïnat de Vall, s/n, 17430 Santa Coloma de Farners (Girona); Tel: 972 840 065; e-mail: info@ termasorion.cat; Web site: www.balneari-termas-orion.com/eng/ index.html. And the Font Vella Hotel Balneari, Passeig de la Font Vella, 57, 17403 Sant Hilari Sacalm (Girona); Tel: 972 868 305; e-mail: info@balnearifontvella.cat; Web site: www.balnearifontvella. cat/eng/index.php.

Vichy Catalán is a delicious, bottled sparkling mineral water, and you can soak your body in the waters at the Vichy Catalán Baths. Balneari Vichy Catalán, Av. Doctor Furest, 32, 17455 Caldes de Malavella (Girona); Tel: 972 470 000; e-mail: balneario@vichycatalan. es; Web site: www.balnearivichycatalan.com. In the same town you can also visit the Balneari Prats, Pl. de Sant Esteve, 7, 17455 Caldes de Malavella (Girona); Tel: 972 470 051.

Sanamolls is an open-air center with natural therapies including massage, clay, and baths. Sanamolls, Castelló d'Empúries; Tel: 972 451 593; e-mail: banysargila@banysargila.com; Web site: www.banysargila.com.

Caldes de Boí Balneari, outside of Lleida, in the Valle de Boí near the Parc Nacional d'Aigues Tortes, is a full-service spa with a variety of massage and thermal water therapies. There are two hotels serving the spa, the Hotel El Manantial and Hotel Caldes. Offices at Caldes de Boí, C/ Pau Clair, 162, 6º 3, 08037 Barcelona; Tel: 932 722 647; e-mail: info@caldesdeboi.com; Web site: www.caldesdeboi.com. Hotel El Manantial, Tel: 973 696 220; Hotel Caldes, Tel: 973 696 230.

Barcelona and Surroundings

Like the other Arab baths around Spain, the appointment times at Aire de Barcelona are at two-hour intervals. Prices start at 20 euros for the baths and then 31 and up for additional massages. There are three pools (cold, warm, and hot) as well as a hammam (steam room). Aire de Barcelona Baños Árabes, Passeo Picasso, 22, 08003 Barcelona; Tel: 902 555 789; e-mail: reservas@airedebarcelona.com; Web site: www.airedebarcelona.com; open 10:00 a.m. to 2:00 a.m.

Outside of Barcelona there are five towns known for their natural mineral and thermal springs. The towns can be reached by car, train, or bus. Suits are required at all the baths, and it is recommended that you bring flip-flops, a bathrobe, and towels.

The town of Arenys de Mar is on the sea. The baths are at the Balneari Titus with water at 100.5ºF. Balneari Titus, Ctra. N-11, Km 655, 08350 Arenys de Mar; Tel: 937 912 076; Web site: www.balnearititus.com; open year-round.

In Caldes d'Estrac, also on the sea, there are two facilities that take advantage of the natural 102ºF mineral water. Banys de Caldes d'Estrac, C/ Riera, 29, 08393 Caldes d'Estrac; Tel: 937 912 605; Web site: www.termalismetotal.org; open year-round. At the Hotel Colón they offer both mineral water as well as thalassotherapy (seawater) treatments. Hotel Colón, Pl. de les Barques, s/n, Caldes d'Estrac 08393 (Barcelona); Tel: 937 910 400; e-mail: info@hotel-colon.net; Web site: www.hotel-colon.net; open year-round.

In Caldes de Montbui the thermal waters have been used since Roman times. The Thermalia Museum is located here. The Balneari Broquetas is in the old part of the town. The water is naturally hot at 158ºF. Balneari Broquetas, Pl. de la Font de Lleó, 1, Caldes de Montbui; Tel: 938 650 100; e-mail: recepcio.b@grupbroquetas.com; Web site: www.grupbroquetas.com/ENG/home.aspx; open year-round. The Termes Victòria is in the main square, near the preserved Roman baths. Termes Victòria, C/ Barcelona, 12, 08140 Caldes de Montbui; Tel: 938 650 150; Web site: www.termesvictoria.com.

In La Garriga the thermal waters are naturally at 140ºF and as in Caldes de Montbui, have been used for centuries. Two spas offer water therapies: La Garriga Gran Hotel Balneario Blancafort, C/ Mina, 7, 08530 La Garriga; Tel: 938 605 600; Web site: www.balnearioblancafort.com; and Termes La Garriga, C/ Banys, 23, 08530 La Garriga; Tel: 938 717 086; e-mail: info@termes.com; Web site: www.termes.com.

The historic town of Tona is near the Montseny massif. The Balneari Codina has been a spa for one hundred years. Balneari Codina, Ctra. de Manresa, 59, 08551 Tona; Tel: 938 870 314; Web site: www.balnearicodina.com.

Madrid

The Baños Árabes has three pools with different temperatures in the typical Arab bath style, a steam room, and a resting room, with prices starting at about 40 euros. Baños Árabes, Medina Mayrit, C/ Atocha, 14, 28012 Madrid; Tel: 902 333 334; e-mail: reservas@medinamayrit.com; Web sites: www.medinamayrit.com/en/ and www.hammamsdealandalus.com; Metro: Sol or Tirso de Molina.

The Balnearia Spa Urbano offers hydrotherapy circuits with thermal baths, massages, wine and chocolate spa therapies, Pilates, and more. Balnearia Spa Urbano, P de la Habana, 33 (enter at Crevillente, 1), 28036 Madrid; Tel: 915 648 267; e-mail: info@balneariaspa.com; Web site: www.balneariaspa.com; Metro: Santiago Bernabéu.

Spa Excellence is in a restored nineteenth-century palace. Spa Excellence, Plaza del Ángel, 6, 28012 Madrid; Tel: 915 234 065; e-mail:

recepcion@spaexcellence.es; Web site: www.spaexcellence.es; Metro: Tirso de Molina or Antón Martín.

Valencia
Calma Balneario Urbano is a full-service spa with thermal baths, a variety of bodywork, beauty and spa therapies, and yoga and Pilates classes, on one corner of the busy and majestic Plaza del Ayuntamiento, within two blocks of the train station (Valencia Estació Nord). Calma Balneario Urbano, Plaza del Ayuntamiento, 29, 46002 Valencia; Tel: 963 941 069; Web site: www.calma.es; open Monday to Saturday 10:00 a.m. to 10:00 p.m. Check Web site for Sunday hours.

Castilla-La Mancha
The Castilla-La Mancha region boasts fifteen balnearios.

Balneario de Benito, Reolid-Salobre, Albacete: www.balneariodebenito.es

Balneario Baños la Esperanza, Reolid-Salobre, Albacete: www.balneariolaesperanza.es

Balneario de Tus, Tus-Yeste, Albacete: www.balneariodetus.com

Balneario Baños de la Concepción, Villatoya, Albacete: no Web site

Spa Alba Naturvida, Albacete: no Web site

Balneario Cervantes, Santa Cruz de Mudela, Ciudad Real: www.balneariocervantes.com

Balneario de Fuencaliente, Fuencaliente, Ciudad Real: no Web site

Balneario Spa Alarcos, Valverde, Ciudad Real: www.spalarcos.com

Balneario Solán de Cabras, Beteta, Cuenca: www.rbsc.es

Balneario Baños de Alcantud, Alcantud, Cuenca: www.relaistermal.com. This Web site is for seven different balnearios. Baños de Alcantud is in the lower right of the page, and you can click on it for more specific information.

Balnearios TermaEuropa Carlos III, Trillo, Guadalajara: www.balneariocarlostercero.com

Hotel & Spa Salinas de Imón, Imón, Guadalajara: www.salinasdeimon.com/ingles/principal.htm

Balneario Las Palmeras, Villafranca de los Caballeros, Toledo: www.paralelo40.org/bpalmeras/

Fontecruz Palacio Eugenia de Montijo, Toledo: www.en.fontecruz.com/eugenia-de-montijo/spa/

Villa Nazules Hotel Hípica Spa, Nambroca, Toledo: www.villanazules.com

Castilla y León
There are ten balnearios in the Castilla y León region. See the helpful Castilla y León tourist page for detailed information on the spas; Web site: www.turismocastillayleon.com.

Galicia
For detailed information about the thirty-eight spas, including two thalassotherapy centers, in the region of Galicia, download the free brochure, *Water for the Senses,* from the Galician tourist page; Web site: www.turgalicia.es/default.asp?cidi=I.

Navarra
South of Pamplona in the lower Navarra region the spa town of Fitero, west of Tudela, has mineral waters historically used to treat tuberculosis. The Baños de Fitero, C/ Extramuros, s/n, 31593 Fitero (Navarra) can be accessed at both the Balneario Bécquer hotel, Tel: 948 776 100; and the Balneario Palafox hotel, Tel: 948 776 275; central reservation number: 948 404 749; e-mail: info@balneariodefitero.es; Web site: www.balneariodefitero.es.

Health

If you want to maintain a treatment plan, explore modalities in a foreign country, or seek out new experiences, you can make use of the following resources to help you find health practitioners and services in the regions you are visiting.

Alternative and complementary health services in Spain are not so widespread as in other European countries although availability is growing rapidly and there are services in all the major cities, with massage and acupuncture being the most prevalent. There is currently no licensing for naturopathic doctors and many other modali-

> Maimonides, also known as Rabbi Moses ben Maimon, was born in Córdoba in 1135 and died in 1204. He was a rabbi, physician, and Jewish philosopher. Among his many writings and theories was *El régimen de salud* (*The Regimen of Health*), which was progressive by modern standards. He recognized the interdependence of body and mind, and he felt that health is attained by a healthy diet, exercise, and general balance in all things.

ties. The following Web guides list practitioners in different regions of Spain and are updated regularly.

A network of English-speaking health care practitioners in Barcelona has a Web site searchable for therapies and practitioners at www.barcelonahealersandtherapists.net.

La Chispa is an alternative health and lifestyle print and Web magazine with good resources for all things natural in the Andalucía region; Web site: www.lachispa.net.

Guía Verde is a Spanish Green Guide covering Spanish-speaking countries. Make sure as you search for modalities of alternative health care that the listings you are exploring say España (Spain). Guía Verde; Web site: www.guiaverde.info.

ANTHROPOSOPHICAL MEDICINE

Anthroposophical medicine, based on the use of natural rhythms and remedies, was developed by the scientist and philosopher Rudolf Steiner. Anthroposophy comes from two Greek words: *anthropos,* meaning human being, and *sophia,* meaning wisdom. Anthroposophy can be translated as "human wisdom."

Dr. Rudolf Steiner (1861–1925), a scientist and artist, developed anthroposophical medicine around 1913 based on his studies of natural, social, and spiritual realms, and his conclusions that plants, animals, humans, the earth, and the cosmos are all living things with vital forces. Greatly influenced by the German philosopher

Goethe (1749–1832), Steiner developed not just theories and systems around health, but also systems of education (Waldorf schools), agriculture (biodynamic farming), astronomy, color, and movement (eurythmy).

Dr. Rudolf Hauschka (1891–1969), an Austrian chemist, worked with Rudolf Steiner to develop remedies using anthroposophical theories and understanding of plants, minerals, and metals, and their interactions and effects on human health and vitality.

Based on in-depth studies of rhythm, and a combination of homeopathic potentiation and rhythmic exposure to elemental polarities, Dr. Hauschka, along with Dr. Ita Wegman, another Steiner associate, developed what were to become the WALA (Warmth/Ash, Light/Ash) remedies. The plant-based remedies are made from wild or biodynamically grown plants.

Dr. Hauschka collaborated with Elisabeth Sigmund (1914–), a cosmetologist, and they cofounded Dr. Hauschka Skin Care products.

In Spain the Association for Anthroposophical Medicine is called the Asociacion de Médicos para la Medicina Antroposófica located at the Instituto para la Formación en Medicina y Terapias Antroposóficas, C/ Manuel Tovar, 3, 28034 Madrid; Tel: 913 580 365; e-mail: ifma@iehost.net and fherrero@institutohygiea.com; Web site: www.ifma.org.es.

Beautiful inner courtyards lie hiding in many Spanish buildings.
Garibola vegetarian restaurant in Bilbao.

Bicing, the city-sponsored bike rental program in Barcelona.

Ecological honey from the mountains is sold at some markets.

Bright boats in the fishing village of Bermeo in the northern Basque region.

Ecomercat health food store in Valencia.

The Alhambra from the picturesque and old part of Granada, the Albayzín.

Oranges and lemons are plentiful at all the markets.

The Gate of Forgiveness (Puerta del Perdon) entry to the Orange Court (Patio de los Naranjos) at the Cordoba Mosque (Mezquita).

Artists love the blue and white town of Cadaques, perched on the Mediterranean at one of the easternmost points of Spain.

Spain is the third largest producer of wind energy in the world, so it is commonplace to see mountaintops lined with windmills.

Herboristeria del Rei, open since 1823, is the oldest herb store in Barcelona.

Fresh fruit and juice stand at La Boqueria market in Barcelona.

The grand indoor Mercado Central, the central market in Valencia.

Espai Visor vegetarian restaurant in Valencia.

Bellcaire: Springtime field of sweet-smelling blossoms in the Costa Brava area.

MASSAGE

Therapeutic massage usually involves a full-body massage, with or without oil. While there are different techniques, the general purpose is to relieve muscle tension, increase circulation, and foster relaxation. Bodywork is a broad term covering many different techniques of physical touch and manipulation. Reflexology, a type of massage focused on the feet (and sometimes hands), is popular in Europe and is based on the reflex zones of the feet and their correlation to the whole body.

Many clinics, spas, and thermal baths offer a variety of massage services; see listings under those headings for other choices. The following list includes only a few of the many massage and bodywork options. Massage is *masaje* in Spanish. See the above-listed Spain-wide Web guides for practitioners.

Barcelona

Instituto Cráneo Sacral offers deep-tissue work, stress-release techniques, and craniosacral osteopathy. Alberto Panizo and Greta Adam are the practitioners and between them they speak English, Spanish, and German. Instituto Cráneo Sacral, C/ Diputación, 224, Barcelona; Tel: 689 786 519 or 977 851 640; Web site: www.craneosacral-panizo.com/Craneo_Sacral_English.html; Metro: Universidad.

Masajes a Mil offers massages, facials, siestas, and other body treatments in their four Barcelona locations. A half-hour siesta runs around 4.50 euros. At the Web site click on "centros multiservicio" for cities and then click on a city for locations. Masajes a Mil, C/ Mallorca, 233, bajo, 08008 Barcelona; Tel: 932 158 585; Web site: www.masajesa1000.net. Other locations are at C/ Sardenya, 529; Travesera Les Corts, 178; and in Sitges at Avenida Sofia, 3.

Mailuna offers massages, spa therapies, and siestas, with prices starting at 36 euros. Mailuna, C/ Valldonzella, 48, 08001 Barcelona; Tel: 933 012 002; e-mail: info@mailuna.net; Web site: www.mailuna.net.

O2 Centro Wellness has fourteen full-service fitness and wellness centers around Spain. In Barcelona they are located at O2 Centro Wellness Pedralbes, C/ Eduardo Conde, 2-6, 08034 Barcelona; Tel: 932 053 976; e-mail: pedralbes@o2centrowellness.com; Web site: www.o2centrowellness.com/corporativa/corp_eng/index.htm.

Masajes a Mil, Mailuna, and O2 Centro Wellness all offer massage as well as relaxing rooms for twenty- to thirty-minute refreshing siestas with possible combination siesta and massage packages.

Chavutti offers a type of Ayurvedic massage using the practitioner's feet rather than hands, and warm oil. Treatments last one to two hours. Chavutti Thirumal at Yoga Bindu, Las Ramblas, 40-42, near Plaça Reial, Barcelona; Tel: 609 176 505; Web site: www.saramalena. net; Metro: Liceu or Drassanes.

At Essential you can receive traditional Thai massage, Ayurvedic treatments, and hair and beauty care with English, French, and Spanish spoken. Essential, C/ Paris, 204 (near C/ Balmes), 08008 Barcelona; Tel: 931 650 587; Web site: www.essentialspahairstyle. com; open Monday to Friday 10:00 a.m. to 8:00 p.m., Saturday by appointment only.

Madrid

Eco Bar & Spa offers full spa therapies and massages using natural products. They have a natural foods restaurant and store around the corner from the spa. Eco Bar & Spa, Paseo Pintor Rosales, 76, 28008 Madrid; Tel: 915 441 716; e-mail: infoecobarspa.com; Web site: www.ecobarspa.com; open Tuesday to Saturday noon to 9:00 p.m.

The Ranvvai Center is a school and health center offering a variety of natural therapies including reflexology, massage, naturopathy, osteopathy, and more. Ranvvai Centro de Terapias Naturales, Casa de las Flores, Argüelles area, Madrid; Tel: 915 501 800; e-mail: info@ranvvai.com; Web site: www.ranvvai.com.

Massage, lymph drainage, sports massage, reflexology, naturopathy, and nutrition consulting are all offered at Alborada. Alborada, Postigo de San Martín, 9, 2o2, 28013 Madrid; Tel: 915 232 571; Mobile: 639 686 847; e-mail: quiroalborada@qmail.com; Web site: www.alboradamasaje.com. Metro: Callao.

Thai and Eastern massage and spa therapies are available at the Yommana Thai Concept. Yommana Thai Concept, C/ Fuencarral, 137, 1oD, 28005 Madrid; Tel: 914 450 891; e-mail: info@yommanathai. es; Web site: www.yommanathai.es; Metro: Quevedo.

Ecocentro is a health center offering Reiki, yoga, and other modalities. It has an adjacent organic foods store and restaurant. Ecocentro Salud, C/ Esquilache, 2 al 12 (at Avda. Pablo Iglesias, 2), 28003 Madrid; Tel: 915 531 299; e-mail: info@ecocentrosalud.com; Web site: www.ecocentrosalud.es; Metro: Ríos Rosas or Cuatro Caminos; open Monday to Thursday 11:00 a.m. to 3:30 p.m./5:00 to 9:30 p.m.

Masaje Tradicional Tailandés is a school and therapy center offering Thai massage, open Monday to Friday 10:00 a.m. to 2:00 p.m./4:30 to 8:30 p.m. with prices ranging from 30 to 50 euros. Masaje Tradicional Tailandés, C/ Conde de Romanones, 16, 1º, 28012 Madrid; Tel: 913 694 539; Web site: www.mthai.es; Metro: Tirso de Molina.

Masajes a Mil offers massages, facials, siestas, and body treatments with eight locations throughout Madrid. At the Web site click on "centros multiservicio" for cities and then click on a city for locations. Masajes a Mil, C/ Alcalá, 127, 28009 Madrid; Tel: 915 783 297; Web site: www.masajesa1000.net. See the Web site for their eight other locations.

Granada
EHOPA offers homeopathy and massage therapies, and a small *herbolario,* by the RENFE train station in Granada. EHOPA, C/ Faisán, 1, Granada; Tel: 958 276 878; Web site: www.ehopa.net; open Monday to Friday 9:00 a.m. to 2:00 p.m./5:00 to 9:00 p.m.

Sevilla
A range of massages are offered at Dharma Sevilla, including reflexology, shiatsu, polarity, craniosacral, Thai massage, Ayurvedic massage, and other modalities. They also have yoga and Pilates classes. Dharma Sevilla, C/ Sánchez Perrier, 4 (behind the Hotel Macarena), 41009 Sevilla; Tel: 954 901 503; e-mail: info@dharmasevilla.es; Web site: www.dharmasevilla.es.

The Centro Gaia offers a range of natural therapies including massage. Affiliated with the health food store and restaurant of the same name. Centro Gaia, C/ Arjona, 5, Sevilla; Tel: 954 561 831; Web site: www.gaiaecosalud.com.

Valencia
Masajes a Mil offers massages, facials, siestas, and body treatments. At the Web site click on "centros multiservicio" for cities and then

click on a city for locations. Masajes a Mil, C/ Isabel la Católica, 6, Valencia; Tel: 963 943 709; Web site: www.masajesa1000.net.

See also the Navarro Spa Catalá under "Clinics and Spas," and the Calma Balneario Urbano under "Thermal Baths."

CHIROPRACTIC

The spinal cord is the primary pathway for the nervous system, hence misalignment and/or pressure on nerves can cause various problems. Chiropractors use spinal manipulation and structural adjustment to correct spinal-nerve problems, joint dysfunction, and other musculoskeletal conditions.

David Perelle is a chiropractic doctor trained in the United States at Life Chiropractic College West. His chiropractic clinic has two locations where Spanish, French, and English are spoken. Centre Chiropractic Diagonal, Avda. Diagonal, 353, 3º 2ª (between Bruc and Roger de Lluria), 08037 Barcelona; Tel: 934 588 597; and Centre Chiropractic Diagonal, Avda. Jaime I, 87, 1º 1ª, 08100 Mollet del Valles; Tel: 639 626 951; Web site: www.chiropracticdiagonal.com; Metro: Verdaguer or Diagonal.

The Quiropractic Remedy Centre has a center in London and one in Sant Cugat, just five minutes from the Sant Cugat train station. The Quiropractic Remedy Centre, Plaça Unio, 1, Bloque A, 5th floor, Sant Cugat del Vallès; Tel: 935 441 916; Web site: www.chiropractor-barcelona.com.

ALEXANDER TECHNIQUE

The Alexander Technique focuses awareness on the importance of using only those muscles necessary to a particular task. F. Matthias Alexander developed the technique in the late 1800s to solve a vocal problem he experienced due to poor posture. Particular attention is placed on the head, which comprises about ten to fifteen percent of the body's weight and can place stress on the neck and spine. The Alexander Technique helps to reeducate the body into healthier postural positions. Alexander Barcelona, C/ Santa Anna, 28, 1º 2ª, Oficina 13, 08002 Barcelona; Tel: 664 252 947; Web site: www.alexander-barcelona.net/English.html.

Orna Genislav has eighteen years' experience as an Alexander Technique practitioner, and twelve years as a Biodynamic Craniosacral practitioner. Orna Genislav, C/ Princesa, Barcelona; Tel: 933 102 460; Mobile: 615 688 847; e-mail: orange@yahoo.com.

NATUROPATHY

Naturopathic medicine treats health conditions by utilizing the body's inherent ability to heal. It involves a variety of therapies, including diet, herbs, homeopathy, and hydrotherapy. There are six basic principles to naturopathic medicine: to work with the healing power of nature; to treat the cause rather than the effect; to do no harm; to treat the whole person; to have the physician be a teacher; and that prevention is the best cure.

In Spain the term naturopathic or natural doctors covers a broad range of practitioners. Web sites about naturopathy and natural health in Spain include: The Federación Española de Profesionales en Naturopatía (FENACO) is working to get naturopaths licensed in Spain; Web site: www.fenaco.net. The National Corporation of Professional Experts in Naturopathy (Corporación Nacional de Profesionales Expertos en Naturopatía); Web site: www.expertosennaturopatia.org. The Association of Complementary Medicine (Asociación de Medicinas Complementarias); Web site: www.amcmh.org.

At the comprehensive Asociación Española de Médicos Naturistas (AEMN) (the Spanish Association of Natural Practitioners) you can search for practitioners by province and modality under the heading "Médicos Naturistas." AEMN; Web site: http://medicosnaturistas.es.

Part of the Manantial de Salud line of *herboristería* stores (see "Herbs and Remedies"), Espai de Salut del Manantial (ESMA) is a day-clinic offering naturopathy, homeopathy, acupuncture, massage, mental health care, and natural esthetic treatments. A rarity, they also offer treatments with the Indiba machine, a local heat treatment good for loosening and softening tissues and joints, as well as for organ stimulation and detoxification. See the Web site www.indiba.es/english for more information about Indiba machines. ESMA, Manantial de Salud, C/ Mercaders, 7, Principal, 1º, Barcelona; Tel: 933 104 054 and 933 191 965; e-mail: herbocat@ manantial-salud.com; Web site: www.manantial-salud.com/web/index.html.

The Institute for Biological Health is run by Dr. Domingo Pérez León, an MD trained in various natural and biological therapies. Institute for Biological Health, C/ General Yagües Bis, 6 Local 9, 28020 Madrid; Tel: 915 974 030 or 915 974 513; e-mail: ibs@institutobiologico.com; Web site: www.institutobiologico.com.

HOMEOPATHY

Homeopathy is a specific healing system in which minute doses of specially prepared natural remedies are used to trigger a healing response in an individual. A homeopath prescribes a remedy based on the pattern of symptoms with which a person presents. Homeopathic remedies can be used for a wide range of conditions, from acute illness and injury to complicated chronic conditions.

Homeopathy was developed more than two hundred years ago by Samuel Hahnemann, a German physician, and it remains in wide use throughout the world. There are two key homeopathic concepts: the Law of Potentiation, which states that medicine can be stronger or more effective when more diluted, and the Law of Similars, which holds that like cures like.

At the Asociación Médica Española de Homeopatía y Bioterapia (AMEHB) (Spanish Medical Association of Homeopathy and Biotherapy) you can search under the heading "Homeópatas" for practitioners throughout Spain. AMEHB; Web site: www.amehb.com.

As in many European countries, most of the pharmacies in Spain sell homeopathic remedies, and in large cities there are pharmacies (*farmacias*) on almost every corner. I am including a couple of pharmacies here but rest assured they are plentiful and easy to find throughout Spain.

The Farmacia Guenechea has a good selection of homeopathics and other natural remedies and products including the Sanoflore organic line of personal care and aromatherapy products from France; Web site: www.sanoflore.es. Farmacia Guenechea, C/ Autonomía Kalea, 41, 48012 Bilbao; Tel: 944 210 501.

The Serra Mandri Pharmacy in Barcelona makes a point of specializing in homeopathy and natural remedies and products, with staff who speak English. Serra Mandri Pharmacy, Avda. Diagonal, 478, 08006 Barcelona; Tel: 934 161 270 for the pharmacy; Tel: 932 173 249 especially for homeopathy; Web site: www.farmaciaserra.com; open every day 9:00 a.m. to 10:00 p.m.

Farmàcia Torres is a pharmacy in Barcelona open twenty-four hours a day every day of the year. They have natural remedies, and staff who speak English. Farmàcia Torres, Aribau, 62, at Aragó, 08011 Barcelona; Tel: 934 539 220; Mobile: 629 044 324; e-mail: info@farmaciaabierta24h.com; Web site: www.farmaciaabierta24h.com.

In Girona, Lluis Cals practices a range of health modalities including homeopathy, craniosacral osteopathy, and traditional Chinese medicine. Lluis Cals, C/ Emili Grahit, 59, 1r 1a, 17002 Girona; Tel: 972 411 100.

AYURVEDIC MEDICINE

Ayurveda means the "science of life." A comprehensive medical system that originated in ancient India, Ayurveda is one of the oldest medical systems in the world, dating back thousands of years. It has common themes with Chinese medicine systems, including working with the life force energy (called Prana in Ayurveda, Chi or Qi in Chinese). It includes working with different body types and personality temperaments called doshas, which are similar to more modern metabolic typing and blood type systems.

Ayurvedic medicine incorporates all five senses into therapies—touch, sound, color, aroma, and taste—so treatments involve a combination of diet, herbs, aromatherapy, bodywork, exercise, and spirit. Yoga is the movement and spirit element of Ayurvedic medicine (see "Yoga" section).

Ayurvedic massage is popular in Spain. A few places offering it include the following.

Chavutti offers a type of Ayurvedic massage using the practitioner's feet rather than hands, and warm oil. Treatments last one to two hours. Chavutti Thirumal at Yoga Bindu, Las Ramblas, 40-42, near Plaça Reial, Barcelona; Tel: 609 176 505; Web site: www.saramalena. net; Metro: Liceu or Drassanes.

At Essential you can receive traditional Thai massage, Ayurvedic treatments, and hair and beauty care with English, French, and Spanish spoken. Essential, C/ Paris, 204 (near C/ Balmes), 08008 Barcelona; Tel: 931 650 587; Web site: www.essentialspahairstyle. com; open Monday to Friday 10:00 a.m. to 8:00 p.m., Saturday by appointment only.

A range of massages are offered at Dharma Sevilla, including reflexology, shiatsu, polarity, craniosacral, Thai massage, Ayurvedic massage, and other modalities. They also have yoga and Pilates classes. Dharma Sevilla, C/ Sánchez Perrier, 4 (behind the Hotel Macarena), 41009 Sevilla; Tel: 954 901 503; e-mail: info@dharmasevilla.es; Web site: www.dharmasevilla.es.

Sisecel offers Naam yoga (using sacred sound), Ayurvedic massage, reflexology, and other body treatments. Sisecel, C/ Muntaner, 157, Ático, Barcelona; Tel: 933 215 062; Web site: www.sisecel.com.

The Ayurvedic Spa is in the Vilarmarxant hills about thirty minutes northwest of Valencia city. The spa offers six different types of Ayurvedic massage, water therapies, and other traditional spa and

Books about Ayurveda

Vasant Lad, *Ayurveda: A Practical Guide* (New Delhi: Motilal Banarsidass, 2002).

Dr. Robert Svoboda, *Ayurveda: Life, Health and Longevity* (Albuquerque: Ayurvedic Press, 2004).

Rudolph Ballentine, MD, *Radical Healing* (New York: Crown Publishers, 1999).

Ayurvedic treatments. Ayurvedic Spa, Font Calenta, Polígano, 38, Parcela, 234, 46191 Vilarmarxant (Valencia); Tel: 600 720 357; e-mail: ayurvedicspa@yahoo.com; Web site: www.theayurvedicspa.com.

ACUPUNCTURE AND TRADITIONAL CHINESE MEDICINE (TCM)

Chinese medicine is a four-thousand-year-old system of health based more on energy than on biochemistry. It has common themes with Ayurvedic medicine, including working with the vital life force energy (called Chi or Qi in Chinese, Prana in Ayurveda). Therapies include herbs, acupuncture, bodywork, exercise, diet, and lifestyle. Assessments include pulse readings, tongue diagnosis, acupuncture point palpation, and health history. The key elements include the interrelationship of all systems and organs of the body, balance within the polarities of yin and yang, as well as the integration of body, mind, and spirit. The eight guiding principles in Chinese medicine include external/internal, cold/heat, excess/deficiency, and yin/yang.

Acupuncture is a healing art that has been used in China for thousands of years. Acupuncturists work with the Chi/Qi energy, which flows through specific pathways in the body called meridians. These meridians form an energetic network that traverses the entire body and joins together all of its organ systems. Along each meridian's course, near the surface of the body, are points at which the Qi is most accessible for stimulation. To stimulate the Qi, thin, sterile needles are inserted at specific points determined by the acupuncturist's examination and diagnosis. The purpose of acupuncture is to move and balance the Qi, thus restoring health and harmony in the body.

Research funded by the National Institutes of Health at the University of Vermont is demonstrating the physiological mechanisms of acupuncture. Findings show that acupuncture stretches connective tissue, creating a cell response that leads to changes in brain chemistry.

The Sociedad de Acupuntura Médica de España (The Spain Society of Medical Acupuncture) allows you to search for acupuncturists throughout the country under "Acupuntores." The Sociedad de Acupuntura Médica de España; Web site: www.same-acupuntura.org.

Valencia

Acupuncture and Shiatsu with Olga Fedina offers sessions of shiatsu and acupuncture starting at 40 euros. Acupuncture and Shiatsu with Olga Fedina, C/ José Aguirre, 27, 1st floor, 2º, 46011 Valencia; Tel: 609 429 678; e-mail: info@acupunturavalencia.com; Web site: www.acupunturavalencia.com; open Monday to Friday 10:00 a.m. to 9:00 p.m.

The Centro de Medicina Tradicional China is a school and clinic for traditional Chinese medicine. They offer acupuncture, Chinese herbal preparations, and Tui Na, a type of Chinese bodywork. Centro de Medicina Tradicional China, Guang An Men, C/ Vinalopó, 14-16, bajos, 46021 Valencia; Tel: 963 561 548; e-mail: mtcvalencia@mtc.es; Web site: www.mtc.es/en.

Madrid

The Kaizo Center of Shiatsu and Acupuncture offers shiatsu (40 euros a session) and acupuncture (20 euros a session), plus group classes in yoga, Chi Kung, and Pilates. Kaizo Shiatsu, C/ Mayor, 4, 2º-4, Madrid; Tel: 915 239 674; Mobile: 652 347 962; Web site: www.kaizoshiatsu.com; Metro: Sol.

At Zenedhu you can find bio-energetic and thermal massages, acupuncture, osteopathy, shiatsu, reflexology, and facials with prices starting at 25 euros. Zenedhu Massage and Therapy Centre, C/ Atocha, 43, 28012 Madrid; Tel: 913 692 235; e-mail: zenedhu@e-tech.es; Web site: www.zenedhu.es.

The Corpore Zenter has a range of modalities including physiotherapy, osteopathy, acupuncture, lymphatic drainage, and Pilates. Cor-

Harriet Beinfield, L.Ac., and Efrem Korngold, L.Ac., OMD, *Between Heaven and Earth: A Guide to Chinese Medicine* (New York: Ballantine Books, 1991).

Paul Pitchford, *Healing with Whole Foods: Asian Traditions and Modern Nutrition* (Berkeley, CA: North Atlantic Books, 2002).

Ted Kaptchuk, OMD, *The Web That Has No Weaver: Understanding Chinese Medicine* (New York, NY: McGraw-Hill, 2000).

pore Zenter, C/ Duque de Alba, 3, 1º5, 28012 Madrid; Tel: 914 291 924; Web site: www.corporezenter.com.

The Centro de Medicina Tradicional China is a school and clinic for traditional Chinese medicine. They offer acupuncture, Chinese herbal preparations, and Tui Na, a type of Chinese bodywork. Centro de Medicina Tradicional China Guang An Men, C/ Jorge Juan, 141, 28028 Madrid; Tel: 902 110 216; e-mail: centromadrid@mtc.es; Web site: www.mtc.es/en.

Acupuncture and traditional Chinese medicine can be found at the Centro de Acupuntura Luna y Sol. Centro de Acupuntura Luna y Sol, Dra. Jing-Xin Liu, C/ Guzmán el Bueno, 93, 1º ext. dcha., 28005 Madrid; Tel: 915 449 821; Web site: www.acupunturalunaysol.com.

Belén Benito Moreno provides acupuncture and osteopathy treatements. Belén Benito Moreno, C/ Dulcinea, 45, 1º, 28020 Madrid; Tel: 660 456 944; e-mail: info@acupunturaymas.com; Web site: www.acupunturaymas.com; Metro: Alvarado.

Barcelona

Joachim Fouret is licensed in acupuncture and Chinese medicine in the UK. He speaks English and French, as well as Spanish. Joachim Fouret Acupuncture, Clinica Tuset, C/ Tuset, 13, atico 2, esc. ext., 08006 Barcelona; Tel: 635 973 807; Web site: www.fouret.es.

Pedro Demicheli holds a doctorate in Traditional Chinese Medicine and acupuncture from the United States. Pedro Demicheli, PhD, Paseo de San Juan, 180, Barcelona; Tel: 934 592 844; Mobile: 629 384 152; e-mail: pedrodemicheli@hotmail.com; Web site: www.pedrodemicheli.com.

The Centro de Medicina Tradicional China is a school and clinic for traditional Chinese medicine. They offer acupuncture, Chinese herbal preparations, and Tui Na, a type of Chinese bodywork. Centro de Medicina Tradicional China, Guang An Men, Avda. Madrid, 168-170, Entlo. A, 08028 Barcelona; Tel: 902 160 942 or 934 901 326; e-mail: intermtc@mtc.es; Web site: www.mtc.es/en.

COLON HYDROTHERAPY

Colon hydrotherapy, also known as colonics, uses special equipment to bathe, flush, and cleanse the colon and large intestine. It washes away old, toxic fecal matter, helping the body with detoxification and cleansing. There are two types of colon hydrotherapy techniques and machines. One uses a pressurized water system. The other uses a gravity, natural-flow water system. A colonic session usually takes from thirty to sixty minutes.

Colon hydrotherapy (*hidroterapia del colon*) is offered at Clínica Fiorela, Center for Pain Treatment, in front of C/ Valderromán, 16, 28035 Madrid; Tel: 91 373 2669; e-mail consultas@clinicafiorela.com; Web site: www.clinicafiorela.com/hidroterapia_eng.htm; open Monday to Friday 10:30 a.m. to 6:30 p.m.; Metro Antonio Machado.

BIOLOGICAL DENTISTRY

For more than a hundred years, many dentists have found connections between oral health, diet, and whole body health. Dr. Weston Price conducted extensive studies in this realm culminating in his 1939 landmark book *Nutrition and Physical Degeneration*. Theories about the relationship between teeth, Chinese meridians, organs, and joints have been developed, including Mouth-Acupuncture developed by a German doctor, Dr. Jochen Gleditsch.

Dr. Josef Issels (1907–1998), a German doctor specializing in cancer treatment, found that ninety-eight percent of cancer patients had

| **Resources about Dental and Body Connections** |

Hans-Ulrich Hecker, MD, Angelika Steveling, MD, and Elmar Peuker, MD, *Microsystems Acupuncture: The Complete Guide: Ear, Scalp, Mouth, Hand* (New York: Thieme Medical Publishers, 2005).

Mark Breiner, DDS, *Whole-Body Dentistry* (Fairfield, CT: Quantum Health Press, 1999). (ISBN: 0-9678443-0-4)

International Academy of Oral Medicine and Toxicology; Web site: www.iaomt.org.

Consumers for Dental Choice; Web site: www.toxicteeth.org.

The American Academy of Periodontology offers a "Perio-Cardio Connection" information section about conventional research concerning the connection between gum bacteria and disease and the health of the whole body including connections with diabetes, heart disease, osteoporosis, and respiratory disease; Web site: www.perio.org/consumer/perio_cardio.htm.

two or more root canals. Dr. Thomas Rau of the Paracelsus Clinic in Switzerland has found similar dental and whole body health correlations, so much so that the clinic has a full, state-of-the-art dental facility as part of its treatment center.

Recent news reports cite mouth-body correlations including periodontitis (gum disease) possibly being connected to stroke, cardiovascular disease, and bacterial pneumonia. Chronic inflammation and high levels of oral bacteria entering the bloodstream (bacteremia) can affect the overall health of the body. People with artificial joints and certain types of cardiovascular disease are recommended to have prophylaxis antibiotics prior to dental work due to the connections between the body and mouth.

Mercuriados is the Spanish association for the effects of mercury amalgams and other mercury sources. The Web site is in Spanish. If you can understand some or all of it, you will find useful information; Web site: www.mercuriados.org.

Mercury-free dentistry by Dr. Federico López-Amo Calatayud, C/ Micer Mascó, 35-1, pta. 1, 46010 Valencia; Tel: 963 390 512;

e-mail: info@odontologia-integral.com; Web site: www.odontolo-gia-integral.com.

Nadal Centro de Odontología Biológica y Tradicional, Dr. Ll. Nadal, C/ Entença, 168 local, 08029 Barcelona; Tel: 933 221 741; also at Av. Costa Brava, 24, 1r, Tossa de Mar (Girona); Tel: 972 342 165.

Biological dentistry using no mercury and employing alternative therapies including homeopathy, neural therapy, and craniosacral therapy: Odontología Bionatural, Dra. Mónica Rodríguez, Plaza Tirso de Molina, 16, 1º, 2, Madrid; Tel: 913 690 003; Mobile: 669 703 981; e-mail: monica.odontbio@hotmail.com; Web site: www.dieteticaexpress.com/spa/item/ART01206.html; Metro: Tirso de Molina or Sol.

Orthodontia and dentistry without metals; homeopathic, osteopathic treatments used: Estomatología Holística Clínica Dental, Dr. Miguel Ángel Recatero, C/ Goya, 38, 1º dcha., 28001 Madrid; Tel: 915 775 468; e-mail: estomatologiaholistica@hotmail.com; Web site: www.estomatologiaholistica.es.

Osteopathy, craniosacral, and ozone treatments: Centro de Odontología Holística, C/ Alfonso XII, 58, 1º izq., 28014 Madrid; Tel: 915 286 614; e-mail: dragelfo@odontologia-holistica.com; Web site: www.odontologia-holistica.com; Metro: Atocha Renfe.

HERBS AND REMEDIES

Called *herbolarios* or *herboristerías* in Spain, herb shops are fairly common. *Herboristerías* tend to be the ones with shelves lined with herbs, tinctures, and oils. Health food stores sell a variety of herbs and remedies as well. For store locations see the "Health Food Stores" section above. In Barcelona there are a number of wonderful *herboristerías* listed here.

The Plantas de la Rebotica Web site lists herbs with their Latin and Spanish names to help you decipher labels or help you find what you are looking for. If you click on "Propiedades medicinales" you can access the Spanish/Latin name list including herbal medicinal properties; Web site: www.bocetos.org/plantas-medicinales/index.htm.

Since 1823, medicinal plants and other health products have been sold in this beautiful old store, supposedly the first herb shop in Catalunya, right off the Plaça Reial, near La Rambla in the old part of Barcelona. It's worth the visit to the store even if you don't need any herbs. L'Herboristeria del Rei, C/ Vidre, 1, 08002 Barcelona, Tel: 933 180 512; Metro: Liceu; open Tuesday to Friday 4:00 to 8:00 p.m., Saturday 10:00 a.m. to 8:00 p.m.

The seven Manantial de Salud stores in Barcelona are full *herboristerías* with herbs and herbal preparations, nutritional supplements, and other health items. Herbalists, as well as naturopathic doctors, are on staff. They also have a health clinic offering massage, acupuncture, homeopathy, and natural medicine; see ESMA under "Naturopathy." Manantial de Salud, C/ Mercaders, 7, Barcelona; Tel: 933 191 965; Web site: www.manantial-salud.com/web/index.html. Another store is near La Rambla at C/ Xuclà, 23, Barcelona; Tel: 933 011 444; Metro: Liceu or Plaça Catalunya; open Monday to Friday 9:00 a.m. to 2:00 p.m./4:00 to 8:00 p.m., Saturday 5:00 to 8:00 p.m. For a list of the other Manatial de Salud stores click on "Las Tiendas" on the left column of their Web site.

Plantis, a division of Artesanía Agrícola, produces a Spanish line of flower remedies based on Dr. Bach's formulas that are produced organically. The Plantis remedies are sold in many health food stores. Plantis, Artesanía Agrícola, Ctra. a Vilafranca, Km 4—Apartado 24, 08810 Sant Pere de Ribes; Tel: 938 962 835; e-mail: info@plantis. net; Web sites: www.artesaniaagricola.com and www.plantis.net.

In Madrid, In-Vitta has two stores selling a range of nutritional and medicinal products. In-Vitta, C/ Fuencarral, 74, 28004 Madrid; Tel: 915 222 967; Web site: www.in-vitta.com; Metro: Tribunal; open Monday to Friday 10:30 a.m. to 8:30 p.m., Saturday 10:00 a.m. to 3:00 p.m. The second store is at C/ Don Ramón de la Cruz, 29, 28001 Madrid; Tel: 914 351 658; Metro: Núñez de Balboa; open the same hours.

CLINICS AND SPAS

Thalassotherapy is the term used for treatments using seawater (from the Greek *thalassa*). For other spas with thermal baths, see "Thermal Baths" in the "Recreation" section above.

Thalassa Sport offers seawater and seaweed therapies plus other complementary therapies from bodywork to diet. Prices for the thermal baths are 15 euros, and additional spa therapies start at 25 euros. They have many price options and special offers including good deals between Monday and Friday. Hotel Spa Thalassa Sport, Jacinto Benavente, 9, Santa Margarita, 17480 Roses (Girona); Tel: 972 253 163; e-mail: thalassasport@thalassasport.com; Web site: www.thalassasport.com/home.php?idm=3; open 8:00 a.m. to 10:00 p.m.

At the Mas Ferran Natural Health Farm rates range from 100 to 320 euros depending on size of room and season. Health treatment programs run from two to seven days with ranges of focus from pain relief, detoxification, and stress relief to weight control and more. The Catalan stone farmhouse is in St. Gregori, next to Girona in northeast Spain about one hour from Barcelona. Mas Ferran Natural Health Farm, Camí de la Bruguera, s/n, 17150 St. Gregori; Tel: 972 428 890; e-mail: info@masferran.com; Web site: www.masferran.com/inici.php?idi=3.

At the regional Web site for Costa Brava click on "Wellness & Spa," where you will find sixteen spas listed; Web site: http://en.costabrava.org/main/home.aspx.

Marítim Esport Talassa is a seawater therapy sports center with pools of various temperatures and saunas. Rates during the week are 13.50 euros; on the weekends 16 euros. Marítim Esport Talassa, Passeo Marítim, 33, 08003 La Barceloneta (Barcelona); Tel: 932 240 440; e-mail: maritim@claror.org; Web site: www.claror.cat/maritim.htm; Metro: Ciutadella-Vila Olímpica; open Monday to Friday 7:00 a.m. to midnight, Saturday 8:00 a.m. to 9:00 p.m., Sundays and holidays 8:00 a.m. to 4:00 p.m.

Hipócrates is a large, fancy "Cur" hotel. Prices are for six- or fourteen-day stays and include access to the pools and saunas. Spa treatments and special health programs are additional. Hipócrates Cur Hotel, Carretera de Sant Pol, 229, 17220 Sant Feliu de Guíxols (Girona); Tel: 972 320 662; Web site: www.hipocratescurhotel.com/web/en/index.php.

Hotel Termes Montbrió has a full spa with thermal baths on the Costa Daurada, one hour south from the Barcelona Airport. Termes Montbrió is a large hotel and spa with 214 rooms. It also has botanical gardens, an outdoor swimming pool, natural hot spring thermal baths, a wellness center with thirty-five therapists, sixty treatment cabins, availability of several health and beauty programs from two to seven days, as well as one-day packages and more than a hundred à la carte services. The price for just the thermal baths is 32 euros. Hotel Termes Montbrió, C/ Nou, 38, 43340 Montbrió del Camp (Tarragona); Tel: 977 814 000; e-mail: HotelTermes@RocBlancHotels.com; Web site: www.RocBlanc.com/index.php?canal=1; open Monday to Friday 10:00 a.m. to 2:00 p.m./4:00 to 8:00 p.m., Saturday and Sunday 10:00 a.m. to 9:00 p.m.

El Gran Hotel Balneario de Puente Viesgo, located in northern Spain, has been a spa and health resort since the 1700s. Rates vary widely from 105 euros/night to 900 euros/week depending on time of year and room choice. Check the Web site for full rates and services. Full spa services include massage, hydrotherapy, and vinotherapy. El Gran Hotel Balneario, C/ Manuel Pérez Mazo, s/n, 39670 Puente Viesgo (Cantabria); Tel: 942 598 061; e-mail: info@balneariodepuenteviesgo.com; Web site: www.balneariodepuenteviesgo.com.

Mas de Torrent Hotel and Spa is an eighteenth-century restored *masía* (farmhouse) with ten rooms, plus an additional twenty-two bungalows, each with a private garden and access to the swimming pool heated by solar panels. The Mas Spa has more than six thousand square feet of therapy space waiting to spoil you. Mas de Torrent Hotel and Spa, 17123 Torrent (Girona); Tel: 902 550 321; Web site: www.mastorrent.com/2006/eng/index.php.

The Galician regional tourist department offers a free downloadable pamphlet with detailed information about the thirty-eight spas in Galicia, including two that offer thalassotherapy treatments. Click on "Brochures" for a list of their informative pamphlets. *Water for the Senses* is the brochure listing Galician spas. Galician Tourism; Web site: www.turgalicia.es/default.asp?cidi=I.

The Navarro Spa Catalá is a natural day spa in Valencia across the street from a wonderful health food store—J. Navarro Terra Verda, and quite close to the train station. It offers a range of spa therapies, bodywork, and hydrotherapy, all done using natural products. Navarro Spa Catalá, Arzobispo Mayoral, 11, 46001 Valencia; Tel: 963 524 334; Web site: www.navarrospacatala.com; open Monday to Friday 10:00 a.m. to 8:00 p.m., Saturday 10:00 a.m. to 2:00 p.m.

Two day spas in Bilbao using natural products are the Ana Carazo

Bioestética offering massages and spa therapies using organic products, and the Naturbell Centro de Estética Integrada. Ana Carazo Bioestética, Centro Zen, C/ Dr. Areilza, 17, 1º dcha., 48011 Bilbao; Tel: 944 273 451; Mobile: 616 006 664; Web site: www.anacarazo. com. Naturbell Centro de Estética Integrada, Plaza Sarrikoalde, 11, 48015 Bilbao; Tel: 944 759 562.

For other spas, resorts, and thalassotherapy centers in the Basque region see the Web site: www.turismoa.euskadi.net/s11-20475/en/.

Ahora Casa Rural of Repose and Center of Natural Therapies offers saunas, massage, Tai Chi, yoga, and other therapies. Ahora Casa Rural of Repose and Center of Natural Therapies, Finca la Vega, Cortes de la Front., Bda. El Colmenar (Est. de Gaucín), 29390 (Málaga); Tel: 952 153 046; Mobile: 696 720 889; e-mail: reservas@ahoraya. es; Web site: www.ahoraya.es.

Bien Estar is a day spa offering massages, facials, beauty treatments, Reiki, and Dr. Hauschka facials. English is spoken. Bien Estar, C/ Marín García, 5, 6º-5 (at ZAEA centro), 29005 Málaga; Tel: 952 609 772 or 655 019 777.

The Hotel Marqués de Riscal, a luxury hotel in the La Rioja wine region, was designed by architect Frank Gehry, who designed the Guggenheim Museum in Bilbao. The hotel design is inspired by the grapes and vineyards indigenous to the area, with purple and silver flowing roofs. The hotel features the Caudalié Vinothérapie Spa offering "wine therapy" massages and other treatments. Hotel Marqués de Riscal is 110 km (about 68 miles) from the city of Bilbao. Hotel Marqués de Riscal, C/ Torrea, 1, 01340 Elciego (La Rioja); Tel: 945 180 880; e-mail: marquesderiscal@luxurycollection.com; Web site: www.starwoodhotels.com/luxury/property/overview/index.html?propertyID=1539.

Shopping
NATURAL, UNTREATED, AND ORGANIC ITEMS

There are a number of Spanish shoe companies manufacturing natural eco shoes. Check out the Web sites for factory visit information and store locations. Elche, in the province of Alicante, is known for their shoe manufacturing. Among the conventional shoe com-

Sale = *rebajas* in Spanish, *rebaixes* in Catalan. From the middle of January through the end of February there are big sales, and summer goods are drastically reduced in price at the end of July and August.

panies you can find a few specializing in natural footwear: Yokono, Web site: www.yokono.es/ing/Index3.htm; Pikolinos, Web site: www.pikolinos.com/default.aspx; and Martin Natur, Elche, Tel: 965 451 639, Web site: www.naturalshoes.es. In Toledo, natural shoes can be found at Bio World, Web site: www.bioworldshoes.com. In Menorca: Nagore, Web site: www.nagore.es; and BioStep, Web site: www.biostep.es/en_index.html.

Note: Camper shoes, known and sold worldwide, are unfortunately no longer made in Spain, but rather in China.

El Naturalista is a Spanish shoe company with a strong environmental commitment using natural and recycled materials and producing divinely comfortable shoes. El Naturalista shoes are sold worldwide. Find stores in any country, including Spain, on the Web site. El Naturalista, Camino de Labiano, 30, 31192 Mutilva Alta (Navarra); Tel: 948 852 767; e-mail: info@elnaturalista.com; Web site: www.elnaturalista.com/index.php/en.

Productos Dippner is a Spanish company making Birkenstock-style shoes using natural leathers. They are located in the northern Navarra region. Dippner Shoes, Paseo Lurbeltzeta, 15, 31190 Zizur Menor (Navarra); Tel: 948 185 500; e-mail: prodippner@abc.bernet.com; Web site: http://export.navarra.net/paghtml/dippe.htm.

Fox Fibre products are made from organically grown cotton that is naturally colored in shades of brown, sometimes green, as well as creamy white, using strains of heirloom cotton varieties, painstakingly researched by Sally Fox. In 1992, Organic Cotton Colours in Barcelona decided to convert their textile company to specialize in products made using Fox Fibre cottons. There are now nineteen stores in Spain specializing in Fox Fibre products, as well as countless other stores such as health food and natural products stores selling the Fox Fibre label. See the Web site for store locations. Organic Cotton Colours, Camí Ral, 578, 08302 Mataró (Barcelona); Tel: 937 576 887; Web site: www.fox-fibre.com/Forms/foxfibre.aspx.

EcoTerry, sold at the Sant Martí Vell monthly organic market, and other venues, offers organic towels and other cotton products. EcoTerry, C/ Unió Europea, s/n, 08540 Centelles (Barcelona); Tel: 938 813 307; Web site: www.terrytowel.biz.

For natural baby and children's items from diapers to toys you can find a list of the more than thirty-five stores of Crianza Natural throughout Spain at www.crianzanatural.com/tiendas.asp.

In La Bisbal d'Empordà, known for its ceramics industry, you can find on the street behind the main ceramic shop thoroughfare the Ekocasa store. Filled with a variety of environmental household products, the store has a very fine selection of natural products for construction—natural paints, flooring, insulation—which you would probably be looking for only if you were renovating a building. A number of the products are German, but one natural paint line is made in Spain—Keim Ecopaint Ibérica. Eko! Ekocasa, C/ Paral.lel, 78, La Bisbal d'Empordà 17100 (Girona); Tel: 972 642 284; e-mail: info@ekocasa.es; Web site: www.ekocasa.es. Keim Ecopaint Ibérica, Octavio Lacante, 55, 08100 Mollet del Vallès (Barcelona); Tel: 932 192 319; e-mail: info@keim.es; Web site: www.keim.es.

The Eco Bar sells the organic cotton and bamboo clothes line Absolute Organic (www.absoluteorganic.es), as well as health food items from Spain and elsewhere. Eco Bar & Spa, Paseo Pintor Rosales, 76, 28008 Madrid; Tel: 915 441 716; e-mail: infoecobarspa.com; Web site: www.ecobarspa.com; Metro: Moncloa.

LOCAL PRODUCTS

In La Bisbal d'Empordà, known for its ceramics industry, the main street has one ceramics shop after another. The stores have some of the same products, but miraculously also have unique items as well. Be sure to ask if the item was "*¿hecho en España?*" (made in Spain?) or "*¿hecho en La Bisbal?*" (made in La Bisbal?) because some are not.

In the Costa da Morte region of western Galicia, the town of Buño has been known for its pottery (*alfarería* in Spanish, *olería* in Galician) since prehistoric times. In Buño and surrounding towns you can find seven ceramic shops and the workshops of fourteen local potters with distinct styles, as well as two museums. For more information see the Web site: www.finisterrae.com/oleria.

Las Moradas sells a mix of souvenirs and lovely handcrafted, artisan goods made in Sevilla and the Andalucía region including inexpensive linen drawstring bags, and ceramic ware from the outstanding Córdoban ceramicist Al-Yarrer. Other stores sell pretty, gay Sevillan ceramics, but this particular company makes especially beautiful wares. Las Moradas, C/ Rodrigo Caro, 20 (at a corner of Plaza Doña Elvira), 41004 Sevilla; Tel: 954 563 917; e-mail: serali@telefonica.net.

If you are looking for traditional espadrille shoes made with hemp and canvas, these are plentiful in Madrid. One store replete with a bounty is on C/ Toledo just off the Plaza Mayor—look for the windows filled with colorful espadrilles in many styles. These are also bountiful in Sevilla with shoe stores galore in the old part of the city.

You can find information about local crafts and artisans, including markets, fairs, products, and special routes in the sun-soaked region of Murcia at the artisan Web cooperative Web site: www.murciartesana.es.

Beautiful inexpensive handmade leather bags and pouches made by Jeno, and other souvenirs, some made in Spain, are sold in this small store owned and run by Jeno y Sidonia right off the Plaza del Mercado: Jeno Souvenirs, C/ Granada, 73, Málaga; Tel: 952 918 357; Mobile: 647 235 744; open 10:00 a.m. to noon/5:00 to 8:00 p.m.

In Granada, the street Calderería Vieja is filled with little bazaar stores selling Middle Eastern wares—scarves, jewelry, and hookahs. Mixed in you can find one or two local artisans selling items. At the top of the street, turn slightly right and continue up the hill on to San Gregori. At the switchback you will find La Casa del Talismán, where the lovely proprietor Silvana Leone sells her handmade jewelry plus other local handcrafts including natural soaps, and fabulous art by a woman named Esperanza Romero (www.esperanzaromero.com). Casa del Talismán, Cuesta de San Gregori, 7 y 9, 18010 Albayzín neighborhood of Granada; Tel: 671 648 463; e-mail: lacasadeltalisman@yahoo.es.

The Patrimonio is a cooperative organization promoting Spanish olive oils. The store is full of olive oils from all over Spain with at least nine organic varieties. It looks as if it would be high-priced, but it is not. The store is a must stop for any olive oil lover or connoisseur. Patrimonio Comunal Olivarero, C/ Mejía Lequerica, 1, 28004 Madrid; Tel: 913 080 505; Web site: www.pco.es; Metro: Alonso Martínez (exit Pl. Santa Bárbara and walk down the street to the end of the Plaza; Olivarero is on the corner). See more local food products under "Eating and Food."

Tierra is a shoe store selling Spanish-brand shoes including the made-in-Spain El Naturalista line with some styles not available in the U.S. Near the Plaza Mayor and the Yerba Buena natural foods restaurant. Tierra, C/ Mayor, 39, 28013 Madrid; Tel: 913 668 799; Web site: www.tierratienda.com; open Monday to Saturday 10:30 a.m. to 2:00 p.m./4:00 to 8:30 p.m.

Regalos Arribas is a souvenir shop in the Plaza Mayor selling made-in-Spain ceramics at good prices. Regalos Arribas, Plaza Mayor, 19, 28012 Madrid; Tel: 915 482 919.

In the beautiful, more than one-thousand-year-old village of Besalú north of Girona in northwest Catalunya you can find the Taller de Cuir, a store full of leather goods and other crafts. They make their own leather bags using vegetable-tanned leather, and sell other products. In the old part of Besalú; Web site: www.tallerdecuir.com. While there you can explore Isis, a lovely little store selling natural foods, body care, health care, as well as some books and esoterica. Isis, C/ Major, 9, Besalú; open Tuesday 9:00 a.m. to 1:00 p.m./5:00 to 8:00 p.m., Wednesday, Friday, and Saturday 10:00 a.m. to 1:00 p.m.

PERSONAL CARE AND NATURAL COSMETICS

There are a number of companies in Spain making natural personal care products, sold in health food stores, *herbolarios,* and some pharmacies. A sampling of companies is listed here. In addition, it seems that most health food stores, *herbolarios,* and pharmacies also sell a number of high-quality natural products made in Germany such as Weleda, Logona, and Sante.

Curiously the made-in-Spain natural wood and bristle brushes, made for the Morrocco Method natural hair care line, do not seem to be sold in Spain, even though they are manufactured in Girona; Web site: www.morroccomethod.com.

There is a plethora of natural soap (*jabón natural*) companies. The Andalucía Natural Soap Company makes a line of natural soaps using an olive oil base. Their Web site lists retail stores where their soaps are sold. Andalucía Natural Soap Company; Web site: www.andalucia-naturalsoap.com. Los Jabones de Mi Mujer sells their handmade soaps online or at their beautiful store outside of Segovia on Saturdays and Sundays. Los Jabones de Mi Mujer; Web site: www.losjabonesdemimujer.com.

Armonía Bio makes skin care creams, using natural and organic ingredients, that are certified as an ecological cosmetic by Ecocert. Armonía Bio, 50720 La Cartuja Baja (Zaragoza); Tel: 976 501 005; Web site: www.armoniabio.com/data/presen.html.

Sanoflore is a French brand of organic personal care and aromatherapy products sold throughout Spain. Sanoflore; Web site: www.sanoflore.es.

Corpore Sano is a very common Spanish brand of organic and natural products for hair, body, face, and mouth found in almost every *herbolario* and health food store. Corpore Sano; Tel: 935 706 292; Web site: www.corporesano.es/en/.inici.

FAIR TRADE

The World Fair Trade Organization defines fair trade as "a trading partnership, based on dialogue, transparency and respect, that seeks greater equity in international trade. It contributes to sustainable development by offering better trading conditions to, and securing the rights of, marginalized producers and workers."

Fair trade is based on fair prices and prompt payment for goods. Fair trade is also based on safe and healthy working environments, and conforms to the United Nations Convention on the Rights of the Child. Fair-trade Web sites include www.fairtrade.org.uk, www.aworldconnected.org, and www.wfto.com.

In Spain, look for the green and blue Fair Trade/Comercio Justo label showing certification by the Asociación del Sello de Productos de Comercio Justo. Products include coffee, tea, bananas, chocolate, fruit juices, sugar, rice, honey, cotton, spices, and crafts. For more information, go to Asociación del Sello de Productos de Comercio Justo, C/ Gaztambide, 50, bajo, 28015 Madrid; Tel: 915 433 399; e-mail: info@sellocomerciojusto.org; Web site: www.sellocomerciojusto.org. IDEAS is a Spanish fair-trade organization at www.ideas.coop.

Fair-trade stores are popular in Spain, and even small towns will often have a store selling fair-trade goods.

In Valencia, the Oxfam store sells a variety of fair-trade products, including fair-trade, Converse-style "No Sweat" sneakers, and products from all over the world. Fundación Intermón Oxfam, C/ Marqués de Dos Aguas, 5, 46002 Valencia; Tel: 963 524 193; Web site: www.intermonOxfam.org; open Monday to Saturday 10:00 a.m. to 2:00 p.m./5:00 to 8:00 p.m.

In the old part of Valencia, not far from the Espai Visor restaurant, there is a store called Namo Buddha, selling beautiful, authentic, and some rare items from Nepal and Tibet, run by a lovely Spanish man named Pablo and his Nepali wife, Goma. Namo Buddha, C/ Danzas, 3, bajo, 46003 Valencia; Tel: 963 916 509; e-mail: gomanepablo@hotmail.com; Web site: www.namobuddha.phpnet.us; open Monday to Saturday 10:00 a.m. to 1:30 p.m./5:00 to 8:30 p.m.

Barcelona has fair-trade stores, two of which are: Xarxa Consum Solidari, Pl. de Sant Agustí Vell, 15, Ciutat Vella, 08003 Barcelona; Tel: 932 682 202; Web site: www.xarxaconsum.org; Metro: Arc de Triomf; and Naidunia Fair Trade Shop, C/ Rocafort, 198, 08029 Eixample; Tel: 934 108 398; Metro: Entença.

In Málaga fair-trade stores include Intermón Oxfam, C/ Nosquera, 2, 29007 Málaga; open Monday to Friday 10:30 a.m. to 1:30 p.m./5:30 to 8:30 p.m., Saturday 10:30 a.m. to 1:30 p.m.; and Comercio Justo, Puerta Nueva, 7, 29008 Málaga; Tel: 952 221 564; Web site: http://malaga.salir.com/comercio_justo; open Monday to Friday 10:00 a.m. to 2:00 p.m./5:00 to 8:30 p.m., Saturday 10:00 a.m. to 2:00 p.m.

Córdoba fair-trade stores are listed under "Health Food Stores."

For people interested in the forbidden fruits of Cuba, you can find plenty of Cuban products in Spain. Especially delicious, fair-trade coffee and rum from Cuba are some of the offerings and are sold in many of the larger health food stores.

THRIFT AND SECONDHAND STORES

Thrift or secondhand stores (*tiendas de segunda mano*) are wonderful places to shop. Often full of clothes, books, art, furniture, kitchen gadgets, and more, they are a treasure trove for travelers interested in recycled items and good prices. Check the hours carefully, as many shops do not keep standard store hours. In addition, local markets sometimes have lots of options for secondhand goods (see "Markets").

For secondhand stores in Barcelona, explore the streets of C/ de la Palla and C/ dels Banys Nous for antique and secondhand stores. Also in Barcelona, in the higher price range, the Bulevard dels Antiquaris is filled with about seventy art and antique stores. Passeig de Gràcia, 55, Barcelona; Tel: 932 155 449; Web site: www.bulevarddelsantiquaris.com; open Monday to Saturday 10:00 a.m. to 8:30 p.m.

There is a good, small secondhand clothing store in Valencia around the corner from a little *herboristería* and the youth hostel: Marropa (ropa de 2a mano), C/ Plaza Cisneros, 5, Valencia; open Monday to Friday 10:00 a.m. to 1:30 p.m./5:00 to 8:00 p.m.

In Bilbao, Koopera/ekorropa sells a large variety of used clothing and accessories at very good prices, plus they offer a small selection of organic and fair-trade food items. They have ten stores total with three in Bilbao: C/ Ronda, 33 (Casco Viejo); C/ Blas de Otero, 11 (Deusto); Koopera Merkatua, C/ Fernández del Campo, 16-18 (same street as Garibolo vegetarian restaurant) (Abando). They have two stores in Getxo: C/ Sarrikobaso, 15 (Algorta); C/ Ibaiondo, 7 (Romo); and five more in nearby towns.

In Córdoba's Plaza de Corredera there are a few flea market and antique stores in the corners of the plaza, which on one end houses the daily covered market.

MARKETS

Most towns have regular market (*mercado* in Spanish, *mercat* in Catalan) days, which rotate and alternate by the day of the week, depending on the region. For example, Mondays there are markets in some towns, and on Tuesdays they are in other towns. Some of the vendors move from village to village, while others stay local. Markets are often held in the central square or a major center of a village, and car traffic is halted in the area. Markets sell a variety of goods, including local meats, fruits, vegetables, cheese, clothes, jewelry, fabrics, shoes, tools, and flowers. Weekends are often the big market days; the earlier you arrive, the better the finds. Please see the "Eating and Food" section for food markets and "City and Regional Highlights" section for other market listings. Listed here are markets with a secondhand or other nonfood emphasis.

In Vitoria, capital of the Basque region, there is a flea market on Sundays in the Plaza de España.

In Sevilla, El Mercadillo del Jueves flea market on C/ Feria opens at 8:00 a.m. Thursday mornings. Also on Sunday mornings near the Roman column of Alameda de Hércules, there is a junk and flea market along the Alameda Boulevard.

In Pamplona in the Navarra region there is a flea market held the first Saturday of every month.

In Oviedo, capital of Asturias, the Rastro open-air "bargain" market is held on Sundays.

El Rastro is a huge market in Madrid with more than one thousand stalls, held every Sunday and feast days from 8:00 a.m. (or 9:00 a.m. depending on the day and the vendors) to 2:00 p.m. (or 3:00 p.m. depending on the day and the vendors). The site has held a market here in one form or another since the fifteenth century. The best Metro stop is La Latina, which delivers you to the top end of the market. This market is not for the crowd-phobic, as you can move only as fast as a shuffle since the crowds are so thick. Historically, this has been known as a flea market, but nowadays the secondhand aspect of it is about flea-size. The market is filled with clothing, household goods, accessories, and music, all of which is maybe ten to twenty percent made in Spain and the rest imported.

The Mercat Fira de Bellcaire, known as Els Encants Vells, is a huge, open-air flea market in Barcelona drawing an estimated one hundred thousand visitors a week. Through the market's eighty-year history there has been talk of moving the site of the market, and now a new proposal is on the drawing board that would provide more space for vendors. If this happens, the market will be located not far from its current location at El Bosquet. Els Encants Vells, Plaza Glòries Catalanes; Tel: 932 463 030; Web site: www.encantsbcn.com; Metro: Glòries or Encants; open Monday, Wednesday, Friday, and Saturday 9:00 a.m. to 6:00 p.m.

Other Barcelona markets include: Plaça Nova antiques and flea market on Thursdays; Plaça de Sant Josep Oriol crafts and local art on the weekends; and Plaça del Pi artisan foods every two weeks from Friday to Sunday.

In Córdoba, Zoco is a city-sponsored permanent market in an old courtyard with workshops in the Jewish quarter that sells crafts handmade by Córdoban artisans. You can see them creating in their workshops and purchase the local goods at excellent prices. Currently there is a jeweler, leather goods, ceramicist, and sculptor. Zoco Mercat, C/ Judíos (across from the synagogue); Tel: 957 204 033.

Girona city has twenty different street fairs and specialty markets throughout the year, many of which are held on Saturday all year except in July and August. These include local artisans and crafts, art, and flowers. These are clustered on streets in and around the old part. On Sunday 9:00 a.m. to 1:00 p.m. you will find the "Collector's Fair" in the Plaça Catalunya.

For Catalunya brocantes markets, selling a mix of antiques and flea market items, look for one the first Sunday of every month in Bàscara; in Figueres, the third Saturday of every month; and in Cadaqués the last Sunday of every month. Secondhand markets are every Saturday in Pals and Palafrugell.

Valencia's Mercado Central is an enormous covered market—see "Farm Stands, Markets, and Local Products." On Sundays check out the Rastrillo flea and bargain market held all morning in Plaza Luis Casanova, next to the Estadio Mestalla (soccer stadium) within walking distance of the old city.

BOOKSTORES

The alternative and political bookstore in Valencia, SAHIRI, sells books in Spanish with many political titles and supports fair trade

George Orwell, *Homage to Catalonia* (New York: Harcourt, 1952). Written by Orwell about his involvement in the Spanish Civil War, with excellent insights into the war and politics. ☞ green earth guide favorite.

Antonio Muñoz Molina, *Sepharad* (New York: Harcourt, 2003). Molina has twice been awarded the national literature award in Spain. In *Sepharad* he interweaves tales of displaced people during World War II.

Javier Cercas, *Soldiers of Salamis* (United Kingdom: Bloomsbury, 2003). Cercas lectures on Spanish literature at the University of Girona. A quick and interesting read, *Soldiers of Salamis* is a novel interweaving historical people and events, offering a glimpse into the Spanish Civil War.

Carlos Ruiz Zafón, *The Shadow of the Wind* (New York: Penguin, 2005). A completely fictional book set in Barcelona, it offers some wonderful glimpses into Barcelona and some glimpses of the Spanish Civil War.

Ildefonso Falcones, *Cathedral of the Sea* (New York: Dutton, 2008). A fictional story based on a real-life cathedral in Barcelona, Catedral del Mar, which when built was on the shores of the Mediterranean, but the sea has receded since then and the cathedral currently stands many blocks from the water.

Miguel de Cervantes, translated by Edith Grossman, *Don Quixote* (New York: HarperCollins, 2003). A 940-page tome, *Don Quixote* (*Don Quijote* in Spanish) is required school reading for Spaniards. This fine translation by Edith Grossman was recommended by a professor of Spanish litera-

and alternative minded authors. SAHIRI Librería Asociativa, C/ Danzas, 5, Valencia; Tel: 963 924 872; www.sahiri.com

J&J has free wifi for all customers. J&J Books and Coffee, C/ Espiritu Santo, 47, 28004 Madrid; Tel: 915 218 576; Web site: www.jandjbooksandcoffee.com; Metro: Noviciado.

ture. Cervantes and Shakespeare were contemporaries and died on the same day in 1616. Scholars believe that Cervantes' *Don Quixote* is the mother (or father) of the modern novel and contains within it all the tools and devices used in modern fiction. ☛ green earth guide favorite.

Miguel de Cervantes, retold by Henry Brook (for children), *Don Quixote* (London: Usborne, 2005). A good retelling and major condensing of the classic tales for children.

Stephen Koch, *The Breaking Point: Hemingway, Dos Passos, and the Murder of Jose Robles* (Berkeley, CA: Counterpoint Press, 2006). Provacative and controversial book about the Spanish Civil War, and the relationship between two star writers of the time, Ernest Hemingway and Dos Passos.

James Michener, *Iberia* (New York: Random House, 1968). Classic book about Spain written by James Michener while Spain was still under Franco rule.

Hugh Thomas, *The Spanish Civil War,* rev. ed. (New York: Modern Library, 2001). 1,120-page history of the Spanish Civil War first published in 1961 and revised to include new information.

Robert Hughes, *Barcelona* (London: Harvill Press, 1992). Art writer Robert Hughes writes about Barcelona, its art, and the city's two-thousand-year history.

Mark Kurlansky, *The Basque History of the World: The Story of a Nation* (New York: Penguin Books, 2001). A political, economic, and cultural history of the Basque people and region dating from pre-Roman to the present day. A worthwhile read for anyone interested in the Basque region and their quest for independence.

Petra's has books in many languages including English, French, German, Italian, Spanish, and more and secondhand books. Petra's International Bookshop, C/ Campomanes, 13, 28013 Madrid; Tel: 915 417 291; Metro: Ópera or Santo Domingo; open Monday to Saturday 11:00 a.m. to 9:00 p.m.

Ecobusinesses, Ecodestinations, and Places of Interest

From the turquoise Mediterranean coast, to the wine regions, to orange and olive groves, Spain offers many natural ecodestinations.

The La Mancha area of Spain, made famous by Cervantes' *Don Quixote* tale and the beautiful windmills, is also the center of Spain's saffron (*azafrán* in Spanish) agriculture. Saffron was once a significant crop in the area, but Spanish production has plummeted as Iranian and Kashmiri sources have grown. The town of Consuegra has a saffron museum and still holds an annual saffron festival: La Fiesta de la Rosa del Azafrán at the end of October in the main square. The crocus flowers from which saffron comes (actually from the yellow stigmas of the purple flowers) are delicate and must be hand plucked. Saffron is sensitive, faring better in straw baskets rather than nylon or plastic. For more information about Consuegra see the Web site: www.aytoconsuegra.es.

BioCultura is an annual exhibition and fair focused on organic products, green lifestyles, and responsible consumerism. In existence for more than twenty-three years, BioCultura is held at the end of November in Madrid and in early May in Barcelona. It is well worth the 5 euro admission price. For more information visit the Web site: www.biocultura.org.

The Wool Routes—Las Rutas de la Lana—Web site offers information about places to visit in the historical wool industry area in the north of Spain, with farms, antique textiles, museums, and maps; Web site: www.rutasdelalana.eu.

ORGANIC FARMS

In Spain, organic agriculture is called *agricultura ecológica* or *biológica,* or *eco* or *bio* for short. Food grown organically is certified as *bio* by one of Spain's organic certification organizations, including: Asociación Comité Andaluz de Agricultura Ecológica (CAAE) (www. caae.es); Asociación Vida Sana (www.vidasana.org); and Sohiscert-Ecocert Spain (www.sohiscert.com). In the Basque region, the organic farming Web site is www.ekonekazaritza.net.

Organic food is not as prevalent in Spain as in France. My own the-

Federación Andaluza de Consumidores y Productores Ecológicos (Andalucian Federation of Organic Consumers and Producers); Web site: www.facpe.org.

Comitè d'Agricultura Ecològica de la Comunitat Valencia; Web site: www.caecv.com.

Three organizations in Spain are members of Vía Campesina, an international peasant movement promoting fair trade, sustainable agriculture, social justice, and environmental integrity; Web site: www.viacampesina.org.

ories about this are that there is such an abundance of inexpensive, beautiful, fresh food grown in Spain (or nearby Morocco and Tunisia) that organic is less compelling, and a number of products are grown as they have been for centuries. I think the Spanish would agree philosophically with using fewer pesticides and other chemicals, but it is not so much in their consciousness as they are surrounded by an absolute bounty of local food. Nevertheless, land farmed organically is increasing every year in Spain. In 2008 the southern region of Andalucía had more than one and a half million acres in organic cultivation. And there are strong organic certification organizations in most regions. As you will see from the list of organic vineyards and available products in all the health food stores, there is plenty of organic food to be had. See "Farm Stands, Markets, and Local Products," "Health Food Stores," and "City and Regional Highlights" for more organic farms and food.

The Parc Agroecològic de l'Empordà is a working farm and educational center just outside the extremely picturesque old stone village of Albons, a few kilometers from L'Escala on the northeast coast. They also have solar electric panels and solar ovens. The little farm stand store, Agrobotiga, is in a building past the fields and by the "Carrer del Sol" demonstrating solar technology. Remember to bring your own bag (*bolsa* in Spanish) to this very eco-minded farm stand. Parc Agroecològic de l'Empordà, Ctra. d'Albons a L'Escala, Km 0.5, 17136 Albons; Tel: 972 765 185; Mobile: 616 693 710; e-mail: info@parcagroecologic.com; Web site: www.parcagroecologic.com; the farm stand is open two days, Tuesday and Saturday, 4:30 to 8:30 p.m.

The Parc Agrari is 5 km south of Barcelona, in the fertile valley of the Llobregat river delta, land that has helped supply the city with fresh food for hundreds of years. Created in response to the encroaching urban sprawl on the rich farmland, the Parc Agrari now encompasses almost 7,500 acres. The Parc's arboretum has sixty-two heirloom varieties of plums, grapes, apples, olives, peaches, and figs, grown to protect the strains using organic farming practices.

Most of the food grown in the Parc goes to Barcelona's wholesale food market, Mercabarna. Some of the farmers are now using a label of origin, "Producte FRESC del Parc Agrari," to denote that it is locally, and in many cases, organically, grown. Restaurants using the products also are displaying the logo on their menus. For more information about the Parc and tours, see the Web site: www.diba.es/parcsn/parcs/plana.asp?parc=9&n=297&0=1. For restaurants and stores selling Parc products see the developing Web site: www.elcampacasa.com.

In the Málaga province of Andalucía you can go to the Guadalhorce Ecológico site and find lists of organic producers in Málaga province as well as organic markets throughout the area, many of which are held once a month. Guadalhorce Ecológico; Web site: www.guadalhorceecologico.com.

ORGANIC VINEYARDS AND WINES

Wine is over the top in Spain—everywhere and cheap! You will not believe your eyes when you see the prices as low as 1 euro a bottle! Organic wines cost more and can run between 2.50 to 10.00 euros a bottle. Also you can refill bottles at local wine stores and even some small grocery stores. Although not organic, this is usually locally produced wine and can be as cheap as almost 1 euro for the bottle refill. In Spain wine is traditionally consumed at both lunch and dinner.

Travel the "Green Coast" with beautiful Atlantic Ocean beaches along the Asturian and Cantabrian coasts, which don't get as crowded as their Mediterranean counterparts, into the region of Galicia. In Galicia, where grapes have grown since Roman times, September is the grape harvest.

The following organic vineyards (*viña* or *viñedo* in Spanish) are just a sampling of the many around Spain. You can find a wide range of organic Spanish wines in both health food and conventional stores. Visits to organic vineyards are often welcome, but call ahead or check the Web site for hours.

Finca Los Frutales is an organic vineyard in the mountains around beautiful Ronda in the province of Málaga. Finca Los Frutales, Paraje de Los Frontones, 29400 Ronda (Málaga); Tel: 951 166 043. Guided visits are available Monday to Friday at 11:00 a.m. Tasting room is open Monday to Friday noon to 2:00 p.m.

The Bodegas Robles winery produces five varieties of Piedra Luenga organic wines, as well as organic vinegars. For more information about the wines and visiting the winery see the Web site. Bodegas Robles, Ctra. Córdoba-Málaga, N-331, Km 47, Apartado de Correos, 55, 14550 Montilla (Córdoba); Tel: 957 650 063; Web site: www.bodegasrobles.com/ingles/indexing.html.

Dionisos Agricultura Biológica makes organic wine, olive oil, and vinegar. Dionisos Agricultura Biológica, C/ Unión, 82, Valdepeñas (Ciudad Real); Tel: 926 313 248; e-mail: info@labodegadelasestrellas.com; Web site: www.agrobio-dionisos.com.

Colonias de Galeón has been making three organic wines in the Parque Natural Sierra Norte de Sevilla since 1998. Colonias de Galeón, Plazuela, 39, 41370 Cazalla de la Sierra (Sevilla); Tel: 607 530 495; e-mail: info@coloniasdegaleon.com; Web site: www.coloniasdegaleon.com.

Bodegas Lezaun makes four organic wines on their vineyard in the Navarra region. Bodegas Lezaun, C/ Egiarte, s/n, 31292 Lakar (Navarra); Tel: 948 541 339; Web site: www.lezaun.com.

Bodegas Tosos Ecológica makes four organic wines in the Aragón region. Bodegas Tosos Ecológica, C/ Cuevas, 2, 50154 Tosos (Zaragoza); Tel: 947 147 040; Web site: www.bodegastososecologica.com/index_en.htm.

Bodegas Langa makes two organic wines as well as *cava* (sparkling wine) in Catalunya. Bodegas Langa, Ctra. Nacional II, Km 241.7, Apartado de Correos, 49, 50300 Calatayud (Zaragoza); Tel: 976 881 818; Web site: www.bodegas-langa.com/?idioma=en&w=home&producto_id=.

Bodegas Tempore makes five organic wines in the Aragón region. Bodegas Tempore, Montalbán, s/n, 50131 Lécera (Zaragoza); Tel: 976 835 040; Web site: www.bodegastempore.com/English/winery.htm.

The Bodegas Paternina makes an organic wine that won the silver medal at the 2009 International BioFach Exposition (BioFach is an annual professional trade show for organic products held in different European countries each year; Web site: www.biofach.de/en/default.ashx). The organic Banda Verde organic wine was awarded the silver medal out of 531 competing wines from thirteen countries. You can visit the winery with advance reservations by phone or e-mail on Tuesday to Sunday at 1:00 p.m., and Saturday and Sunday at 11:00 a.m. and 1:00 p.m. Paternina, Avda. Santo Domingo, 11, 26200 Haro (La Rioja); Tel: 941 310 550; e-mail: visitas@paternina.com or vinoteca@paternina.com; Web site: www.paternina.com/home/default.php.

For organic *cava* go to the organic winery and vineyard of Can Vendrell de la Codina, Albet i Noya. Albet i Noya makes a range of red and white wines, and the Catalunya specialty, *cava*. Tours are available at this organic vineyard for 5.50 euros/person and last about ninety minutes. Albet i Noya, Can Vendrell de la Codina, 08739 Sant Pau d'Ordal, about 45 km west of Barcelona city; Tel: 938 994 812; Web site: www.albetinoya.com/eng/index.html.

For more organic wines in Spain visit the Eco-Bacchus Web site, choosing Spain from the country choices to find forty-two organic wineries in Spain. Eco-Bacchus; Web site: www.eco-bacchus.com.

BIODYNAMIC WINES

Biodynamic farming is based on the agricultural philosophies of Rudolf Steiner. While biodynamic farming includes organic farm

> Maria Thun and Angelika Throll-Keller, *Gardening for Life—The Biodynamic Way: A Practical Introduction to a New Art of Gardening, Sowing, Planting, Harvesting* (United Kingdom: Hawthorn Press, 2000).
>
> Hugh Lovel, *A Biodynamic Farm* (Austin, TX: Acres USA, 2000).
>
> Nicholas Joly, *Wine from Sky to Earth: Growing and Appreciating Biodynamic Wine* (Austin, TX: Acres USA, 1999).

management practices, i.e., including no synthetic pesticides and fertilizers, it also uses specially prepared, natural treatments, incorporating natural rhythms and cycles of the moon and sun, light and warmth.

Iberum is an organic and biodynamic vineyard in Beire near Olite, in the Navarra region. See the Web site for more information: www.iberum.com/wineries.html.

Visit Wine Alchemy, a UK-based Web site about biodynamic wines from around the world. They have a downloadable directory to biodynamic wine producers worldwide. Spain has seven producers listed on page 30 of the guide; Web site: www.winealchemy.com.

SPECIALTY LIQUOR

Founded in 1934, La Alcoholera de la Rioja, Ebro y Duero, S.A. uses the brand name Morillón for their brandy and various types of *orujo*, liqueur made from grape skins. They pride themselves on making natural liquors made from grape products, and some are certified organic. Morillón, La Alcoholera de la Rioja, Ebro y Duero, S.A., Cenicero, La Rioja; Tel: 941 454 261.

BEER AND BREWERIES

In Spanish, beer is *cerveza* and brewery is *cervecería*. Producers of the Spanish beer Estrella Damm (www.damm.es) make a gluten-free version of their beer, with the same name but with "Apta para Celíacos" on the label, sold in gluten-free stores and in some supermarkets including the Mercadona and Bon Preu chains. Producers of San Miguel, another Spanish beer, make their own organic beer called San Miguel Eco (www.sanmigueleco.es), usually sold in health food stores.

In Madrid, the Naturbier brewery and bar makes organic and *artesanal* beers. You can sample them at their bar and restaurant in the heart of Madrid. Naturbier, Plaza Santa Ana, 9, 28012 Madrid; Tel: 913 600 597; Web site: www.cervecerianaturbier.com/en/intro_en.html.

In the Catalunya region there are a few microbrewed beers. Keks/ Gbech *artesanal* brewing is in the volcanic Garrotxa mountains. Gbech, C/ Major, 12, 17257 Fontanilles; Tel: 902 934 569; Web site: www.gbech.com/keks.

Cap D'Ona makes six *artesanal* beers including one *cerveza biológica,* certified organic by Ecocert. Cap D'Ona, Brasserie Artisanale des Alberes, Avenue des Flamants Roses, 29, 66700 Argeles sur Mer; Tel: 468 957 909; Web site: www.cap-dona.com; open Monday to Friday 8:00 a.m. to noon/2:00 to 6:00 p.m.; for visiting and tasting call ahead.

The Cervesera del Montseny makes unfiltered ales, stout, and beer. Companyia Cervesera del Montseny, C/ Del Feu, 15, 08554 Sant Miquel de Balenya; Tel: 938 123 217; Web site: www.ccm.cat/index.php?lang=en.

In Sevilla, La Fábrica has been serving up microbrews since 1992 in a former train station. La Fábrica, Centro Comercial Plaza de Armas, Torreón Princesa, Plaza Legión, 1, 41001 Sevilla; Web site: www.lafabrica-cerveceros.com/eng/index.htm.

Cervezas Alhambra has been making beer since 1925. Cervezas Alhambra, Avda. de Murcia, 1, Granada; Tel: 958 185 050; Web site: www.cervezasalhambra.com.

La Cervesera Artesana is a brew-pub serving up microbrews. La Cervesera Artesana, C/ Sant Agustí, 14, 08012 Barcelona; Tel: 932 379 594; Web site: www.lacervesera.net.

Calvin's beer is microbrewed in Madrid. Calvin's Beer, C/ Luis I, n° 71, nave 22, Madrid; Web site: www.calvinsbeer.es.

Also in Madrid is Cervecería Magister, making *artesanal* beers. Cervecería Magister, C/ Príncipe, 18, 28012 Madrid; Web site: www.naturalbeer.net.

Les Clandestines makes five beers including one that is *biológica* (organic). Les Clandestines; Web site: http://lesclandestines.net.

MINERAL SPRINGS

Although Spain is often thought of as a dry country, there are numerous mineral springs and more than one hundred brands of bottled water. The majority of the springs are in Spain's northeast corner. Brands include: Vichy Catalán, Font D'or, Font del Regàs (in the Montseny Natural Park), Sant Aniol (in La Garrotxa Volcanic Park), Font Selva, Les Creus, Lunares, Malavella, Aguas de Benassal, and Mondariz (from Galicia).

WIND AND SUN ENERGY

In Spanish, windmill is *molino de viento* and wind (*viento*), or wind energy, can be translated as *energía eólica.* It is a majestic sight when you see a row of windmills from the window of your train seat. See the *Green Earth Guide* Map to Windsites on page 146 to give you an idea of where windmills are situated in Spain. Solar energy is huge in Spain. Spain is the fourth largest manufacturer in the world of solar power technology, and what isn't used in Spain is exported, mostly to Germany. The Spanish Wind Energy Association can be found at www.aeeolica.es/en/.

Renewable energy buffs will be amazed at the solar and wind energy work going on in Spain. A research and demonstration site with a visitor center for solar energy can be found at www.psa.es/webeng/index.html. Other informative sites include: www.censolar.es for solar energy, and www.infoeolica.com for wind energy.

Ecotècnia is a designer, manufacturer, and operator of wind farms with forty-two wind farms currently operating in Spain and nine more under construction. The company's newest wind farm has nineteen wind turbines in Villafranca Montes de Oca in Burgos. Ecotècnia, C/ Roc Boronat, 78, Barcelona; Tel: 932 257 600; e-mail: ecotecnia@ecotecnia.com; Web site: www.ecotecnia.com.

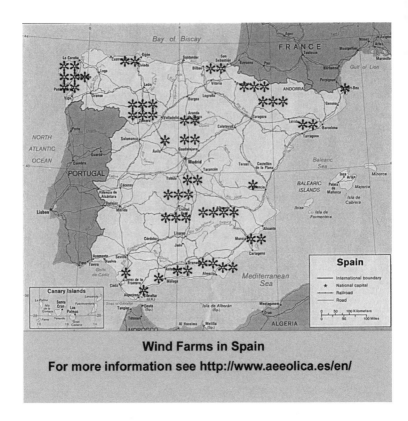

Wind Farms in Spain
For more information see http://www.aeeolica.es/en/

Windmills in Spain are plentiful. Pictures can be viewed at the Windmills! 2/23/08 post at: http://travelingnaturally.blogspot.com/2008/02/windmills.html.

In the Galicia region there are windmills on every mountaintop. It is a vision to see them working within view of farmland, ruins, the ocean, and ancient villages—the old with the new with the old.

In the solar arena there are a number of solar electric power stations in Spain, ten of which generate more than 20 megawatts, powering thousands of homes. See the Solar Plants in Spain map on page 147.

Beneixama, a small town in the Alicante province of southeastern Spain, is home to the Parque Solar Beneixama, a 124-acre "park" containing one hundred thousand solar electric photovoltaic panels, powering twelve thousand homes.

In Sanlúcar la Mayor, in the province of Sevilla, the PS10 Solar Power Tower is located in a field of 624 large, rotating mirrors generating

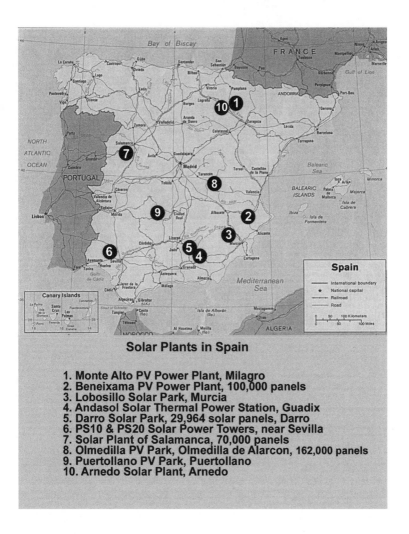

Solar Plants in Spain

1. Monte Alto PV Power Plant, Milagro
2. Beneixama PV Power Plant, 100,000 panels
3. Lobosillo Solar Park, Murcia
4. Andasol Solar Thermal Power Station, Guadix
5. Darro Solar Park, 29,964 solar panels, Darro
6. PS10 & PS20 Solar Power Towers, near Sevilla
7. Solar Plant of Salamanca, 70,000 panels
8. Olmedilla PV Park, Olmedilla de Alarcon, 162,000 panels
9. Puertollano PV Park, Puertollano
10. Arnedo Solar Plant, Arnedo

11 megawatts of power. In Guadix in the province of Granada the Andasol 1 solar power station generates solar electricity and stores it in molten salt as a type of thermal storage. Greenpeace is a proponent of this thermo-solar technology. The Planta Solar Fuente Álario in Los Mayordomos covers one hundred and fifty acres generating electricity for thirteen thousand homes.

UNESCO World Heritage Sites

Spain boasts more than forty sites on the United Nations Educational, Scientific, and Cultural Organization (UNESCO) list, and the most World Heritage designated cities in any one country in the

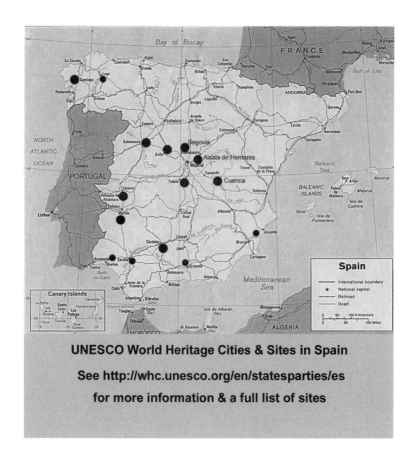

UNESCO World Heritage Cities & Sites in Spain

See http://whc.unesco.org/en/statesparties/es

for more information & a full list of sites

world. The eight World Heritage cities of Spain are Ávila, Cáceres, Córdoba, Cuenca, Salamanca, Santiago de Compostela, Segovia, and Toledo. Some are highlighted below and more are included under "City and Regional Highlights." See the UNESCO Web site for all the Spain sites: http://whc.unesco.org and the map of UNESCO World Heritage Cities and Sites in Spain above.

In Cuenca, east of Madrid, in the Castilla-La Mancha region, there are the *casas colgantes* (hanging houses) built in the fifteenth century, which seem to hang from cliffs six hundred feet over two river canyons. Cuenca is also home to the Ciudad Encantada, the "enchanted city," named for the unusual natural forms that have been created due to erosion.

Toledo's first vegetarian and organic restaurant is Madre Tierra, a smoke-free, beautiful restaurant in the old town serving Spanish and international dishes made with organic ingredients, and without microwave ovens—a rarity in this day and age. Madre Tierra, Bajada de Tripería, 2 (junto Plaza San Justo, near the cathedral), 45001 Toledo; Tel: 925 223 571; open Monday to Sunday 1:00 to 4:00 p.m./8:30 to 11:00 p.m.

There is a tiny health food store directly across from the Mezquita de Tornerías on C/ Las Tornerías between Plaza Mayor and Plaza del Solarejo.

The Jewish quarter has two remaining synagogues out of an estimated original twelve in Toledo—Sinagoga Santa María la Blanca, built in the thirteenth century, with a Jewish information center to the side (www.jewishtoledo.com); and the Sinagoga del Tránsito, built in 1366, which also houses the Museo Sefardí. La Mezquita del Cristo de la Luz is a tenth-century mosque. The doors (*puertas*) and gateways to the walled city are magnificent. Toledo is quite overrun with tourist shops, but most sell goods made in Toledo—namely knives and swords—it is the knife and sword capital of the world where these weapons are made for famous films and storied armies. Other local products include ceramics and jewelry.

The sobering and excruciating exhibit, Ancient Instruments of Torture, a joint effort of the government of Toledo and Amnesty International, displays truly gruesome tools used to torture people by the Inquisition and beyond—a bleak and stark reminder of the horrors of torture and the venomous cruelty that humans can inflict on one another. Antiguos Instrumentos de Tortura, C/ Alfonso XII, 24 (junto C/ Sant Tomé), Toledo; Tel: 925 253 856; Web site: www.t-descubre.com/en/activities/show/744; open Monday to Friday 10:00 a.m. to 2:00 p.m./4:00 to 9:00 p.m., Saturday 10:00 a.m. to 9:00 p.m.

In the Catheral of Toledo you can see the Virgen Morena—La Esclavitud de Nuestra Señora del Sagrario—see "Black Madonnas."

Segovia is considered to be a little less touristy than Toledo but no less beautiful. It was declared a UNESCO city in 1985, for its two-thousand-year-old Roman aqueduct, an old Jewish quarter, Alcázar, and "green Segovia," a walled area in the confluence of the two rivers Eresma and Clamores. You can get to Segovia from Madrid by train, line C8 Cercanías, or by bus.

The Altamira caves and museum 2 km southwest of Santillana del Mar in Cantabria have cave paintings dating back to 25,000 BC and include the famous bison wall and ceiling paintings drawn with ochre and charcoal. The real caves are closed to the public but the museum has replicas. Museum of Altamira; Web site: http://museo-dealtamira.mcu.es/ingles/index.html.

The Alhambra, meaning "The Red One" in Arabic, in Granada is one of the finalists for the new Seven Wonders of the World. Built from the thirteenth to fifteenth centuries, the Alhambra was built by the Nasrid kings. The original fortified city covered around twenty-five acres, but only thirty percent of the structures still exist today—what is left is extraordinary. See Granada in "City and Regional Highlights" for more information.

Santiago de Compostela: see "Sacred Sites" below for a description of the El Camino trails to Santiago de Compostela.

Córdoba and Salamanca: see "City and Regional Highlights."

Doñana National Park in Andalucía, 50 km southwest of Sevilla, is Europe's largest sanctuary for migrating birds. The UNESCO Web site for Doñana is http://whc.unesco.org/en/list/685.

The Urdaibai Reserve area, almost sixty acres in size, near Bilbao in the Basque region was recognized in 1984 as a biosphere reserve by UNESCO. The Santimamiñe caves with Paleolithic drawings dating from 35,000 BC are in Kortezubi within the reserve; Web site: www.ingurumena.ejgv.euskadi.net/r49-12892/en/.

Historical Sites and Other Sites of Interest

Consuegra, south of Madrid, in the La Mancha area of Spain, has been made famous by Cervantes' *Don Quixote* tale and the beautiful windmills. There are eleven windmills and one castle on a hill in the town. If you take one of the ten paths of the Ruta de Don Quijote you can see other traditional windmills. Full route information can be found at www.castillalamancha.es/viajeros/SP/contenidos/Rutas/. On Route #7 from Campo de Criptana to La Solana there are ten more windmills, as well as nature reserves and old villages. In the village of Esquivias, you can visit the sixteenth-century house where Cervantes is reported to have written part of *Don Quixote*. The windmills are quite magnificent on their own, but make for an especially wonderful visit if you are a *Don Quixote* fan.

Spain has a number of caves with prehistoric paintings. In the region of Cantabria there are two caves near Santander in Puente Viesgo—see "City and Regional Highlights."

The Altamira caves: see "UNESCO World Heritage Sites."

In the Basque region in the Urdaibai Reserve there is the Cueva de Santimamiñe—see "UNESCO World Heritage Sites" and "City and Regional Highlights."

You need advance booking to see the Paleolithic drawings in the Cueva de Ekain, near Deba, between Bilbao and San Sebastián.

The Tito Bustillo Cave has 120 cave paintings from as long ago as 22,000 BC including one room with images of the female body. The cave is open March 15 to September 14, Wednesday to Sunday, 10:00 a.m. to 4:30 p.m. with admittance every twenty-five minutes. The cave is closed on Monday and Tuesday. General admission: 4.00 euros with half price for seniors and children, but children under seven are not permitted. Tito Bustillo Cave, Ribadesella, Asturias; Tel: 985 861 120.

Also in Asturias there is La Peña de Candamo cave in Candamo, 28 km from the capital Oviedo, where you will find rock art from 18,000 to 3000 BC. You must contact the Town Hall to schedule a visit; Tel: 985 828 056.

Near Cangas de Onís, 72 km from Oviedo, there is the Buxu cave with paintings. Visitors are limited to twenty-five people per day so you must call ahead to schedule a visit; Tel: 985 940 054.

You can *skip* the museum and mine tour in Almadén, west of Ciudad Real, where the world's largest mercury mine existed and where there are still vast reserves of cinnabar, from which mercury is extracted (and yes, used as a red paint pigment in Vermillion red).

City and Regional Highlights

So much to see and so little time—this is the truth about Spain. The cities and regional highlights included here are just a taste of all that Spain has to offer. Please see the *Green Earth Guide* Map to Highlighted Sites on page 152 to give you a visual sense of where these sites are located within Spain.

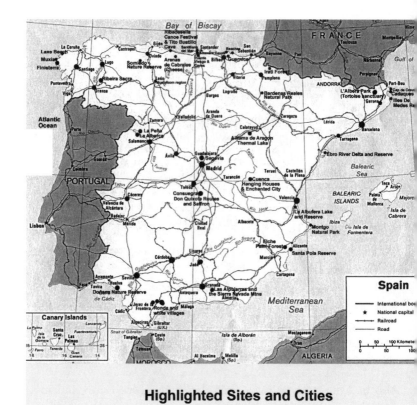

Highlighted Sites and Cities

CATALUNYA

In Catalunya (in Spanish it is Cataluña; in English, Catalonia), towns are fairly close together. Villages and towns are usually no more than 3 to 6 km apart. This makes for easy touring. Trains run from Barcelona up to the city of Girona and then up through the western edge of the Costa Brava from Flaçá up to the French border. The train is inexpensive and runs every thirty to sixty minutes. For towns off the train route, there are buses, but the schedules are limited, especially in the winter months. There are copious biking and walking routes. If you are feeling not entirely athletic and want to visit many of the small villages, you may have to resort to renting a small, efficient car for some of your jaunts. If you do this, remember that most rental cars are a standard stick shift.

BARCELONA-SPECIFIC

Barcelona definitely has a beat and vibe different from Valencia and Madrid. I found it to be the most full of tourists, less subdued for sure than Valencia, but also light and airy, which may be a factor of being on the sea. Barcelona is in the province of Catalunya, which has an independent and proud history. The native language is Catalan, but Spanish is also spoken. Signs and menus are usually in both languages.

Barcelona's dominant tourist attractions are the buildings designed by the architect Antoni Gaudí, who lived from 1852 to 1926. His buildings contain many elements drawn from nature and with many similarities to Rudolf Steiner (1861–1925) inspired architecture. In fact, Gaudí and Steiner were contemporaries and died within a year of each other. Some of Gaudí's famous buildings include La Sagrada Família, a massive cathedral, Casa Batlló and La Pedrera, used as apartment and office buildings along Passeig de Gràcia, and Parc Güell, a magical park in northern Barcelona originally commissioned as a utopian village, which was never realized. Güell Palace (Palau Güell) is another magnificent structure off of La Rambla.

All the Gaudí sites are often crowded and have entrance fees—go early before the lines get too long. La Sagrada Familia, Mallorca, 401, Barcelona; Tel: 932 073 031; Web site: www.sagradafamilia. org; Metro: Sagrada Família; open October to March 9:00 a.m. to 6:00 p.m., April to September 9:00 a.m. to 8:00 p.m.; entry fee 8 euros. Casa Milà/La Pedrera, Passeig de Gràcia, 92, Barcelona; Tel: 934 845 995; Metro: Passeig de Gràcia; open Monday to Sunday 10:00 a.m. to 8:00 p.m.; entry fee 8 euros. Casa Batlló, Passeig de Gràcia, 43, Barcelona; Tel: 932 160 306; Web site: www.casabatllo. es; Metro: Passeig de Gràcia; open Monday to Sunday 10:00 a.m. to 8:00 p.m.; entry fee 16.50 euros. Parc Güell, C/ Olot, Barcelona; Tel: 932 193 811; Metro: Lesseps; bus #24; open Monday to Sunday 10:00 a.m. to 7:00 p.m.; entry fee 4 euros. Palau Güell, C/ Nou de la Rambla, 3-5, 08001 Barcelona; Web site: www.palauguell.cat; Metro: Liceu; entrance free; open Tuesday to Saturday 10:00 a.m. to 2:30 p.m.

Health food stores and restaurants are plentiful, and the huge La Boqueria market, just off La Rambla, is not to be missed (see "Farm

The Fútbol (soccer) Club Barcelona, founded in 1899, has long been associated as the club of the people and stood for the independence and freedom of the Catalan region. In 1936 the president of the club, Josep Suñol, known for his slogan, "Sports and Citizenship," was murdered by Franco's troops. The club was consistently harassed by Franco, from bombings, to intimidation of players, and came to embody resistance to Franco's regime. Its motto, "more than a club," was first coined in 1968 to illustrate the club's commitment to social justice and democratic rights. Despite times of economic hardship, the club resisted commercial logos on its jerseys, breaking with that more than one-hundred-year-old tradition in 2006 to promote the humanitarian work of UNICEF worldwide.

Stands, Markets, and Local Products"). Barcelona is in general a bicycle-friendly city, with many bike lanes and promenades. The inexpensive citywide bike rental system, Bicing, is visible and used by many people (see "Transportation" section).

City information can be found at Barcelona Turisme Web site, available in English, where they sell a "Barcelona" card with discounts on tour buses, museums, and cultural and entertainment venues including the zoo and aquarium; Web site: www.barcelonaturisme.com. Metro information is at the Transports Metropolitans de Barcelona (TMB) Web site: www.tmb.cat/en_US/home.jsp.

La Rambla, the major pedestrian walkway and tree-lined boulevard that stretches 1.25 km, is busy every day but especially crowded on Saturday nights. Enjoy the bustling atmosphere and street entertainers, but make sure your wallet is somewhere on your person and is pickpocket-proof.

The Gardens of Montjuïc, filled with tropical and desert plants, are open 10:00 a.m. to sunset. The Magic Fountain, a water and light show put to music—much better than fireworks in my opinion—has been put on in the evenings at the Montjuïc gardens since 1929. It makes for a delightful way to pass an hour or so on a lovely evening.

Magic Fountain, Montjuïc Park, Barcelona; Metro: Plaça Espanya; open in the winter from October to April on Friday and Saturday with shows every half an hour from 7:00 to 8:30 p.m.; in the summer from May to September shows are Thursday, Friday, Saturday, and Sunday every half an hour from 9:30 until 11:30 p.m.

The Castell de Montjuïc affords great views of the city, but be forewarned, there are no bank machines within what seems like miles, so go prepared with cash. You can take in the view without entering what is now a military museum, but if you want to wander in and walk on the ramparts you will need the 3 euros cash. There is a funicular that runs up to the castle, but it is hardly worth the fare since the bus runs up there for about 1.20 euros. Castell de Montjuïc, Carretera de Montjuïc, 66, Barcelona; Tel: 933 298 613; open Tuesday to Friday 9:30 a.m. to 8:00 p.m., Saturday and Sunday 9:30 a.m. to 7:00 p.m.

For soccer fans, the FC Barcelona Camp Nou (pronounced "no") stadium is fun to visit. The stadium museum is open Monday to Saturday 10:00 a.m. to 6:30 p.m., Sundays only until 2:30 p.m., and there is a 6 euro entry fee. Tours of the stadium run Monday to Saturday 10:00 a.m. to 5:30 p.m., Sundays until 1:30 p.m., with a 10.50 euro fee. Tickets for games range from 30 to 120 euros and you should buy well in advance. The stadium also has a large souvenir and gear store. For those who must have some FC Barcelona (soccer) team souvenirs, but who can't or don't want to go to the stadium, check out the FC Botiga in the old part of the city, or at the Estació de Sants (Sants train station). Note that for bargains you will have to go to the gift shop at the stadium. FC Barcelona, Camp Nou Stadium, C/ d'Aristides Maillol, Les Corts neighborhood, Barcelona; Tel: 902 189 900; Web site: www.fcbarcelona.com/web/english/; Metro stop: Collblanc; box office for game (match) tickets open Monday to Friday 9:00 a.m. to 1:30 p.m./3:30 to 6:00 p.m.

The Museu de la Xocolata (Chocolate) is a small museum with amazing models of monuments and characters in chocolate! It was developed by the Confectionary Guild and Pastry School of Barcelona. At the entrance to the museum you can purchase delectable chocolates from the chocolate bar. Museu de la Xocolata, Comerç, 36, 08003 Barcelona; Tel: 932 687 878; e-mail: museu@pastisseria.cat; Web site: http://pastisseria.com; Metro: Jaume I; open Monday and

Wednesday through Saturday 10:00 a.m. to 7:00 p.m., Sunday 10:00 a.m. to 3:00 p.m., closed Tuesday; entry fee 3.90 euros.

Barcelona has a medieval Jewish Call tucked into its old part near Plaça Sant Jaume. *Call* is a Catalan word used to mean quarter or neighborhood, derived from the Latin *callis,* meaning street. Here there is an old synagogue and a museum of sorts. The Call Association of Barcelona (Asociació Call de Barcelona), C/ Marlet, 5, 08006 Barcelona; Tel: 933 170 790; Web site: www.calldebarcelona. org/eindex.html; open Monday to Saturday 11:00 a.m. to 6:00 p.m., Sunday 11:00 a.m. to 3:00 p.m.

For information about the famous La Boqueria market see "Farm Stands, Markets, and Local Products." For other markets in Barcelona see "Markets."

Thursday evenings at 7:00 p.m. in the Plaza Sant Jaume along the wall of the Palau de la Generalitat de Catalunya you can join Artisans for Peace standing in silence for thirty minutes holding placards with images and words invoking peace.

GIRONA-SPECIFIC AND THE COSTA BRAVA

Girona is a small university city about one hour northeast of Barcelona, known in the biking world as a base training home for Tour de France contenders. Of note in Girona are the great biking trails in the region for various training levels; the fortified wall that overlooks the city; the Arab baths from the twelfth century near the cathedral in the old part of the city; and the Call with narrow, cobblestone streets, one of the best preserved ninth- to fifteenth-century Jewish neighborhoods in Europe, now with museums, stores, and cafés including the Museum of the History of the Jews.

The Jewish Call is where for centuries Jews and Christians lived harmoniously until the fifteenth century when the Call became not just the Jews' neighborhood, but the only place they could live in Girona. In 1492 the Catholic monarchs expelled the Jews from Spain and they were forced to leave this warren of stone buildings and streets. Today the Museum of the History of the Jews is housed on the site of a former synagogue. The Call makes for wonderful walking. Museum of the History of the Jews, C/ de la Força, 8, Girona; Tel: 972 216 761; e-mail: callgirona@ajgirona.org; Web site: www.

ajuntament.gi/call/; open Monday to Saturday 10:00 a.m. to 6:00 p.m.; entry fee 2 euros. Hours in winter are slightly shorter. The Arab baths ruins are open in the summer from April to September, Monday to Saturday, 10:00 a.m. to 7:00 p.m., Sunday 10:00 a.m. to 2:00 p.m. In the winter they are open every day from October to March 10:00 a.m. to 2:00 p.m.

The wrought-iron footbridge over the Onyar River was designed by Gustave Eiffel. There are two markets in Girona on Tuesdays and Saturday mornings. One market is a mini version of La Boqueria in Barcelona, where produce stalls line the outside of the daily covered market. Mercat del Lleó has thirty permanent booths, you can find many fresh fish stalls (so fresh nothing smells like fish), more fruits and vegetables, and my favorite, the 0% Gluten booth. What a thrill—gluten-free goodies of all kinds from croissants, baguettes, cookies, and cakes to pizzas and pastas. 0% Gluten, Plaça Mercat del Lleó, nº 200, 17002 Girona; Tel: 972 200 814; e-mail: girona@zeropercentgluten.com; Web site: www.zeropercentgluten.com. Mercat del Lleó is open Monday to Friday 5:30 a.m. to 1:30 p.m., and Saturday 5:00 a.m. to 2:00 p.m.

The other market, Mercat de les Ribes del Ter, is huge and takes place in the park in northwestern Girona. There you can find all sorts of food as well as what feels like miles of clothes and household goods. This too is open Tuesday and Saturday mornings. In the winter Mercat de les Ribes del Ter is held on the banks of the Ter River at the northwest side of the Parc de la Devesa. In the summer months the market is along the south end of the Parc de la Devesa. Winter and summer the market is open Tuesday and Saturday mornings until 1:30 p.m.

For more information about Girona see the Girona Tourist Office Web site, where you can choose English at the bottom of the page; Web site: www.ajgirona.org/web/.

At the Costa Brava tourism page you will have access to pages of biking routes for the area. You can travel over the same routes Lance Armstrong and others have used to train for the Tour de France. There are posted trails and "greenway" trails built over old railroad tracks. Click on "Sports," then on "Cycling and mountain biking," and then click on "See all" for biking routes. Costa Brava Web site: en.costabrava.org/main/home.aspx.

The Cap de Creus nature reserve is breathtaking, but not for the faint of heart since the route through it is a twisty mountain road through seemingly endless terraced olive trees. The village of Cadaqués, at the end of the road, is sublime—a visual feast of white and blue set against mountains and the Mediterranean. Park in the lot at the entrance to the village and wind your way through the stone-studded alley-like streets. Cadaqués is well worth visiting for a day or a month—feast your eyes and your soul.

The Empúries ruins and beach just the north side of L'Escala are a great excursion. You can park for free on the bridge by the Olympic Torch monument and walk along the beautiful beaches or the wooded path for bikes and pedestrians. Or you can drive to the parking lot for the ruins and walk from there. One and a half miles (2.4 km) down the trail you will come to the ruins of a large Greek settlement. Remains of an ancient stone jetty are in the sea in front of the ruins. You can walk to Sant Marti d'Empúries, an old cobble-stoned village on top of a hill overlooking the sea. A few restaurants serve visitors, and in the summer a few little stores are open. Museu d'Arqueologia de Catalunya—Empúries; Tel: 972 770 208; Web site: www.mac.es. The ruins are open from July to the end of September 10:00 a.m. to 8:00 p.m., and in the winter from October until the end of June 10:00 a.m. to 6:00 p.m.

The beach at L'Estartit (Girona/Costa Brava) is sandy and long. You can walk almost 10 miles (16 km) down the beach if you desire. Off the shore of L'Estartit are small rocky islands called Les Illes Medes, a protected underwater nature reserve, where all the different sea life throughout the Mediterranean can be found around the islands. In the warm months, this is a hot spot for snorkelers and divers.

La Bisbal d'Empordà, known for its ceramics production, makes for a good visit and has an excellent market on Friday mornings—see "Farm Stands, Markets, and Local Products." Pals, a restored medieval stone village in the corner of an otherwise working-class town, makes for great walking. Peratallada is a wonderful thirteenth-century village that is still inhabited, and looks much like it did eight hundred years ago. For accommodations see the Històric Hotel and Apartments in Girona and L'Hostal Blau in Peratallada under "Accommodations."

Begur is a beautiful village northeast of Palafrugell. The remains of an eleventh-century castle battlements are the highest point of the town and afford spectacular 360° views. The village of Begur is enticing with its lovely narrow streets and numerous walking trails to idyllic beaches and coves. The tourist office has a handy *Begur on foot* (*A peu per Begur*) pamphlet with all the trail details; Web site: www. visitbegur.com.

Ciutat Ibèrica d'Ullastret is the protected remains of the Indiket indigenous settlement dating from 600 BC in Ullastret with a small museum and extensive grounds filled with unearthed remnants of walls, foundations, silos, wells, and more. The site is part of the Museu d'Arqueologia de Catalunya. It is in the town of Ullastret off the main road, and is well signposted. Museu d'Arqueologia de Catalunya—Ullastret; Web site: www.mac.es; open in the summer from June 1 to September 30, Tuesday to Sunday 10:00 a.m. to 8:00 p.m., closed Monday. In the winter from October 1 to May 31 the site is open Tuesday to Sunday 10:00 a.m. to 2:00 p.m./3:00 to 6:00 p.m., closed Monday.

The area northwest of Girona city—the towns of Besalú, Olot, and Vic—makes for great adventuring, and there is beautiful walking and biking through the natural park of the Garrotxa volcanoes. South of Barcelona, in the Tarragona area, you can visit the Castillo de Miravet (Miravet Castle). Miravet Castle is open Tuesday to Sunday 10:00 a.m. to 1:30 p.m./3:00 to 5:30 p.m. with a 3 euro entry fee. Miravet Castle; Tel: 977 407 368; Web site: www.riberadebre.info/english/miravet.htm. The nearby city of Tarragona is light and airy, is full of great Roman ruins, and overlooks the turquoise sea.

VALENCIA-SPECIFIC

Valencia is a spacious, relaxed city on the Mediterranean, less crowded and expensive than Barcelona and Madrid. There are many artists' galleries and venues, as well as cafés and other fun and alternative businesses. Valencia has beautiful city beaches where you can easily walk for miles, accessible by their sparkling new tram. The plazas are plentiful and filled with majestic old buildings from government offices to churches.

Valencia has numerous health food stores and good natural foods restaurants throughout the city, and is home to the largest health food store I found in Spain—J. Navarro Terra Verda, C/ Arzobispo Mayoral, 20, Valencia—the closest you will find to a Whole Foods market in Spain. Across the street from the store is the Navarro Spa Catalá, using natural products and offering a variety of spa therapies. And a few blocks from that is the Calma Balneario Urbano, a spa with thermal baths, body treatments, and yoga classes. See the "Health Food Stores" and "Restaurants" sections for listings including the Kimpira restaurant. The owners of Kimpira offer classes and workshops in specialty food preparation such as sushi and various vegan and macrobiotic meals.

There is a good-size community in Valencia focused on alternative lifestyles. A handy little print and Web eco-guide is published called *Revista Eina;* Web site: www.revistaeina.net with an extensive directory and an "EcoMapa," accessible by clicking on the left-hand side of the Web page, with listings of health food stores, restaurants, exercise centers, and more. Other free, alternative mini guides in print are *Guía Verde* and *Gamana.*

The old part of Valencia is quite large and differs from some other cities in that the old part is not so precious, but rather very much a living, working neighborhood of the city, a little funky, and beware, not pedestrian only. Be on alert for cars and motorbikes on miniscule streets. You will find grand medieval towers and arches at different corners of the old city borders.

The Turia River, which once ran along one border of the old city, was diverted for irrigation purposes decades ago, and the dry riverbed is now home to more than 6 miles (9.6 km) of parks and soccer (*fútbol*) pitches for children and adults alike. Stand on one of the many bridges crossing the Turia and you can often watch great soccer games below.

Valencia is a market city with twenty-four municipal markets and scores of street markets on any day of the week. The largest is Valencia's Mercado Central, a beautiful and enormous covered market in the old part of the city, open Monday to Saturday 7:30 a.m. to 2:30 p.m. Look for the organic stall, La Morhada; Web site: www.lamorhada.com. Mercado Central Web site: www.mercadocentralvalencia.es. On Sundays check out the Rastrillo flea market held in Plaza Luis Casanova right next to the Estadio Mestalla, Valencia's *fútbol* (soccer) stadium, within walking distance of the old part.

Just 15 km south of Valencia city is the Parque Natural de la Albufera, almost fifty-two thousand acres of park including a huge freshwater lake, as well as beaches along the Mediterranean Sea; Web site: www.albufera.com.

Elche, in the province of Alicante, is known for its shoe manufacturing (see "Shopping"). It also has 9 km of white sand beaches, a Neolithic site and museum, and Europe's largest palm forest with close to two hundred thousand palm trees in the Elche Oasis. The local tourist page has information in English; Web site: www.turismedelx.com/en. Nearby is the Santa Pola nature reserve. See information about the Santa Pola nature reserve, two hours south of Valencia, in the "Wild and Natural Resources" section.

Agua de Valencia is a local drink made with fresh-squeezed orange juice and sparkling white wine, served chilled. Oranges in general are abundant and delicious.

The Montgó Nature Reserve in the Valencia region covers more than 5,300 acres around the almost 2,500-foot-high Montgó mountain that dominates the skyline. Hundreds of plant species and wildlife can be found in the reserve, as well as the Migdia cave with rock paintings. Climbing the mountain takes all day, almost eight hours round-trip. At the top of the mountain there are the remains of a 700 BC indigenous Iberian village called Casa de Biot. The information center is in the town of Denia. Montgó Park Information Center, C/de Sant Joan, s/n, Parc del Bosc de Diana, Apdo. 492, 03700 Denia; Tel: 966 423 305; e-mail: parque_montgo@gva.es; open every day 9:00 a.m. to 2:00 p.m.

Between Valencia and Barcelona, the coastal town of Peñíscola makes for great walking and touring. There is the beach, Playa del Pebret, south of the city, a 10 km circular walking route, castle remains, the Sierra de Irta with Mediterranean vegetation, and more. Accommodations possibilities include the Hostal Aranda and the Hostería del Mar. The Hostal Aranda is shielded by the walls surrounding the Templar castle with double rooms for 50 to 75 euros/night. Hostal Aranda, Tel: 606 222 917. The Hostería del Mar, with views of Playa del Norte, offers doubles between 68 and 133 euros. Hostería del Mar, Tel: 964 480 600. See the city Web site for more information: www.peniscola.org.

Very useful city information, including city and Metro maps, lists of rural accommodations, and more in Spanish can be found online at the Guía del Tiempo Libre (Free-Time Guide); Web site: www.gtlvalencia.com. For an online English guide see www.thisisvalencia.com.

MADRID-SPECIFIC

Madrid is Spain's largest city, and quite majestic with its broad boulevards and grand buildings. If you are in the downtown business and shopping district it can seem that there are street musicians at almost every turn and Metro stop. Thursday evening is the night people can put out all manner of unwanted items like furniture to be collected by the city trash trucks, so keep your eye out for treasures. Madrid reminds me of New York City although it is much more airy and grand without the extremely tall buildings closing in on the city. It is easy to navigate with more to see than is possible during a short trip. Highlights include the museums and the majestic parks, filled with wonderful paths for walking and biking, cafés, and coveted summer shade. There are plentiful health food stores and restaurants throughout Madrid, and I find something interesting at every turn. Look for a display of Goya's *Caprichos* at the Goya Metro stop.

Madrid is home to a number of large, world-famous museums, including the Thyssen-Bornemisza Museum, the Prado Museum, and the Reina Sofía Museum, where the original of Picasso's *Guernica* hangs, surrounded by rooms filled with paintings and photographs illustrating the painting's context and history. All three museums are within walking distance of each other and are near the Atocha train station in downtown Madrid. Thyssen-Bornemisza Museum, Paseo del Prado, 8, Madrid; Tel: 913 690 151; Web site: www.museothyssen.org//THYSSEN/home; open every day except Monday. Museo Nacional Centro de Arte Reina Sofía, Santa Isabel, 52, Madrid; Tel: 914 675 062; Web site: www.museoreinasofia.es/index_en.html. The Reina Sofía is closed Tuesday. Entry fee is 6 euros. Prado Museum, Paseo del Prado, Madrid; Tel: 913 302 800; Web site: www.museoprado.es/en/. It's best to purchase your tickets to the Prado in advance to avoid huge lines. The Prado is closed Monday.

Madrid's eight parks include the large Casa de Campo, covering close to 4,500 acres, and the smaller Parque del Retiro, with about three hundred acres, both excellent for walking and biking, or taking in the scenery.

A quick half-hour AVE train ride from Madrid brings you to the UNESCO designated walled city of Toledo. Toledo is the handcrafted sword manufacturing capital and for anyone with knife and sword fetishes this is your idea of heaven. Swords and knives made in Toledo fill the sea of souvenir stores and you can just picture Íñigo Montoya's father toiling in a workshop. See "UNESCO World Heritage Sites" for more information.

For a different and fun way to see Madrid you can try a Madrid Segway tour. See the Web site for more information: www.madsegs.com.

There are a number of books about Guernica. See Gijs van Hensbergen, *Guernica: The Biography of a Twentieth-Century Icon* (London: Bloomsbury, 2004).

BILBAO AND THE BASQUE REGION

The landscape in the Basque region reminds me of Switzerland—lush and mountainous with lots of farmland. Local food specialties in the Basque region include sheep cheeses, one of which is Idiazábal, apples and cider, and *txakoli,* a sparkling wine. Look for the Eusko label of origin for authentic, locally produced food. Eusko Label; Web site: www.euskolabel.net/in_index.asp.

In Bilbao, Txorierri, in the old part of the city (Casco Viejo), is one of the many stores selling gourmet and local foods. Txorierri, C/ Artekale, 19, Bilbao; open Monday to Friday 9:00 a.m. to 2:30 p.m./4:30 to 8:30 p.m., Saturday 9:00 a.m. to 2:30 p.m.

Bilbao is in the Basque region of Spain where both Spanish and Basque are spoken. I found Bilbao to be vibrant and easy to get around. The RENFE train station is right in the heart of it. There is a simple Metro, a sleek new tram, and city buses. Sites are all within walking distance of the city center, as are multiple health food stores and restaurants. Everyone I encountered was friendly. The city felt very hip, international, and lively.

The old part of Bilbao, called Casco Viejo, dating from the fifteenth to eighteenth centuries, still has the original seven streets (Siete

The village of Guernica, in the Basque region of northern Spain, was the site of a devastating bombing attack by the Germans and Italians on April 26, 1937, during the Spanish Civil War. Picasso created a huge black and white painting entitled *Guernica,* eleven feet high by twenty-three feet wide, as a testament to the horrors of war and as a tribute to the victims of the Guernica bombings. Although various theories have circulated through the decades as to why Guernica was bombed, recent information suggests that Franco orchestrated the attack with Nazi Germans and Fascist Italians to terrorize and break down the strong resistance to his nationalistic ideology in the Basque region, and the Germans used it as a testing ground for their carpet-bombing tactic. In 1997 the German government officially apologized to the people of Guernica and Spain for their involvement in the bombing. The story has it that when a German soldier burst into Picasso's studio in France and saw Picasso's *Guernica* painting, he asked, "Did you do that?" and Picasso replied, "No, you did."

Calles) that made up the medieval city and are now chockablock full of little stores and cafés. On one end of the old part is the Mercado de la Ribera, a huge covered market filled with every kind of food, including an organic stall by one of the entrances. *Pintxos (pinchos),* offered at many restaurants, are an appetizer-like snack similar to tapas. In the evening and into the night, people stroll along the river and in the old part of the city.

The Frank Gehry designed Guggenheim Museum is in the heart of Bilbao. The structure is amazing—a work of art all unto itself. The atrium is 180 feet tall, and the museum covers six acres. Built of limestone, glass, and titanium, the museum's design is elemental. The museum is an important stop—allow time to savor the ins and outs of the museum. Guggenheim Bilbao Museum, Avda. Abandoibarra, 2, Bilbao; Tel: 944 359 080; Web site: www.guggenheim-bilbao.es/?idiom=en; open Tuesday to Sunday 10:00 a.m. to 8:00 p.m., closed Monday (except July and August), admission charge 10.50 euros.

There are numerous day-trip options from Bilbao including numerous beaches, natural areas, as well as the town of Guernica (Gernika in Basque), made famous by Picasso's painting of the same name.

Getxo is a suburb of Bilbao with three beaches and is a quick twenty-five minutes on the Metro from the heart of Bilbao. Take note that there are six Metro stops covering Getxo. Areeta gets you to the Pont Bizkaia (the UNESCO hanging bridge, or Puente Colgante); Neguri and Algorta will both lead you to the *playa* (beach) d'Ereaga; and Bidezabal is near the Arrigunaga beach. See the town Web site for more information: www.getxo.net.

Plentzia is a beach town with a medieval quarter and is about a forty-five-minute Metro ride from Bilbao, and a steal for only 1.60 euros one-way. To get to the beach and port, a roughly twenty-minute walk from the Metro, go straight over the bridge, then left onto the promenade by the river. Follow the river down to a mini circle and go right, following the street, and you will come to the beach and port. There is a shuttle bus from Plentzia to Gorliz, where there are six-thousand-year-old petrified dunes.

Gernika

The town of Gernika (Guernica in Spanish) is the site of the April 26, 1937, bombings, killing an estimated 1,650 people, that inspired Picasso's famous painting.

The Gernika sites are all within blocks of each other and all are within walking distance from the train station. There are three train stops for Gernika—take the middle stop simply called Gernika, and hold on to your train ticket as you need it to exit. The Gernika tourist office is across the street from the Peace Museum and they are very helpful. Gernika Tourist Office, C/ Artekale, 8, Gernika; Web site: www.gernika-lumo.net/in_index.asp.

If you happen to be in Gernika on a Monday, that is the big market day when Basque local products are sold. The market is a few blocks

In Bilbao you can take the fast Metro or the new tram to the Termibús bus station. Both cost in the 1.20 to 1.40 euros range. The Metro to the northern beaches of Getxo and Plentzia costs 1.60 euros/trip. For Bilbao Metro information see www.metro-bilbao.net/eng/home.jsp.

The RENFE train station in Bilbao is called Abando. Next door to the RENFE station is the Concordia train station for the regional FEVE trains; the Atxuri station, 1 km into the old part (Casco Viejo), is where the EuskoTren trains leave for local excursions to Gernika and other towns including Durango, Deba, Zumaia, Zarautz, and San Sebastián/Donostia.

The EuskoTram runs between the city and the Atxuri train station. Stops include the Ribera market, the bus terminal, the Guggenheim, RENFE station, and more. Some stops have ticket machines—some don't. The Abando stop (RENFE station) does not and you must go into the BBK bank at the corner. Since you must enter the bank's ATM room to access this particular tram ticket machine, you will need your credit card to enter; look for the machine in the far right corner for tram tickets. The price is 1.20 euros/ride and you can pay with cash or credit card. The tickets need to be validated, which you can do at the metal signpost at the stop.

For more information about Bilbao you can explore the tourist information Web site: www.bilbao.net; for information about the Basque region see the Web site: www.euskadi.net. Both sites have English versions.

from the Peace Museum and the train station. Look for the "Eusko" label of origin.

The Museo de la Paz de Gernika (Guernica Peace Museum) has a powerful, striking floor display with debris under glass that you walk over as if you were walking over bombing wreckage. Although it does have some artifacts from the bombing of Gernika, it is not a museum in the traditional sense, but rather designed to trigger thought and reflection about the past, present, and future state of war and peace,

Gernikako Arbola Song (Two of the Twelve Verses)

Gernikako arbola
Da bedeinkatua
Euskaldunen artean
Guztiz maitatua:
Eman ta zabal zazu
Munduan frutua,
Adoratzen zaitugu
Arbola santua.

Arbolak erantzun du
Kontuz bizitzeko,
Eta bihotzetikan
Jaunari eskatzeko:
Gerrarik nahi ez dugu
Bakea betiko,
Gure lege zuzenak
Emen maitatzeko.

Translated this reads: The tree of Gernika is blessed among the Basques, absolutely loved, with deep love. Give and deliver the fruit unto the world. We adore you, holy tree. The tree answered that we should live carefully and in our hearts ask the Lord: We do not want wars [but] peace forever, to love here our fair laws.

conflict and human nature, including a provocative and I am sure controversial exhibit and commentary about the Basque campaign for independence. The museum is an excellent companion visit to what I consider to be the other important sites in Gernika. Museo de la Paz de Gernika, Plaza Foru, 1, Gernika; Web site: www.peacemuseumguernica.org/en/initiate/homeeng.php; open Tuesday to Saturday 10:00 a.m. to 2:00 p.m./4:00 to 7:00 p.m., Sunday 10:00 a.m. to 2:00 p.m.

Four blocks north on C/ Allende Salazar is a tile replica of Picasso's *Guernica* painting.

West on the same street as the tile *Guernica* replica is the Basque history museum, Euskal Herria Museoa. In front of the museum and downstairs is an open area near where many of the bombs hit, with a memorial to the bombing victims on the wall. Behind the museum is the Parque de los Pueblos de Europa, a small, pretty park that will bring you to the oak tree if you have been wandering through the park paths. Euskal Herria Museoa, C/ Allende Salazar, 5, Gernika; Tel: 946 255 451; Web site: www.bizkaia.net/euskalherriamuseoa/; open Tuesday to Saturday 10:00 a.m. to 2:00 p.m./4:00 to 7:00 p.m., Sunday 11:00 a.m. to 3:00 p.m., closed Monday.

Gernika's famous oak tree, symbolizing peace and freedom, came from the seedling of an ancient oak, and now a tall stump of the tree is protected within a gazebo in the yard of the government building (Casa de Juntas). A new tree has been planted in the rear. The laws of the land were declared and sworn to under the tree. A popular folk song was written in the 1800s by José María Iparraguirre that illustrates the tree's significance and is an unofficial anthem of the Basque people.

Although most famous, Gernika was not the only town to endure practice saturation or carpet-bombing by the Nazis. In the town of Durango south of Gernika, a 1937 German Condor Legion used the town for target practice prior to Gernika. The Luftwaffe destroyed the stone streets and churches, killing more than 238 people. Irún, on the French border, suffered carpet-bombing by the Nazis after Gernika.

Other Day Trips from Bilbao

Other day trips from Bilbao, some of which are within minutes of Gernika, include Bermeo, Mundaka, the Urdaibai Reserve area, and the Urkiola forest.

Bermeo is a large fishing port, known for ancient whaling expeditions. It is said that in the year AD 1000 Bermeo fishermen followed whales up to the Arctic! Minutes south from Bermeo is Mundaka, famous to surfers for having the longest left-hand break in Europe. Mundaka is at the mouth of the estuary that is part of the protected Urdaibai Biosphere (see "UNESCO World Heritage Sites"). There are promenades along the water and beaches. At the Mundaka train station go right a few blocks and then left down the hill to get to the water. Web site: www.mundaka.org.

The Urdaibai Reserve area, almost sixty acres in size, was recognized in 1984 as a biosphere reserve by UNESCO. Beaches and the environmental center for the reserve are in Sukarrieta, but the train stop is called Busturia-Itsasbegi; Web site: www.ingurumena.ejgv.euskadi.net/r49-12892/en/.

The Paleolithic Cueva (cave) de Santimamiñe, with drawings dating from 35,000 BC, is just outside Kortezubi, in the Urdaibai Reserve. Unfortunately there is no public transportation to this cave site. Guided tours are available Monday to Friday 10:00 a.m. to 6:00 p.m.

The Parque Natural Urkiola is a birch tree forest (*urkia* means birch tree in Basque, and *ola* means place) with hiking trails throughout.

The town of Vitoria (Gasteiz in Basque), south of Bilbao, is the capital of the Basque region. Cars are minimized and pedestrians rule. The medieval old part of the city and the pedestrian zone are within a few blocks' walk of the RENFE train station. Named for the philosopher Francisco de Vitoria (1486–1546), a theologian sometimes referred to as the father of international law because he was opposed to the colonizing of the New World and converting the "pagans." He defended human rights of native peoples and believed that war was never justified. Vitoria is home to the Basque University with a center for Basque language and history.

Some of the beautiful coastal towns en route between Bilbao and San Sebastián include Bakio, Elantxobe, Lekeitio, Ondarroa, Mutriku (on an inlet 3 km from the beach at Saturra, linked with Deba and Zumaia by a clifftop path), Zumaia, Getaria (church of San Salvador with a menorah), and Zarautz (the beach is 1.5 miles—2.4 km—long). Unfortunately the bus takes the fast route along the highway, so it does not go past any of these towns. The EuskoTren local train goes to Deba, Zumaia, and Zarautz. For the other towns you need a car.

San Sebastián, called Donostia in Basque, is about an hour northeast of Bilbao on the coast and is known for its beautiful city beach. The Bahía de la Concha is a large, crescent shaped beach, flanked by a long, pleasant promenade, which seems to always be filled with people enjoying the scene. The old part of the city (Parte Vieja) is filled with shops and cafés. The Centro Romántico has again more

The bus "station," really just a parking plaza for the buses, between Plaza de Pío XII and the river, is a thirty-minute walk south of the old part (Parte Vieja). Take bus #28 or any that stop at *Boulevard,* which is Alameda Boulevard and will place you by the beaches, the old town, and generally where you will find the action. The PESA bus company runs buses to Bilbao every thirty to sixty minutes depending on the day and season, and it takes about one hour. The ticket office is a small storefront on the avenue just up the street from where the buses park; Web site: www.pesa.net. The RENFE train station is Estación del Norte on Paseo de Francia with the track canopy designed by Gustave Eiffel. The local and regional FEVE and EuskoTren trains run from Estación de Amara.

shops. There are other city beaches, the Playa Ondarreta and Playa Gros-Zurriola on Paseo la Zurriola. With the promenades along the beaches and river, San Sebastián has seemingly endless city walking options.

NAVARRA

Pamplona is a lively, "green" university city and is on the French route to Santiago de Compostela. The remains of the city's old walls are on the east side of the city, and the old part is called Casco Antiguo. Pamplona has almost one thousand acres of parks with a 7-mile (11.26 km) pathway along the Río Arga. In the old monastery of San Pedro there is the Environmental Education Museum of San Pedro, promoting sustainable use of energy and natural resources. Environmental Education Museum of San Pedro, Monasterio Viejo de San Pedro, C/ Errotazar, s/n, Pamplona; Tel: 948 149 804; open Tuesday to Friday 10:00 a.m. to 1:00 p.m./4:00 to 6:00 p.m., Sunday 10:00 a.m. to 1:00 p.m.; free entry.

See "Sacred Sites" for dolmens and magic caves in Navarra, and see "Wild and Natural Resources" for parks in the region.

CASTILLA Y LEÓN REGION

The Castilla y León region boasts three UNESCO World Heritage cities, Segovia, Ávila, and Salamanca; see "UNESCO World Heritage Sites." The region has numerous pure water springs where the waters are bottled for sale, ten *balnearios,* and numerous hiking routes, all of which can be explored on the helpful tourist Web site: www.turismocastillayleon.com. This region of Spain is also well known for being particularly conducive to mushrooms, with more than 1,500 mushroom species, many of which are edible. You can find full information about mushrtoom picking routes at www.myas.info/micoturismo/sendas.php.

"THE GREEN COAST": CANTABRIA AND ASTURIAS

Cantabria

Cantabria and Asturias are known as the Green Coast because they are lush from large amounts of rainfall. Rural accommodations can be found at these Web sites: www.cantabriarural.com/eng/home/84-eng.html and www.tourismcantabria.com. The Turismo Cantabria site also lists the twenty magnificent beaches along the Cantabrian coast.

Local Cantabrian food specialties include Cantabrian white bean stew; and *sidra,* a fizzy cider that waiters pour from high above, known as "throwing the cider," with the theory that the cider absorbs oxygen along the way, which makes it taste better. Ciders are served at taverns called *siderias* or *chigres.* Cantabria runs from Santander on the Basque border to San Vicente de la Barquera on the Asturias border. Santander has some nice beaches that are about a forty- to fifty-minute walk from the train station, but otherwise it is best as a base. San Vicente de la Barquera is at the mouth of an estuary. In addition to a beautiful coast, Cantabria's highlights include interesting villages and prehistoric caves.

About 25 km south of Santander in Puente Viesgo are the Cuevas de El Castillo, two caves with prehistoric drawings. El Castillo and La Moneda are open from October to April, Wednesday to Sunday, 9:30 a.m. to 5:00 p.m. Buses run from Santander to Puente Viesgo. El Gran Hotel Balneario spa is in Puente Viesgo too—see "Clinics and Spas." In Liérganes, Cantabria, also about 25 km from

The regional FEVE train runs on a narrow gauge track, Europe's longest, originally designed to haul workers and minerals through the mountains. It is a wonderful way to see the countryside as the train often goes through areas with no roads. The train follows various Santiago camino routes. The train snakes its way through the Picos de Europa mountains, farmland, and forests, with tiny glimpses of the ocean. It makes you feel as though you could be walking or biking through the bucolic setting. This is mountainous terrain—Spain is said to be second only to Switzerland in being the most mountainous country in Europe. The train surpasses the bus for me in comfort, because even if you are not prone to carsickness, the buses can make you woozy as they twist and turn around the sometimes hairpin curves of the mountain roads. Rail passes are not valid on the FEVE independent train line (www.feve.es) and it is not designed for long-distance travel. Few people ride from one end of the line to the other.

I chose to take all three legs. The best way to do this is to stop overnight along the way, and get on a train a day or two later after exploring. You have to buy tickets for different legs of the journey; you can't buy one for Bilbao to Ferrol. If you are traveling east to west, the Yellow line from Bilbao to Santander takes about three hours making about thirty-two stops, with three trains a day, and costs about 8 euros. The Blue line goes between Santander and Oviedo and going the full trip takes about five hours making around forty stops, costing 14 euros with only two trains a day. This leg of the trip includes many poten-

Santander, is the Balneario Liérganes with tiled rooms and luxury treatments. Balneario Liérganes, C/ José Antonio Primo de Rivera, s/n, Liérganes, 39727 Cantabria; Tel: 942 528 011.

In Santillana del Mar only cars of residents may drive into the city; the rest must park in car parks at the city limits; Web site: www.santillana-del-mar.com/English/index-i.htm. Sixteen km from Santillana, Gaudí enthusiasts, who I will assume have covered Barcelona, can go to the town of Comillas to the Capricho de Gaudí ("Gaudi's

tial stops including Cabezón de la Sal, San Vicente de la Barquera, Llanes, Ribadesella, and Arriondas. The Red line between Oviedo and Ferrol has the most coastal vistas, takes a full seven hours, and costs 20 euros. Only two trains run the full route every day, making more than seventy stops. Stops include Cudillero, Navia, Ribadeo, and Viveiro. If you are making your way to Santiago, there are one-hour bus rides between Ferrol and Santiago. Please note that the bus station in Ferrol is about a one-block distance from the train station but neither have ATMs and you will need cash if you are buying a bus ticket. Be prepared or you will have to hoof with your luggage a few blocks into the Plaza de España for a bank machine.

If you are traveling between Easter and October and are looking for an Old World, luxury experience, the El Transcantábrico train travels from León to Santiago de Compostela (or vice versa) over eight days. The train stops in Luarca, Gijón, Llanes, Santander, Bilbao, and Cistierna, making excursions from the train, more in the style of a cruise. The train does not travel at night, but rather stops in stations with the thought that passengers will sleep more soundly that way (personally I love sleeping on a moving train). The train is equipped with perks such as a sauna and wifi. Up to fifty-two passengers can enjoy this trip (there are twenty-six double rooms), and pay from 2,600 euros per person for a double or 3,500 euros for a single. This includes meals and accommodations (but not drinks) and does not include connecting transportation. See the Web site for departure dates. El Transcantábrico Train; Web site: www.transcantabrico.feve.es/index.asp.

whim") and see his brightly colored building with wild designs including rows of sunflowers. Two km southwest of Santillana del Mar is the Altamira Museum with the Neocueva replica caves; Web site: http://museodealtamira.mcu.es/ingles/index.html. See "UNESCO World Heritage Sites" for more information.

Cabezón de la Sal is where salt has been mined since Roman times. For more information go to the town Web site: www.cabezondelasal.net/.

Asturias

Local food specialties in Asturias are similar to those in Vermont. Cheese and cider are local staples in this part of Spain, as well as delicacies. There are goat and sheep farmers tucked into the hills who make small quantities of divine cheeses from their animals that they milk by hand. Cabrales is a blue cheese made from cow milk that is carefully aged in bat-filled caves in the mountains. Spanish regulations require the cheese to age at least two months to be called Cabrales. South of Arenas there is an exhibition cheese cave, Cabrales Exhibition Cave (or La Cueva Exposición Cabrales). From October to March the cave is open only on Saturday and Sunday, 10:00 a.m. to 2:00 p.m., 4:00 to 8:00 p.m. In the summer the cave is open every day with the same hours. For information on guided tours of the cave contact the Fundación Cabrales, Barrio Cares, s/n, Arenas de Cabrales, 33554 (Asturias); Tel: 985 846 702; Web site: www.fundacioncabrales.com/. You can find the local cheeses for sale at the store La Casa del Quesu, Ctra. General, s/n, Arenas de Cabrales. The last Sunday in August is the Feria del Cabrales celebrating the local cheese (www.cabrales.org). Nava, 31 km from Oviedo, is considered the cider capital and has a cider museum.

Asturias, like everywhere else in Spain, is filled with beautiful and interesting towns and natural sites. In Ribadesella you can visit the Cueva de Tito Bustillo (see "Historical Sites and Other Sites of Interest"), and consider attending the International Canoe Festival (see "*Green Earth Guide* Spanish Festival Events Calendar). Oviedo is the capital of Asturias and is a pleasant city with parks, and an old part within easy walking distance from the RENFE train station. Honoring Woody Allen's praise of the city, there is a statue of him in a small plaza. There are thirteen *herbolarios* in Oviedo, and the El Corte Inglés *supermercado* on C/ Uría, just blocks from the train station, has a good selection of natural foods. Nearby Gijón on the coast has ruins of old Roman thermal baths (see www.gijonasturias.com). Llanes is on the coast and has three city beaches, plus one accessible by a path—the Playa la Ballota, which has an area for nudists. You can find local cheeses at Casa Buj, C/ Mercaderes, 13, Llanes; Tel: 985 401 072; Web site: www.casabuj.com.

In Navia there is a 19 km path along the coast, and an archeological park with the ruins of an ancient Celtic settlement, the Navia Coaña. Archeological Park Navia, Carretera AS-12, 33795 Coaña; Web site:

www.parquehistorico.org; open from April to September, Tuesday to Sunday, 11:00 a.m. to 2:00 p.m./4:00 to 7:00 p.m.; from October to March, Tuesday to Sunday, 11:00 a.m. to 2:30 p.m.; entry fee 2 euros, free on Wednesday. See the same Web site for information about the coastal path under "Rutas." Cudillero is a particularly picturesque village 55 km from Oviedo (see Web site: www.cudillero.org/indexingles.htm). Ribadeo, on the border of Galicia and Asturias, is on the Río Eo estuary with large beaches on the Bay of Biscay. The Picos de Europa are tall mountains with lakes and rivers full of endless hiking opportunities. You can take a curvy road to Lake Enol from Arriondas.

There are two nature reserves around Cangas del Narcea, one of which has the largest oak forest in Spain—see "Wild and Natural Resources" for more information.

The L'ayalga Posada Ecológica is an ecological guesthouse in a small, inland Asturias village—see "Eco-Accommodations."

SALAMANCA REGION

The city of Salamanca is known for its university and old city. Language schools and courses of all kinds are plentiful. The city is alive with young students from all over the world. More than three hours from Madrid, Salamanca is accessible from Madrid by bus, or by train from the Chamartín (not Atocha) train station in Madrid. Trains take about two and a half hours and there are five a day.

La Alberca is a historic village located in the Salamanca region of Spain, about an hour's ride from Salamanca city. The tiny, cobblestone streets are lined with buildings dating from Columbus's time and before. In this tiny village you can find traditional life mixed with modern-day. Off the northwest corner of the main square you will find a store specializing in fair-trade goods and some organic treats. Donkeys carting manure-filled baskets walk down the streets, as do men carrying tools to work the land. Numerous stores sell the famous local delicacy, *pata negra,* meaning black leg or hoof, a special "ham" from Spanish black pigs that eat only acorns from cork oak trees. This meat really should not be called ham as it is not remotely similar to American ham; rather, it is closer to prosciutto. It is a dark meat with a rich and unusual taste, and is very expensive (about $100 to $170/pound).

There are biking and walking trails in the area, and nearby, the monastery of La Peña de Francia, which sits about 5,200 feet high on a mountain, with amazing views. It is known for its Black Madonna and sanctuary, as well as its guesthouse and café.

It takes almost four hours to reach La Alberca from Madrid, but it is worth it for the time travel experience.

GALICIA

Spring in Galicia brings people out with their hoes, spades, pitchforks, and carts, tilling the deep, dark, rich soil that has supported them for millennia. *Hórreos,* ancient stone structures (granaries) used for storing the harvest—corn, potatoes, and more—dot every village. Galicia is truly spectacular—somewhat of a well-kept secret, which is probably its saving grace. It is easy to gasp at every turn in the road, as the coast is stunning, and the hillsides pastoral. Fortunately, the laws regarding development are strict in this region of Spain, particularly in Carnota, which boasts a 7-km-long white sand beach, the longest in Galicia. The land is full of ancient history and Celtic myths. The northwest has some lesser traveled routes to and from Santiago de Compostela, where all the routes converge in the Plaza (*praza* in Galician) do Obradoiro.

The Galicians are delightful, friendly people. Galicia, with half of Spain's fishing fleet, is known for its fish and seafood. One specialty is octopus, commonly prepared by boiling or grilling, served with olive oil and paprika (made from red bell or chili peppers), called *pulpo a la Gallega.* Another Galician delicacy is small pancakes filled with apple cream and sorbet made from *orujo* (grape skin liqueur) called *filloas rellenas de crema y manzana con sorbete de orujo.* In the Ribeiro wine region in Galicia, covering about 7,500 acres, the vineyards produce eight varieties of red wine and ten of white, including the common Albariño white wine. *Queimada* is a Galician ritual involving a very strong alcoholic drink made with lemon peel, apple, sugar, and *orujo* (grape skin liqueur—for the Morillón natural brand see page 143) that is lit on fire and an incantation recited to rid evil spirits and keep witches away. Local seaweeds are used in soups and garnishes. Porto-Muiños, in A Coruña, packages seaweeds free of preservatives and coloring; Web site: www.portomuinos.com. For information about the local wine (Ribeiro) and vineyard routes (not organic), see the Web site: www.ribeiro.es/?seccion=portada&idioma=en.

In 2002 the oil tanker *Prestige* sank, spilling sixty-four thousand tons of oil and killing more than twenty thousand birds, ruining beaches, wildlife, and fish on the Galician coast. The organization Nunca Máis ("Never Again," in Galician) has been instrumental in cleanup and prevention activities. Jean-Michel Cousteau made a film of the same name, *Nunca Máis,* about the disaster.

Finisterre (Fisterra in Galician) means land's end, and it sits on a peninsula at the end of that part of Spain, with the Atlantic Ocean crashing around the rocks at the bottom of the mountain. This was the destination of my pilgrimage—not Santiago. The beach as you approach Fisterra seems like heaven, and must certainly seem so to any pilgrims making their way through the spiny gorse and forest paths. With turquoise green water and white sand stretching for 2 km, it is littered with shells, many of which are like the shell symbol that marks the way to Santiago. On the westernmost coast of Fisterra there is another spectacular beach, rougher since it is on the open Atlantic, with a boardwalk through the sand.

The walk from the village of Fisterra to the lighthouse is about 2 km up part of a mountain. You can drive this as well if you have a car. For a real hike and more history, there is an optional walking route up to the top of Monte San Guillermo and Monte Facho, where there are large stones; one is purported to help infertile couples conceive, others are believed to involve solar and lunar rituals, and the views are incredible.

Another leg of the camino is between Fisterra and Muxía, also breathtaking. A single stone cross sits up among rocks at the highest point in Muxía overlooking the stone-lined descent toward the Santuario de Barca and the crashing sea. From there a lovely promenade follows the bay line back to the parking area and village.

In addition to Fisterra and Muxía, there are numerous towns with outstanding beaches and coastline including the beaches at Laxe and Razo. Corcubión is a historic village between Cee and Fisterra with a sweet old part, a port, and an exceptionally helpful tourist office with a free wifi zone—see www.corcubion.info/en/. O Pindo has a port, the Xallas falls, trails up A Moa, and a fabulous lookout (*mirador*)—see "Sacred Sites." Between O Pindo and Corcubión is the small city of Cee, where you can find a market and a small health food store—see "Eating and Food."

The city of Ferrol is known for its surfing beaches including Doniños and Pantin, where international surfing championships have been held.

Galicia has numerous dolmens—see "Sacred Sites."

Inland Galicia is overflowing with farmland. The Río Miño has natural thermal waters. In the city of Orense (Ourense in Galician) the As Burgas fountains surge with the local medicinal mineral waters in the Praza das Burgas. Near Orense is what is known as the Sacred Riverbank (Ribeira Sacra), where the rivers Miño and Sil converge, thought to be named for the monasteries that lined the river. I suspect the name is really for the natural magnificence of the river and canyon. A site in Spanish has been developed for information and cultural sites of interest in the area; Web site: www.ribeirasacra.org. Lugo is a walled city, with Roman walls dating from the first century AD. You can walk the 2 km around the walls for views of the city and surrounding area. Castropol is a picturesque whitewashed village near Lugo. Of course, the inland focus of Galicia is Santiago de Compostela—see "Sacred Sites."

See "Accommodations" for numerous Galician guesthouses in historic buildings.

ANDALUCÍA

Málaga

Tourism is big in Málaga. Even in the off-season, when everyone is donning winter coats, not swimsuits, there are plenty of tourists—so during the high season the streets and beaches are overflowing. This is understandable as Málaga has some beautiful and interesting sites. Be forewarned: many things are closed on Monday. The beaches and beach promenades are beautiful along the turquoise water. The Plaza de la Constitución in the old part is large and busy; look for the bronze newspaper replicas in the pavement commemorating Spain's becoming a democracy.

Sites include the remains of the Castle Gibralfaro, where there is nothing much left except excellent views. The castle is open in the winter 9:00 a.m. to 5:45 p.m., and in the summer 9:00 a.m. to 7:45 p.m.

The Alcazaba de Málaga has buildings mostly from the eleventh century, the interior palace from the eleventh to fourteenth centuries. At the time this fortification was built, the sea actually came up to the lower walls, which you will find amazing when you see where the sea is now. Closed Monday. In the summer the Alcazaba is open 9:30 a.m. to 8:00 p.m., and in the winter 8:30 a.m. to 7:00 p.m.

The natural foods scene in Málaga is fairly slim. The stores I found either were miniscule or had closed. I did find a few vegetarian and natural foods restaurants, but only two were decent. There are some towns within 20 to 60 km of Málaga that seem to be more hip to the health food scene and they have much better quality options. Málaga seems to have more esoteric stores than health food stores—maybe a result of the centuries of fluctuating dominant religions.

Picasso was born in Málaga so there are two museums in his honor. Casa Natal Picasso, Plaza de la Merced, 15, Málaga; Web site: www.fundacionpicasso.es; open Monday to Saturday 10:00 a.m. to 8:00 p.m., Sunday 10:00 a.m. to 2:00 p.m. And the Picasso Museum (Museo Picasso Málaga), San Agustín, 8, Málaga; Tel: 952 602 731; Web site: www2.museopicassomalaga.org/i_home.cfm; open Friday and Saturday 10:00 a.m. to 9:00 p.m., Tuesday, Wednesday, Thursday, and Sunday 10:00 a.m. to 8:00 p.m., closed Monday.

Málaga has endless day-trip possibilities as it is surrounded by nine natural parks—Parque Natural de los Montes de Málaga; Torcal de Antequera; Laguna de Fuente de Piedra; Desfiladero de los Gaitanes; Sierra de las Nieves; Sierra de Tejeda y Almijara; Sierra de Grazalema; Los Alcornocales; and Acantilado de Maro-Cerro Gordo in Nerja. There are also buses to beautiful coastal and mountain towns, including some of the famous "white villages" like Ronda.

Natural resources, mountains, and rivers abound in Andalucía. Although Andalucía is thought of as a dry, hot area, it is blessed with special limestone aquifers that store massive amounts of water. Remarkable rivers include the Río Alaminos—Barranco Blanco (for the white limestone) in Alhaurín el Grande and Coín. La Fuente (the fountain) is the name for where the river comes to the surface from an underground reserve in the Mijas Mountains. The water is so clean that it can support otters and barbel, an endangered fish. Other notable rivers are the Río Guadaiza, Río Guadalmina, and

Río Guadalmansa. In Benahavis you can walk along the banks of Río Guadalmina. In the town of Istán you can see the Río Verde, clean enough to support otters as well as trout and the endangered, but protected Andalucían river tortoise, *Galápagos leprosos.* The Río Genal comes out of the ground in Pujerra and is also home to the above critters.

It is an hour-plus bus ride from Málaga, and costs just over 3 euros, to the seaside city of Nerja. Nerja is not immune from growth and tourism, but rather than high-rises they have opted for smaller, whitewashed buildings that are more pleasing to the eye. The water is a magnificent turquoise. The main part of the village is fairly large, filled with restaurants, shops, and souvenir stores. Nerja has seven beaches and the Balcón de Europa, a beautiful balcony overlooking the Mediterranean. In nearby Maro, 4 km away, you can explore caves. The Río Chillar is 6 km from Nerja and, unlike many rivers in Andalucía, runs all year despite drought conditions. In Cahorros, the river has carved the rocks over thousands of years in the Sierra Almijara. The river runs under- and aboveground and provides drinking water for Nerja. La Tahona bakery makes fresh breads and has some gluten-free options in their freezer. La Tahona, C/ El Barrio, 43, Nerja; Tel: 952 521 645. The Tetería Jardín de Al-Andalus serves fifty different teas, as well as smoothies, and has wifi, with a terrace and a Moroccan tent. Tetería Jardín de Al-Andalus, C/ Carabeo, 87, Nerja; Tel: 952 528 313; open 4:00 p.m. to midnight, closed Monday and Tuesday.

Granada

The university students give Granada a very hip pulse. You can hear magnificent flamenco music in one plaza, find little artisan shops up a tiny stone street, and finish your day with a trip to the Hammam—the Arab baths. There are different sections to the city. The old Albayzín area is filled with young people with dreadlocks, mixed in with Spanish families. The Albayzín has numerous old sites, but many are not regularly open to the public. Moving down into the old Jewish quarter, now teeming with Middle Eastern stores and cafés, the Calderería Vieja street is pedestrian only, with mini bazaar-like stores, Arabic teterías (tea shops), and travelers.

Mixed in with the tourist shops you can find one or two local artisans selling items. At the top of the Calderería Vieja street, turn slightly right and continue up the hill on to San Gregori. At the switchback you will find La Casa del Talismán, where lovely Silvana Leone sells her handmade jewelry plus other local handcrafts from natural soaps to fabulous art by a woman named Esperanza Romero (www.esperanzaromero.com). Casa del Talismán, Cuesta de San Gregori, 7-9, 18010 Albayzín (Granada); Tel: 671 648 463; e-mail: lacasadeltalisman@yahoo.es.

The Realejo area is nearby below the Alhambra area, with a very hip, student scene. The traditional old part is around the cathedral with lots of shops. Nice places to hang out are numerous throughout Granada, which has plenty of plazas with public seating as well as café seating. The Paseo del Padre Manjón is particularly lovely in the afternoon, with a fountain, below the Alhambra. Up on a hill in the Albayzín is the Plaza San Nicolás, which is near the mosque and looks across at the Alhambra. This is a hangout for young people, live music, and people selling handcrafts. For information about the Arab baths see "Thermal Baths."

The Alhambra is almost straight up the hill from the Plaza Nueva. In peak season six thousand people a day visit the Alhambra, so at any time other than midwinter it is best to purchase tickets in advance. There is a lot to the complex. The Alhambra, meaning "The Red One" in Arabic, was built between the thirteenth and fifteenth centuries by the Nasrid kings. The original fortified city covered around twenty-five acres with only thirty percent of the structures still existing today. What is left is extraordinary and is designated a UNESCO World Heritage Site.

There are five main areas to the Alhambra. The Generalife, with its numerous gardens, was a palace used for rest and relaxation. On the walk toward the main Nasrid palace you can see the small but interesting *mezquita* (mosque) baths. The super attraction is the Nasrid palaces, for which you have an assigned visit time on your ticket—the rest of your visit is either all morning or all afternoon. The palaces are filled with jaw-dropping, unfathomable architectural and artistic detail on every wall and ceiling. The palace of Carlos V is newer than the Nasrid palaces and houses a small but wonderful museum that is part of your full ticket price. The *alcazaba* (fortress) remains are quite impressive and you can go up to the top of the towers for great city views. You can and should spend hours at the complex, so allow

Tales of the Alhambra, by Washington Irving, animates the palace and the area as the author recounts legends he learned while he lived at the palace in the early 1800s.

plenty of time. The official bookstores have the best book selections, but the tourist places have basic information books. Alhambra, open in the summer 8:30 a.m. to 8:00 p.m., in the winter until 6:00 p.m.; advance tickets Web site: www.alhambra-tickets.es.

Hostal Venecia is a little *pensión* on the street that leads up to the Alhambra. Just delightful Sergio (pronounced Serhio) is the proprietor and couldn't be better. My room was spotless, tiny, and colorful, with a cotton bedspread instead of the kind you don't want to touch, much less sleep under, usually found in hotels. The shared showers were clean as were the bathrooms. It is two flights up with no elevator so be forewarned if you are carrying heavy bags. Compact energy efficient bulbs are used in the lovely Spanish ceramic light fixtures, tiles line the floors, and bright colors are throughout. My room was yellow! Hostal Venecia, Cuesta de Gomérez, 2, 2nd Floor, 18009 Granada; Tel: 958 223 987; Mobile: 656 903 057. If you are not up too early, Sergio will bring you a hot cup of herbal tea (*infusión*).

A sister *pensión* is a guesthouse located in the old center below the cathedral. Casa de Huéspedes Patagonia, C/ Buensuceso, 52, 18002 Granada; Tel: 958 223 987; Mobile: 655 903 057.

If you are arriving in Granada by bus, the station is away from the old area and the Alhambra so you will need to take city bus #3—buses cost 1.20 euros and you can buy tickets on the bus. The RENFE train station is closer to the action, but you will probably still want to take a bus. You have to walk up one block to the main Avenida de la Constitución to catch a city bus toward the Plaza de Isabel la Católica.

Córdoba

About one million people lived in Córdoba from the ninth to thirteenth centuries with the three religions—Christians, Muslims, and Jews—living and working together cooperatively. Córdoba promotes their local artisans, specializing in beautiful ceramics, leather, and silver work. Zoco is a city-sponsored permanent market in an old courtyard in the Jewish quarter, steps from the synagogue, where there are the workshops of local craftspeople, so you can see them creating their wares and purchase the handmade products. Currently there is a jeweler, leather goods, ceramicist, and sculptor.

For fresh fruit and vegetables, flowers, and other items at reasonable prices, go to the Sunday street market at El Arenal.

Córdoba's main attraction is the impressive *mezquita* (mosque)-cathedral, a UNESCO World Heritage Site in the old part of the city. The *mezquita*-cathedral is believed to have originally been the site of a Visigoth basilica, then the mosque was built starting in AD 785, and conversion to a cathedral occurred between the thirteenth and fifteenth centuries. Covering 252,000 square feet, the *mezquita* is the third largest in the world. *Mezquita*-cathedral; opening hours vary through the year from 10:00 a.m. to 5:30 to 7:00 p.m. closing; entry fee 8 euros.

Sites close to the *mezquita* include the much-restored Roman bridge, water wheel, and the Tower of la Calahorra, now a museum at the far end of the bridge. The museum is small but has some interesting displays of Córdoban history including surgeons' tools from the tenth century, astronomy and mapping instruments, and water engineering. Torre de la Calahorra; open Monday to Sunday 10:00 a.m. to 6:00 p.m.; Web site: www.torrecalahorra.com.

Córdoba has a museum about baths on the site of unearthed ancient Arab and Roman baths. At its height of wealth and population, Córdoba had hundreds of baths, a sign of wealth and prosperity. Baños del Alcázar Califal; underground at Campo Santo de los Mártires; open Tuesday to Saturday 10:00 a.m. to 2:00 p.m./4:30 to 6:30 p.m., Sunday 9:30 a.m. to 2:30 p.m., closed Monday; entry fee 2 euros, free on Wednesday.

The old synagogue in Córdoba, built in 1315, is the only preserved synagogue in Andalucía and is one of only a few synagogues left in Spain—hard to believe—with two others in Toledo, and one in Barcelona. In 1885 it was declared a national monument and saved from any further destruction.

Casa de Sefarad/Casa de la Memoria is a small museum and cultural center dedicated to sharing knowledge about the Sephardic (Spanish) Jews with artifacts and history, housed in part in what is believed to be the old *mikvah* (bath house) for the synagogue across the street. The collection includes relics and information about Jewish holidays, music, Córdoba's Jewish quarter, domestic life in the tenth to fifteenth centuries, and prominent Jewish women from that period. The Casa de Sefarad is an excellent companion visit to the synagogue and worth the 4 euro entry fee. A tiny gift shop sells a small selection of lovely items, many of which are made in Córdoba, including silver *hamsas,* a hand symbol shared by Muslims and Jews that is professed to protect from evil and misfortune. Casa de Sefarad/Casa de la Memoria, on the corner of C/ Judíos and C/ Averroes, 14004 Córdoba; Tel: 957 421 404; Web site: www.casadelamemoria.es. At this Web site click on "Enlaces" (links) to find a link to the Casa de Sefarad in Córdoba.

The Subbética mountain area is a natural park near Córdoba with twelve towns including Carcabuey, a beautiful village great for walking, with an old castle and fortress ruins and fountains.

The Mezquita Hotel is a five-star hotel with Motel 6 rates. A true gem, it is housed in a restored sixteenth-century mansion across the street from Córdoba's famed *mezquita.* The twenty-one rooms have marble floors and private baths, phones, but no wifi, but the unbelievable rates make that perfectly acceptable. My room had a view of the mosque. Breakfast is optional for an extra charge in the elegant courtyard. Hotel Mezquita, C/ Plaza Santa Catalina, 1, 14003 Córdoba; Tel: 957 475 585; e-mail: hotelmezquita@wanadoo.es; Web site: www.hotelmezquita.com.

Luna de Cristal has apartments for rent by the week or longer in a restored stone building in a small plaza behind the Plaza de la Corredera in the historic old part of Córdoba. Luna de Cristal, Plaza de las Cañas, 1, 14002 Córdoba; Tel: 957 492 353; e-mail: info@lunadecristal.com; Web site: www.lunadecristal.com.

In Córdoba there are buses right outside the RENFE train station—look for #16 and #3, both of which stop on the street between the river and the *mezquita.*

Sevilla
Sevilla is a delight. A city filled with youth and vibrance, and a hot spot for flamenco, not to mention health food stores, and an open,

airy feeling, Sevilla makes for great touring. On sunny days every square and plaza is filled with joyous Spaniards partaking in their afternoon lunches and *cervezas* (beers). Orange trees line the streets and the perfume from fallen, crushed oranges fills the Sevillan air. Sevilla's famous cathedral is massive and the Alcázares Reales spectacular, with extensive gardens and Moorish architecture to rival the Alhambra. I would put the Alcázar Real (Royal Palace) at the top of any Sevilla must-see list. Built in the ninth century and evolving through the fourteenth century, the Alcázar Real shared artisans, architecture, and inspiration with the Alhambra and was a cultural center. The gardens of the Alcázar are extensive, as is the nearby María Luisa Park. Sevilla seems to have square miles of parks and gardens.

There are plazas large and small at every turn in Sevilla, including the large Plaza San Francisco and the smaller Plaza San Salvador. Sevilla has its own version of cheap bicycle renting called Sevici. Sevici bikes are available to rent in the large Plaza Nueva. Flamenco is big in Sevilla and the Triana neighborhood is considered the Flamenco hot spot.

Other sites in Sevilla include the massive cathedral and the old Jewish quarter with tiny streets now filled with shops and cafés. La Casa de la Memoria is in an eighteenth-century palace, with parts of it from a fifteenth-century Jewish house. The patio is host to dance and music performances, while the palace can be visited. The gift shop has arts and crafts from the area. At 9:00 p.m. there are flamenco and other performances; tickets are 15 euros and it is recommended that you book in advance. Casa de la Memoria Cultural Center, C/ Ximénez de Enciso, 28, Sevilla (in the Santa Cruz neighborhood); Tel: 954 560 670; e-mail: memorias@terra.es; Web site: www.casadelamemoria.es.

In the old part is the Flamenco Dance Museum, C/ Manuel Rojas Marcos, 3, 41004 Sevilla; Tel: 954 340 311; e-mail: info@museoflamenco.com; Web site: www.flamencomuseum.com; open daily 9:00 a.m. to 7:00 p.m.

The Sevilla tourist office provides free wifi 8:00 a.m. to 3:00 p.m. Monday to Friday on the corner of Plaza San Francisco. For more information about Sevilla see the tourist office Web site: www.turismosevilla.org/index.php?idi=en; and for accommodations, which are by the score, see the Web site: www.hotelesdesevilla.com. *El Giraldillo* is a monthly guide of events in Sevilla in print for free at many locations in Sevilla or online; Web site: www.elgiraldillo.es.

Sevilla is surrounded by many notable natural areas including the UNESCO Doñana National Park, and the mountains Sierra Norte de Sevilla and Sierra Nevada. Nature reserves include La Cañada de los Pájaros and Dehesa de Abajo, and natural monuments include Cascadas del Huéznar and Cerro del Hierro.

JAÉN PROVINCE

Jaén province in the eastern region of Andalucía has four national parks and other protected areas. The cities of Úbeda and Baeza are new UNESCO World Heritage Sites. The Jaén province is the largest olive oil producer in the world, producing about twenty percent of the world's olive oil, close to Italy's entire production, and around fifty percent of Spain's total olive oil production. The olive groves in Jaén have been producing for generations and are often family operations of ten acres or less. In the town of Cambil every family owns on average two to three hundred trees. Often on steep slopes accessible only by mules, the olives are in many cases still collected by hand using poles and baskets.

Alcaudete Calidad is a small store selling local and organic products. Alcaudete Calidad, C/ Carmen, 1, 23660 Alcaudete (Jaén); Tel: 953 561 439.

Look for cave houses in southern Spain—a clever way to naturally beat the heat. Typical in the *altiplano* (high plateau), the clay soil and climate are conducive to cave dwelling. Many of the caves are hundreds of years old and are naturally cool in the overbearing heat of southern Spain, usually maintaining even temperatures of between 60 and 70°F year-round. Originally homes for poor agricultural workers, the caves have been renovated into comfortable, modern homes.

Sacred Sites

In addition to the sacred beauty of Spain's bountiful natural resources, Spain is host to innumerable old churches and cathedrals, at least one in every village. Spain also has a staggering number of an-

Santiago de Compostela Routes

1. Portugese Road/ Camino Portugués
2. Silver Route/ Via de la Plata
3. Connecting Madrid Route
4. French Way/ Camino Francés
5. Northern Way/ Camino del Norte
   and Coastal Route
6. English Way/ Camino Inglés
7. Connecting French Routes from Paris,
   Vezelay & Le Puy
8. Connecting French Route from Arles

cient stone structures, many dating back thousands of years. Below you will discover a few more unusual sites to visit and enjoy.

El Camino de Santiago, known as The Way of St. James or The Pilgrim's Way, is a thousand-year-old series of routes from parts of France and Spain to Santiago de Compostela in the northwest region of Galicia north of Portugal. There are seven routes in Spain that lead to the pilgrimage site of the tomb of Saint James the Apostle in Santiago de Compostela. See the map of Santiago de Compostela Routes above. You can walk on any section of the routes, but if you want to be considered an official pilgrim, and be granted the official certificate of pilgrimage, there is a minimum distance you must travel—100 km (62 miles) on foot or 200 km (124 miles) on bicycle. There are low-cost, and sometimes free, accommodations along all the routes for pilgrims only. Hiking, bicycling, and horseback are common along the road. The Galician tourism office has a free downloadable pamphlet in English, *Way of St. James,* describing the Santiago routes, which are the French Road, the English Road, the Aragón Road, the Portuguese Road, the Silver Route (Vía de la Plata), the Northern routes, both coastal and inland, and the Fisterra-Muxía route. It lists hostels on the routes where pilgrims can sleep. Galician Tourism; Web site: www.turgalicia.es/default.asp?cidi=I.

The different routes to Santiago are filled with all sorts of ancient and historical sites, as well as remarkable natural beauty. Legends and mysteries pervade the routes. On the Santiago route west of Pamplona there is a stretch of road with monuments purported to have secret messages. In the village of Obanos, 15 km or so from Pamplona, and about 1.6 km past the village, is the Church of Santa María de Eunate (meaning one hundred doors) built by the Knights Templar. West of Pamplona on a Santiago route there seems to be a confluence of mysticism and the sacred with monuments having secret or undeciphered messages. In Puente la Reina two Santiago roads (French and Aragón) converge at an eleventh-century bridge. The Iglesia del Crucifijo de Puente la Reina has scallop shell (symbol of the Santiago route) and Celtic designs.

Santiago can be reached from Madrid by bus (www.alsa.es for routes and hours) or train. From Bilbao in the northern, Basque region of Spain, you can travel by either day or overnight transit. There are northern coast train routes on the independent train line FEVE (www.feve.es [rail passes not valid]) with three lines—the Yellow line running between Bilbao and Santander; the Blue line between Santander and Oviedo; and the Red line between Oviedo and Ferrol. There are one-hour-long bus rides between Ferrol and Santiago. And there are buses to Santiago from every city in Galicia.

An exhaustive guidebook focused on the Spain "French Road" to Santiago, *The Road to Santiago* includes information about the Coast road, the Aragón route, Vía de la Plata, the Northern roads, the Portuguese roads, the English roads, and some of the extension roads, complete with maps and photographs. José María Anguita Jaén, *The Road to Santiago: The Pilgrim's Practical Guide*, 3rd ed. (León, Spain: Everest, 2005) (www.everest.es).

The Vía de la Plata (Silver Route) Web site provides detailed information about the Spanish southern route to Santiago and has links to information about the other routes; Web site: www.theviadelaplata.com.

From Santiago you can bus or walk to Fisterra, meaning "land's end" or "end of the world," on the dramatic Atlantic coast. The Fisterra Web site offers different phases of the route from Santiago to Fisterra as well as other information about the town; Web site: www.concellofisterra.com/en. A handy guide to this leg of the Santiago Camino is *A Pilgrim's Guide to the Camino Fisterra: A Practical and Mystical Manual for the Modern Day Pilgrim* by John Brierley (Forres, Scotland: Findhorn Press, 2003) (www.findhornpress.com).

Hiking on El Camino can conjure all sorts of adventures and friendships. I have heard of people meeting on El Camino, falling in love, and getting married—a lifetime of journeying.

O Pindo is a fishing village east of Fisterra where you can hike to A Moa, the highest point of Monte Pindo, considered to be the Celtic "Mount Olympus" and a mysterious and magical area. You can also hike to the canyon of the Xallas River, the only river in Europe that ends as a waterfall into the ocean, although it is now controlled for power purposes.

A guesthouse in O Pindo is Pensión Rústica A Laxe, a renovated stone house with three rooms—Mar (sea), Río (river), and Monte (mountain)—named for their respective views. The fully equipped kitchen has an old stone sink. The guesthouse is 2 km away from the Xallas waterfalls. Also nearby is the hiking trail that goes to A Moa and takes about five-plus hours. Fisterra is about an 18 km drive from O Pindo. Pensión Rústica A Laxe, O Pindo; Mobile for José: 617 889 641; Web site: www.pensionrusticaalaxe.com/english.

Other guesthouses in the area include two other renovated stone homes: Hotel Rústico Dugium is north of Fisterra, Web site: www.dugium.com/en/index.php; and Casa de Trillo is in Santa Mariña, Muxía, Web site: www.casadetrillo.com/welcome.htm.

Spain has a large number of ancient stone structures, most of which date back thousands of years. Many of these stone structures are not listed in guidebooks; however, depending upon the town, some are listed as historical monuments and are on local tourist maps, and many regional tourist offices offer information about megalith sites. The word "megalith" is a general term from the Greek, meaning "great stone." Many single and grouped stones, and stone structures, dot the Spanish countryside. Dolmens are megalithic stone structures that look like a giant table, with two standing stones and one stone resting horizontally across the top. Dolmens are thought to have been built as passageways or tombs. Menhirs are large, upright stones, usually standing alone, whose purpose remains a mystery. Menhirs may have been used as territory markers or for religious ceremonies.

For megalith buffs, go to www.megalitos.es for extensive information about and photographs of megalith sites throughout Spain. For a general idea of megalith locations in Spain see the Megaliths-Dolmens in Spain map on page 191.

The Dolmen Route in Galicia is a somewhat marked route from just south of the town of Baio down along a beautiful, pastoral road to Baíñas. With six dolmen sites and a seventh up a different road from Baíñas, there is plenty to see. The actual dolmens are not so well marked, so leave plenty of time if you choose to explore this route. The Dolmen of Dombate, a large, impressive dolmen, is not on this route, but is outside Cabaña de Bergantiños. It is protected by a fenced-in park and is currently under repair. Within a couple of kilometers is another site called the Castro de Borneiro, a series of round stone foundations. The sole remaining circle of stones in the area is on Monte Neme in the Carballo area, known as Eira das Meigas ("land of witches" in Galician). At the Costa da Morte Tourism page you can download a free brochure in English about the megaliths in the area; Web site: www.turismocostadamorte.com/en/web/index.php.

In Fisterra you can climb to the top of Monte Facho and see the stone Ara Solis, believed to be the remains of stones used for Celtic solar and lunar rituals.

In the Basque area there are countless dolmens and other megalithic sites. There is a Dolmen Route due south of Vitoria-Gasteiz in the area of Elvillar and Laguardia where there are outstanding dolmens

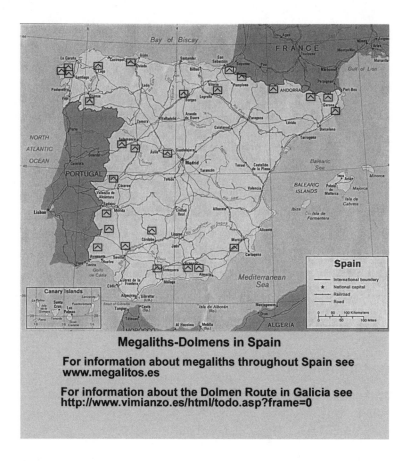

Megaliths-Dolmens in Spain

For information about megaliths throughout Spain see www.megalitos.es

For information about the Dolmen Route in Galicia see http://www.vimianzo.es/html/todo.asp?frame=0

including the Dolmen de la Hechicera on highway A-3228, and more off highway A-124.

In the Catalunya region there are dolmens and menhirs in the Serra de l'Albera mountains, and southeast of Girona there is the Dolmen d'en Daina in Santa Cristina d'Aro; Web site: www.santacristina.net/turisme/en/index.html. The Pedralta rocking stone is considered to have been a site for pagan worship and is the second largest rocking stone in Europe. Majestically perched on another giant rock, it no longer rocks due to restoration work after an enormous storm a few years ago, but still makes for an impressive site. Between Sant Feliu de Guíxols and Santa Cristina, it is about a 12 km round-trip hike to reach the enormous stone. The best directions can be found on the Costa Brava tourism page; Web site: http://en.costabrava.org/main/home.aspx.

In Cangas de Onís, about 72 km from Oviedo in the Asturias region, there is the Santa Cruz dolmen beneath the Santa Cruz Chapel. Nearby is the Buxu cave—see "Historical Sites and Other Sites of Interest."

The Navarra region is said to have forty-four dolmens. The Aralar dolmen routes can be found in northwestern Navarra, with a 15 km hiking trail from the parking lot of the Etxarri campgrounds. For details see the Web site: www.turismo.navarra.es/eng/home/.

Also in Navarra is the magical Cave of Zugarramurdi near the French border. The cave is filled with legends of witches, wizards, and pagan rituals; people from this area were killed by the Spanish Inquisition for being witches. Situated four hundred meters from the village, a stream has cut a natural four-hundred-foot-long tunnel with walls as high as forty feet in some places, making way for the mystical cave area including the "Sorginleze" witches' cave. For more information see the Web site: www.turismo.navarra.es/eng/home/.

BLACK MADONNAS

Black Madonnas, also called Black Virgins, hold a fascination for people. Spain has a large number of Black Madonnas (or *madona negra, Nuestra Señora Negra*), and each one is unique.

The monastery of La Peña de Francia sits about 5,200 feet high on a mountain, with amazing views, near La Alberca, an old village designated as a national monument in the Salamanca region. La Peña is known for its Black Madonna and sanctuary, as well as its guesthouse and café. La Alberca and La Peña are almost four hours northwest from Madrid and a car is recommended.

Montserrat, northwest of Barcelona, is home to a twelfth-century Black Madonna. An operating monastery, the basilica where the Black Virgin sits is closed in the winter from October to June, so plan your visit in the summer months. There are also trails around the mountain. You can get to Montserrat by train from Barcelona, connecting with either another train or a funicular or cable car to get up the mountain and to the thousand-year-old Benedictine monastery, park, and museum. Montserrat, Tel: 938 777 701; e-mail: informacio@larsa-montserrat.com; Web site: www.montserratvisita.com.

Other Black Madonnas in Spain include the Black Virgen de la O in

Estella, on one of the Santiago routes, open only in the summer. For more information about the beautiful town of Estella see the Web site: www.turismo.navarra.es/eng/home/. In the village of Ujué (derived from the Basque word *usoa,* meaning dove) south of Pamplona there is a Black Virgin in the thirteenth-century Santa María church. In Madrid, Our Lady of Atocha has a Black Madonna, and in Andújar, Jaén, Our Lady of la Cabeza houses a Black Madonna. The Cathedral of Toledo has the Virgen Morena: La Esclavitud de Nuestra Señora del Sagrario, Cathedral of Toledo, C/ Cardenal Cisneros, Toledo; open Monday to Saturday 10:00 a.m. to 6:30 p.m., Sunday 2:00 to 6:30 p.m.; entry fee 7 euros.

Color and Art

Through the ages, Spain has been known for its great artists and artwork.

There are museums dedicated to Pablo Picasso in many cities. In Madrid, the Reina Sofía Museum houses Picasso's *Guernica*—see "Madrid-Specific" in the "City and Regional Highlights" section. In Málaga, Picasso's birthplace, there are two museums, the Museo Picasso Málaga and Casa Natal Picasso—see "Málaga" in the "City and Regional Highlights" section. In the old part of Barcelona is the Museu Picasso, C/ Montcada, 15-23, 08003 Barcelona; Tel: 932 563 000; Web site: www.museupicasso.bcn.cat/en/; Metro: Jaume I; open Tuesday to Sunday 10:00 a.m. to 8:00 p.m.; entry fee 9 euros.

Works by Francisco Goya (1746–1828) can be seen in almost every city in Spain. Museums in Bilbao, Zaragoza, Huesca, Oviedo, Valencia, and Sevilla all have Goya's work. In Madrid his works are in the Prado; at the Metro station named Goya; at the Basílica de San Francisco el Grande; and at the Museo Lázaro Galdiano, C/ Serrano, 122, Madrid; open Wednesday to Monday 10:00 a.m. to 4:30 p.m. Admission is free to see the frescoed ceilings painted by Goya in the Ermita de San Antonio de la Florida. Goya is buried here by the altar. Ermita de San Antonio de la Florida, Glorieta de San Antonio de la Florida, 5, Madrid; open Tuesday to Friday 10:00 a.m. to 2:00 p.m./4:00 to 8:00 p.m., Saturday and Sunday 10:00 a.m. to 2:00 p.m. In Goya's birth town you can visit two museums: Casa Natal de Goya, C/ Zuloaga, 3, Fuendetodos (Zaragoza); open Tuesday to

Sunday 11:00 a.m. to 2:00 p.m./4:00 to 7:00 p.m.; and the Museo del Grabado de Goya, down the street.

The Miró museum in Barcelona exhibits work by Joan Miró as well as other artists. Fundació Joan Miró, Av. Miramar, Parc de Montjuïc, s/n, Barcelona; Tel: 934 439 470; Web site: www.fundaciomiro-bcn.org/; Metro: Paral.lel; buses #50 and #55; open in the winter from October to June, Tuesday to Saturday, 10:00 a.m. to 7:00 p.m., Sunday 10:00 a.m. to 2:30 p.m.; open in the summer from July to September, Tuesday to Saturday, 10:00 a.m. to 8:00 p.m., Thursday until 9:30 p.m., Sunday 10:00 a.m. to 2:30 p.m.; entry fee 7.50 euros.

The art and architecture in all the Moorish palaces are not to be missed—see "Granada," "Sevilla," and "Córdoba" in the "City and Regional Highlights" section.

The Guggenheim Museum in Bilbao is a spectacular building and museum—see "Bilbao and the Basque Region" in the "City and Regional Highlights" section for more information.

Titan is a made-in-Spain brand of paints. Titan makes artists' oil and acrylic paints, sold in art supply stores throughout Spain. Titan Paints; Web site: www.titanlux.com/index_eng.asp.

Wild and Natural Resources

As I mentioned in the beginning of the book, I could fill large tomes with the wild and natural resources of Spain. There are thirty-seven designated biosphere reserves in Spain, and nearly ten percent of the land is in some sort of national park or protected area. Spain has close to 5,000 km of coastline and is second only to Switzerland for mountainous terrain in Europe. Mountain ranges include the Picos de Europa, the Pyrenees, and the Sierra de Guadarrama in northern Spain; toward the south are the Sierra Nevada and Las Alpujarras near Granada, and the Sierra de Grazalema; west of Madrid is the Sierra de Gredos. See the map of National Parks in Spain on page 195.

Many of the Web sites I have listed are for the respective tourist office. This is because the sites either do not have Web sites of their own or do not have English versions.

For those who really like to go *au naturel,* the Naturist Association of Asturias lists all the beaches (*playas*) on their Web site that have nud-

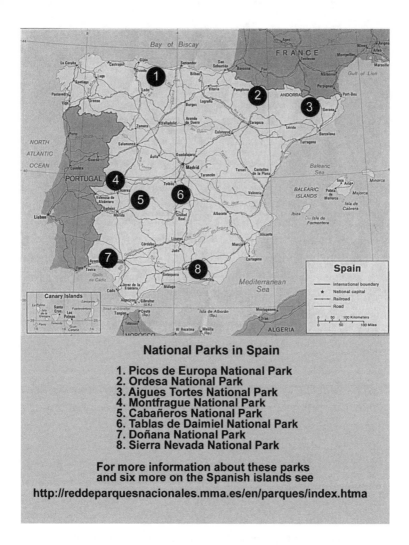

National Parks in Spain

1. Picos de Europa National Park
2. Ordesa National Park
3. Aigues Tortes National Park
4. Montfrague National Park
5. Cabañeros National Park
6. Tablas de Daimiel National Park
7. Doñana National Park
8. Sierra Nevada National Park

For more information about these parks and six more on the Spanish islands see
http://reddeparquesnacionales.mma.es/en/parques/index.htma

ist areas; Web site: www.naturismo.org/anapa. North of Bilbao in Sopelana, La Salvaje (Barinatxe) beach is clothing optional.

Spain has fourteen national parks and numerous natural parks. The Cabo de Gata Natural Park, designated as a biosphere reserve by UNESCO, covers almost 113,000 acres on the southeastern coast of Spain, making it the largest protected coastal area in Andalucía; Web site: www.parquecabodegata.com.

The following four natural parks and reserves are in Catalunya.

The beach from L'Estartit (Girona/Costa Brava) heading south is sandy and long—you can walk almost 10 miles (16 km) down the beach if you desire. Off the shore of L'Estartit are Les Illes Medes, a protected underwater nature reserve, where all the different sea life throughout the Mediterranean can be found around the islands. In the warm months, this is a hot spot for snorkelers and divers. At the Costa Brava tourism page, click on "Nature" and you can access long lists of other beaches and coves, nature parks, parks and gardens, and protected natural areas; Web site: http://en.costabrava.org/main/home.aspx.

Parc Natural dels Aiguamolls de l'Empordà, El Cortalet (Castelló d'Empúries); Tel: 972 454 222.

The Cap de Creus nature reserve is breathtaking, but not for the faint of heart since the route through it is a twisty mountain road through seemingly endless terraced olive trees. The village of Cadaqués, at the end of the road, is sublime—a visual feast of white and blue set against mountains and the Mediterranean. Park in the lot at the entrance to the village and wind your way through the stone-studded alley-like streets. You can hike to the Cap Creus lighthouse on the *camí antic* (ancient road) from the north part of Cadaqués—the only access to this easternmost part of the Spanish mainland coast—which is a rugged 8 km trail. Parc Natural del Cap de Creus, Palau de l'Abat, Monestir de Sant Pere de Rodes (El Port de la Selva); Tel: 972 193 191.

Parc Natural de l'Albera comprises two areas in the northernmost part of Spain along the Pyrenees. It is a sanctuary for the endangered Mediterranean tortoise. The area also boasts 115 dolmens and fifteen menhirs, most of which are connected by paths. An information center is at Espolla, where you can find maps and more information. Rectoria Vella, C/ Amadeu Sudrià, 3, Espolla, Tel: 972 545 079; and Can Laporta, C/ Major, 2, La Jonquera, Tel: 972 555 250.

Thousands of birds pass through the Ebro (Ebre) river delta on their seasonal migration and almost two hundred thousand of them choose to overwinter right there. It is reported that nearly sixty percent of the bird species found in Europe can be seen in this area. Local rice is grown in the delta, accounting for close to twenty percent of Spain's rice production. Isla de Buda (Buda Island) is the nature reserve of the delta where you can see up to three hundred species of seabirds.

The Santa Pola nature reserve is two hours south of Valencia on the Mediterranean coast. It is home to Spain's permanent flock of flamingos and many other birds including overwintering storks. There are also historical ruins and a small aquarium. The Santa Pola Web site provides travel information and much more: www.santapola.com/turismo/guia_ing.htm. For more information about birds and birding in Spain visit the Spanish Ornithology Society at www.seo.org.

The national parks in the Castilla-La Mancha region are Parque Nacional de Cabañeros, Pueblonuevo de Bullaque; and Parque Nacional de las Tablas de Daimiel: the visitor center is 12 km from Daimiel. Natural parks are Lagunas de Ruidera, Ruidera; Barranco del Río Dulce, Guadalajara; Calares del Río Mundo y de la Sima, Riópar; Alto Tajo, Molina de Aragón; Hayedo de Tejera Negra, Guadalajara. Mountains include Sierra de Alcaraz and Sierra del Segura.

Málaga is surrounded by nine natural parks: Parque Natural de los Montes de Málaga; Torcal de Antequera; Laguna de Fuente de Piedra; Desfiladero de los Gaitanes; Sierra de las Nieves; Sierra de Tejeda y Almijara; Sierra de Grazalema; Los Alcornocales; and Acantilado de Maro-Cerro Gordo in Nerja. As with other natural parks, there are extensive hiking routes through these parks and detailed information can be obtained from any of the Málaga tourist offices.

The Sierra Nevada mountains, east of Granada, are a national park and biosphere reserve that have the highest peaks in Spain, sixteen of which are over nine thousand feet high; the highest is Mulhacén at over 11,400 feet. More than two thousand of Spain's eight thousand plant species can be found there. There are seemingly endless hiking routes and some sleeping huts (*refugios*). The majority of the Alpujarras lie within the Sierra Nevada National Park and there are thirty villages with white houses made with local clay built into the hillsides; Web site: www.juntadeandalucia.es.

Other natural parks around Granada are the Sierra de Huétor, Sierra de Baza, and Sierra de Castril. All offer numerous walking routes from half an hour up to eight hours depending on the park and trail. Andalucía Tourism offers information at these Web sites: www.andalucia.org/index_en.html and www.juntadeandalucia.es.

The Basque region is teeming with wild and natural resources, both coastal and mountain. The Basque part of the Atlantic Bay of Biscay has breathtaking coastline and seaside villages including the six-thousand-year-old petrified dunes of Gorliz, and beaches at Lekeitio, Mundaka (www.mundaka.org/English.asp), Bakio (1-km-long beach), and Sopelana. For more information about these and other beaches see the Web site: www.bizkaiacostavasca.com/index_en.aspx. In Zarautz just west of San Sebastián the Iñurritza protected biotope is a dune field on the Bay of Biscay. The Web link with English information for Iñurritza is www.turismoa.euskadi.net/s11-12375/en/contenidos/g_naturaleza/0000004912_g2_rec_turismo/en_4912/4912-ficha.html. For more information about the bounty of amazing natural sites in the Basque region explore the Web site: www.bizkaianatural.net/eng/home.html.

Natural parks and nature reserves abound in the Basque Country including the Valderejo, Izki, Entzia, Aralar, Aizkorri, Gorbeia, Urkiola (beech forest), Aiako Harria, Pagoeta, and Armañón. The Urdaibai Biosphere Reserve in the Guernica-Mundaka estuary is a UNESCO biosphere—see "UNESCO World Heritage Sites." Protected biotopes are the Lakes of Laguardia, San Juan de Gaztelugatxe, Itxina, Leitzaran, Iñurritza, and the Tidal Platform. For information about any of these parks click on "Nature," then on "Natural Areas," at the Basque Tourism Web site: www.turismoa.euskadi.net/s11-18805/en/.

Northeast of Pamplona in the Pyrenees is the Forest (*Bosque*) of Irati, the largest primeval beech and yew forest in Spain, full of wildlife and rare birds, covering forty-two thousand acres. In the area, southeast of the forest, look for the village of Orbaitzeta, where close by you can find the dolmen Azpegi I, encircled by 123 standing stones. Forest of Irati; Web site: www.irati.org. Southwest of Pamplona is the Arbayún Gorge (Foz), a 3.5-mile-long (5.6-km-long) canyon with sheer, vertical limestone walls, some as high as nine hundred feet, rising from the Salazar River.

Due south of Pamplona, wedged between the regions of La Rioja and Aragón, lies the Bardenas Reales, a wild, desert-like place, likened to the southwestern United States, shaped by erosion with rocks atop pyramid-shaped earth and other unusual forms. The Bardenas Reales covers more than one hundred thousand acres in southeastern Navarra with the long-distance GR13 walking path passing through a portion of it. The Bardenas Reales Web site is www.bardenasreales.es.

The Doñana Nature Reserve and National Park (Parque Nacional de Doñana) in Andalucía, 50 km southwest of Sevilla, is Europe's largest sanctuary for migrating birds, covering almost 134,000 acres. The park contains wetlands, beach, sand dunes, as well as some scrub and woodlands. Needless to say, there are countless hiking and touring possibilities. The UNESCO Web site for Doñana is http://whc.unesco.org/en/list/685.

In Asturias near Cangas del Narcea, about 99 km from Oviedo, the capital of Asturias, you can find the Muniellos Nature Reserve, more than 113,000 acres encompassing the largest oak forest in Spain. Visitors are limited to twenty people a day and you must call the Regional Natural Resources Authority to schedule a visit at 985 105 545. In the same vicinity, about 85 km from Oviedo, in Pola de Somiedo there is the Somiedo Nature Reserve with woodland and lakes. Somiedo Park Reception Center, Tel: 985 763 758.

There are twenty-nine botanical gardens in Spain including in all the major cities: Jardí Botànic, C/ Doctor Font i Quer, 2, Parc de Montjuïc, Barcelona; Tel: 934 264 935; Web site: www.jardibotanic.bcn.es/index_eng.htm. Real Jardín Botánico (Royal Botanic Gardens of Madrid), Plaza de Murillo, 2, 28014 Madrid (opposite Museo del Prado); Tel: 914 203 017; Web site: www.rjb.csic.es/infov_eng.php.

Wildlife enthusiasts will find a wealth of information at Iberia Nature: a guide to the environment, climate, wildlife, geography, and nature of Spain at: www.iberianature.com, where birds, trees, flora, and wildlife information can be found—English/Spanish glossaries, nature, geography, and much more. Excellent guidebooks on natural sites in Spain are *Spain: Travellers' Nature Guide,* by Teresa Farino, Mike Lockwood, and Martin Walters; and *Wild Spain: The Animals, Plants and Lanscapes,* by Teresa Farino.

Volunteer Tourism

If you want to work as a volunteer there are two organizations that have ongoing projects in Spain. You can search the following Web sites for current selections and find more information in the "Europe-Wide Information and Resources" section in the beginning of the book.

For opportunities to volunteer on organic farms, explore the World Wide Opportunities on Organic Farms (WWOOF), an international association with many participating farms in Spain. Farm choices can vary between large and small operations, and from vineyards to vegetables to goats. The Spain WWOOF is at WWOOF España—www.wwoof.es.

In Spain there is a very special opportunity to spend seven nights with all meals included for free in exchange for your willingness to speak in English-only with Spanish-speaking people. The program, Pueblo Inglés (full information at: www.morethanenglish.com/anglos/index.asp), has four sites in Spain and one in Italy. You can get to know a great deal about the culture and the area you are staying in with free accommodations and meals in exchange for your English language skills. During the seven days there are group and one-on-one speaking sessions, meals, and a little free time. You must pay for and make your own travel arrangements to Madrid, where a bus will bring you to your designated site: Valdelavilla, La Alberca, Cazorla, or Pals. Valdelavilla is in Soria north of Madrid. The old village has been restored as a mini campus, with twelve stone houses and cobblestone streets. Accommodations are simple but comfortable and sessions run from April to October. La Alberca, west of Madrid in the province of Salamanca, has a "campus" of twenty-five chalets. Sessions at the La Alberca site run from mid-January until the end of November. Cazorla is in the Jaén region, south of Madrid in the heart of olive oil production. Thirty-two villas constitute this "campus." This site has limited dates. The Pals site, in the northeastern corner of Spain, is the newest location with very limited dates as this takes place in a hotel resort. You must apply for any of the programs.

I met the most wonderful people, made lifelong friends, and had a week full of laughter when I volunteered at the Pueblo Inglés program.

four resources

Language Resources

The BBC Languages Web site offers free courses in Spanish, French, Italian, German, and other languages. For more information, go to www.bbc.co.uk/languages. The Deutsche Welle Radio Web site at www.dw-world.de offers free German language courses.

There are also a number of free language podcast series available for download, including Spanish, French, German, and Italian.

Listed below are important phrases and words for traveling naturally, not usually found in conventional phrase books. Pronunciation tips follow some words in parentheses.

ENGLISH	CATALAN	BASQUE	SPANISH
herbs	herbes		hierbas
herbalist	herbolari		herboristería/ herbolario
homeopathic	omeopatic		homeopático
naturopathic doctor			médico naturista
massage therapy	massatge		masaje
acupuncture	acupuntura		acupuntura
traditional Chinese medicine			medicina tradicional China
drugstore/pharmacy	farmàcia	farmazia	farmacia
thrift store/ secondhand	segona mà		2a mano/ segunda mano

ENGLISH	CATALAN	BASQUE	SPANISH
organic	biològic	ekologikoaren	biológico/ ecológico
street	carrer/passeig	kalea	calle
train track	via/vies		vía/vías

The Jewels: Please, Thank You, Excuse Me

ENGLISH	CATALAN	GALEGO/ GALICIAN	BASQUE	SPANISH
Hello/Hi	Hola	Ola	Kaixo (kaisho)	Hola
Good morning	Bon dia	Bom día	Egun on (egoo non)	Buenos días
Goodbye	Adéu (a the oo)	Adeus or Até logo (a de oos)	Agur (agoor)	Adiós
Please	Si us plau (sees pla oo)	Por favor	Mesedez (s)	Por favor
Thank you	Gràcies	Graciñas/ Grazas	Eskerrik asko (eske reek kasko)	(Muchas) Gracias
Excuse me	Perdona	Perdoe	Barkatu	Perdóneme/ Discúlpe
You are welcome	De res	De nada	Ez horregatik (es ore ga teek)	De nada

More Information about Traveling Naturally

We welcome your comments, suggestions, and insights.

Please visit the Traveling Naturally Web site at www.travelingnaturally.com and the Traveling Naturally blog at http://travelingnaturally.blogspot.com for Traveling Naturally updates as well as news about other Green Earth Guides including to France, Switzerland, Britain, and other countries.

index

Bold page numbers indicate maps.

A

accommodations, xvii–xviii, xix, 14–17, 37
  bed-and-breakfasts, 16, 38, 40, 43, 45, 47
  camping, 14–15, 16, 38
  eco-, 15, 37, 42–47
  farm stays, 16
  guesthouses, 38–41
  home exchange, 15
  homestays, 17
  hostels, 14, 37–38
  hotels, 37, 38–42
  house-sitting, 15–16
  Paradores, 38
  pensiónes, 37
  rentals, 16, 42
  sublets, 16
acupuncture, 117–20
addresses, 24
air travel
  airports, 28–29
  environmental impact of, 2, 3
Alaminos, Río, 178
Alcazaba de Málaga, 179
Alexander Technique, 112–13
Alhama de Aragón, 100
Alhambra, 150, 181–82
Alpujarras, 197
Altamira caves, 149–50
A Moa, 177, 189
anchovies, 70
Ancient Instruments of Torture, 149
Andalucía
  biking, 93–**94**
  health food stores, 59–63
  highlights, 178–86
  markets, 66
  restaurants, 83–85
  thermal baths, 100–102
anthroposophical medicine, 107–8
Antiguos Instrumentos de Tortura, 149
Aragón route, 188
Ara Solis, 190
Arenys de Mar, 103
art, 193–94
As Burgas fountains, 178
Asturias
  festivals, 27
  highlights, 174–75
  markets, 68
ATMs, 9
AVE trains, 29, 32
Ávila, 148
Ayurvedic medicine, 115–17

B

backpacks, 10
Baeza, 186
Bakio, 169
Baños del Alcázar Califal, 183
Barcelona
  acupuncture, 119–20
  airport, 29
  bicycling, 34–35
  festivals, 26
  health food stores, 50–51
  herbs and remedies, 122–23
  highlights, 153–56

Barcelona, *continued*
  local specialties, 68
  markets, 63–64, 134–35
  massage, 109–10
  rail travel, 31–32
  restaurants, 75–78
  thermal baths, 103–4
  traditional Chinese medicine,
    119–20
  yoga, 95–96
Bardenas Reales, 199
Basque Country
  beaches, 198
  dolmens, 190–91
  health food stores, 58–59
  highlights, 163–70
  hiking, 90
  language, 27, 165, 201–2
  markets, 66–67
  parks, 198
  spas, 126
baths, thermal, 99–106. *See also* spas
beaches, 158, 161, 165, 169, 171, 174,
    177–78, 194–96, 198
bed-and-breakfasts, 16, 38, 40, 43, 45,
    47
beer, 143–45
Begur, 159
Benahavis, 180
Bermeo, 168
Besalú, 130, 159
Bicing, 34–35
biking, 34–36, **91,** 91–94, **94,** 157
Bilbao
  health food stores, 58
  highlights, 163–65
  markets, 66–67
  restaurants, 85
  transportation, 166
BioCultura, 26, 27, 138
biodynamic farming, 142–43
biosphere reserves, 194, 195, 197,
    198
birds, 150, 197, 198, 199
Biscay, Bay of, 175, 198
Black Madonnas, 192–93
Blasco Ibáñez, Vicente, 24
books, 135–37
botanical gardens, 199
brandy, 143
breweries, 143–45
Buddhism, 98–99
Buño, 128–29
buses, 13, 29, 33–34
Buxu cave, 151

C
Cabañeros National Park, 197
Cabezón de la Sal, 173
Cabo de Gata Natural Park, 195
Cabrales Exhibition Cave, 174
Cáceres, 148
Cadaqués, 158, 196
Cahorros, 180
Caldes de Montbui, 104
Caldes d'Estrac, 103–4
Call Association of Barcelona, 156
calling cards, 13–14, 28
Cambil, 186
camping, 14–15, 16, 38
Cangas el Narcea, 175
canoeing, 27
Cantabria, 171–73
Cap de Creus Nature Reserve, 158, 196
Capricho de Gaudí, 172–73
Carbonfund.org, 3
carbon-offset programs, 3–4
Carcabuey, 184
Carnaval, 26
car rentals, 11–12, 28
Casa Batlló, 153
casa colgantes, 148
Casa de Biot, 161
Casa de la Memoria Cultural Center,
    185
Casa de Sefarad/Casa de la Memoria,
    183–84
Casa Natal de Goya, 193–94
Casa Natal Picasso, 179
Castell de Montjuïc, 155
Castilla–La Mancha, 105–6, 197
Castilla y León, 106, 171
Castle Gibralfaro, 178
Castro de Borneiro, 190
Castropol, 178
Catalunya
  dolmens, 191
  highlights, 152
  local specialties, 68, 70
  markets, 64–66, 135
  parks and reserves, 195–96
  thermal baths, 102–3
Cathedral of Toledo, 193
cava, 70–71, 142
caves, 149–50, 151, 169, 171, 180,
    186, 192
Cazorla, 200
Cee, 177
cell phones, 28
ceramics, 128–29
Cervantes, Miguel, 24, 136–37, 150

cheese, 27, 68, 174
cherries, 26
Chi, 117
Chillar, Río, 180
Chinese medicine, traditional, 117–20
chiropractors, 112
chocolate, 73–74, 155–56
cider, 27, 171, 174
cities, largest, 22. *See also individual cities*
Ciudad Encantada, 148
Ciutat Ibèrica d'Ullastret, 159
Climate Counts, 5
clinics, 8, 123–26
clothing, 11, 127–28
C-N-Do Scotland, 3
colon hydrotherapy, 120
Comillas, 172–73
Conservation International, 4
Consuegra, 27, 138, 150
Corcubión, 177
Córdoba
  bicycling, 36
  health food stores, 60–61
  highlights, 182–84
  markets, 66, 135
  restaurants, 84
  thermal baths, 101
  World Heritage Site, 148
cosmetics, 130–31
Costa Brava
  biking, 93
  health food stores, 55–57
  highlights, 156–59
  hiking, 90
  spas, 124
cotton, 127–28
CouchSurfing, 16
credit cards, 9, 25
Cuban products, 132–33
Cudillero, 175
Cuenca, 148
Cueva de Ekain, 151
Cultura Natura, 25

D
dairy allergies, 88–89
debit cards, 9
Denia, 161
dentistry, biological, 120–22
dolmens, 190–92, **191**
Doñana National Park, 150, 199
Donostia (San Sebastián), 58–59, 169–70
Don Quixote, 136–37, 150

dry-cleaning, 11
Durango, 168

E
EarthFuture, 4
eating and food
  fair trade, 48
  health food stores, 48–63
  local specialties, 68–74
  markets, 63–68
  organic food, xviii, 48, 49, 138–40
  restaurants, 74–86
  Slow Food movement, 17, 47, 48
  special diets, 86–89
  supermarkets, 48–49, 50
  vegetarians, 16, 17, 48
Ebro River, 197
ECEAT (European Centre for Ecological and Agricultural Tourism), 16, 45
eco-accommodations, 15, 37, 42–47
ecobusinesses and destinations, 138–47
Eco-Sí Fair, 27
Eira das Meigas, 190
Elantxobe, 169
El Camino de Santiago, **187,** 187–89
El Castillo, 171
Elche, 126, 161
El Corte Inglés, 48–49
El Transcantábrico train, 173
Empúries, 158
Environmental Education Museum of San Pedro, 170
environmental footprint, 1–3
Ermita de San Antonio de la Florida, 193
escarola, 68
Esquivias, 150
Estella, 193
Eurail passes, 13
EuroVelo routes, **94**
Euskadi. *See* Basque Country
EuskoTren, 31, 33
Experiment in International Living, 17
Expo EcoSalud, 26

F
Facho, Monte, 190
fair trade, 48, 131–33
farms, organic, 16, 138–40
Federation EIL, 17
Ferrol, 178
festivals, 26–27
FEVE, 31, 33, 172–73
FGC, 31

FGV, 31
Fira de les Herbes, 26
Fisterra, 67, 177, 189, 190
Fitero, 106
Flamenco Dance Museum, 185
flea markets, 134–35
food. *See* eating and food
Fox Fibre products, 127–28
Franco, Francisco, 22, 154, 164
FreeCycle, 18
French Road, 188–89
Fundació Joan Miró, 194
Fútbol Club Barcelona, 154, 155

G
Galicia
    dolmens, 190
    festivals, 26
    health food stores, 59
    highlights, 176–78
    local specialties, 70, 176
    markets, 67
    spas, 125
    thermal baths, 106
García Lorca, Federico, 24
Gaudí, Antoni, 24, 153, 172–73
Genal, Río, 179
Gernika (Guernica), 67, 164, 165–68
Gernikako Arbola Song, 167, 168
Getaria, 169
Getxo, 165
Gijón, 174
Girona
    airport, 29
    health food stores, 54–55
    highlights, 156–59
    markets, 64–66, 135, 157
    restaurants, 78
Gleditsch, Jochen, 120
global warming, 1, 4–5
gluten-free foods, 9, 86–88
Goya, Francisco, 24, 193–94
Granada
    health food stores, 59–60
    highlights, 180–82
    massage, 111
    parks, 197–98
    restaurants, 83–84
    shopping, 129
    thermal baths, 100–101
Gran Recorrido (GR) trails, 89, **92**
Green Coast, 171–75
Greenpeace, 25, 147
Greenways, 90, **91,** 92–93
Guadaiza, Río, 178
Guadalmansa, Río, 179

Guadalmina, Río, 178, 179
Guernica (Gernika), 67, 164, 165–68
Guernica Peace Museum, 166–67
guesthouses, 38–41
Guggenheim Museum, 164

H
Hahnemann, Samuel, 114
hand sanitizers, 10
Hauschka, Rudolf, 108
health, xviii–xix, 8, 106–7
    acupuncture, 117–20
    Alexander Technique, 112–13
    anthroposophical medicine,
        107–8
    Ayurvedic medicine, 115–17
    chiropractic, 112
    clinics and spas, 8, 123–26
    colon hydrotherapy, 120
    dentistry, 120–22
    herbs and remedies, 122–23
    homeopathy, 8, 114–15
    massage, 109–12
    naturopathy, 113–14
    traditional Chinese medicine (TCM),
        117–20
    travel kit, 8
health food stores, 48–63
herbolarios, 49
herbs, 26, 122–23
hiking, 89–91, **91, 92,** 187–89
historical sites, 150–51
history, 22, 24, 164
holidays, 24
Holy Week, 26
home exchange, 15
homeopathy, 8, 114–15
homestays, 17
hórreos, 176
hostels, 14, 37–38
hotels, 37, 38–42
house-sitting, 15–16

I
Iberia Nature, 199
Intergovernmental Panel on Climate
    Change, 5
Iparraguirre, José María, 168
Irati, Forest of, 198
Irving, Washington, 182
Issels, Josef, 120–21
Istán, 180

J
Jaén province, 186
jaywalking, 36

K

knives, 163

L

La Alberca, 175–76, 192, 200
La Bisbal d'Empordà, 128, 158
La Fuente, 178
La Garriga, 104
La Moneda, 171
languages, 27, 201–2. *See also* Spanish
    language
La Pedrera, 153
La Peña de Candamo cave, 151
La Peña de Francia, 176, 192
La Sagrada Família, 153
Las Fallas de Valencia, 26
laundry, 11
Laxe, 177
leather goods, 129, 130
left luggage, 34
Lekeitio, 169
L'Escala, 70
Les Illes Medes, 196
L'Estartit, 158, 195–96
Lick Global Warming campaign, 5
Liérganes, 171
liquor, 143
Llança, 93
Llanes, 174
local products, 68–74, 128–30
Lugo, 178

M

Madrid
    acupuncture, 118–19
    airport, 28–29
    bicycling, 35
    health food stores, 51–52
    herbs and remedies, 123
    highlights, 162–63
    markets, 134
    massage, 110–11
    meditation, 99
    Metro, 34
    museums, 162
    parks, 162–63
    rail travel, 31–32
    restaurants, 80–83
    thermal baths, 104–5
    traditional Chinese medicine,
        118–19
    yoga, 96–97
Magic Fountain, 154–55
Maimonides, 107
Málaga
    airport, 29

biking, 93–**94**
    health food stores, 62–63
    highlights, 178–80
    markets, 66
    organic food, 140
    parks, 179, 197
    restaurants, 83
    thermal baths, 102
maps, 25
markets, 63–68, 133–35
Maro, 180
massage, 109–12
meditation, 98–99
megaliths, 20, 190–92, **191**
menhirs, 190, 191
mercury mining, 151
Metro, 34
mezquita-cathedral, 183
mind-set, 7–8
mineral springs, 145
Miño, Río, 178
Miravet Castle, 159
Miró, Joan, 24, 194
money, 9, 25
Montgó Nature Reserve, 161
Montjuïc gardens, 154–55
Montserrat, 192
Morillón, 143
mountain ranges, 194, 197
Mulhacén, 197
Mundaka, 168
Muniellos Nature Reserve, 199
museums
    Altimira, 149–50
    Baños del Alcázar Califal, 183
    Casa de Sefarad/Casa de la Memoria,
        183–84
    Casa Natal de Goya, 193–94
    Casa Natal Picasso, 179
    Environmental Education (San
        Pedro), 170
    Flamenco Dance, 185
    Fundació Joan Miró, 194
    Grabado de Goya, 194
    Guernica Peace, 166–67
    Guggenheim, 164
    History of the Jews, 156–57
    Lázaro Galdiano, 193
    Picasso (Barcelona), 193
    Picasso Málaga, 179
    Prado, 162
    Reina Sofía, 162
    Thyssen-Bornemisza, 162
    Tower of la Calahorra, 183
    Xocolata (Chocolate), 155–56
mushrooms, 70, 171

Mutriku, 169
Muxía, 177

N
national parks, **195**
 Cabañeros, 197
 Doñana, 150, 199
 Picos de Europa, 175
 Sierra Nevada, 197
 Tablas de Daimiel, 197
*Native*Energy, 4
natural parks, 195–99
Natural Resources Defense Council
 (NRDC), 4
naturopathy, 113–14
Navarra
 dolmens, 192
 highlights, 170
 markets, 67
 thermal baths, 106
Navia, 174–75
Neme, Monte, 190
Nerja, 180
newspapers, 24
nudist beaches, 174, 194–95
number machines, 25
Nunca Máis, 177

O
Obanos, 188
olive oil, 71–73, 130, 186
Olot, 159
Ondarroa, 169
Onyar River, 157
O Pindo, 177, 189
Ordizia, 67
Orense, 178
Organic Consumers Association
 (OCA), 49
organic food, xviii, 48, 49, 138–40
Orwell, George, 21, 136
Oviedo, 68, 134, 174

P
packing, 9–10
paint, 128
Paiosaco, 26
País Vasco. *See* Basque Country
Pals, 158, 200
Pamplona, 67, 134, 170
paprika, 70
Paradores, 38
Parc Agrari, 140
Parc Agroecològic de l'Empordà,
 139–40
Parc Güell, 153

Parc Natural de la Albufera, 161
Parc Natural de l'Albera, 196
Parc Natural del Cap de Creus, 158,
 196
Parc Natural dels Aiguamolls de
 l'Empordà, 196
Parque Natural Urkiola, 169
passports, 25
pata negra, 68, 175
Peaceful World Travel, 18–19
peak travel times, 25
pedestrians, 36
Pedralta rocking stone, 191
Peñíscola, 161
pensiónes, 37
Pequeño Recorrido (PR) trails, 89
Peratallada, 158
perchloroethylene, 11
personal care products, 130–31
phones, 13–14, 27–28
Picasso, Pablo, 24, 162, 164, 165, 179,
 193
Picos de Europa National Park, 175
Pilgrim's Way, **187,** 187–89
pimentón peppers, 70
Pindo, Monte, 189
Plentzia, 165
politics, 22
pottery, 128–29
Prado Museum, 162
preparations, 8–11
Price, Weston, 120
Pueblo Inglés, 200
Puente la Reina, 188
Puente Viesgo, 171

Q
Qi, 117

R
rail travel, 12–13, 29–33, 172–73
Rau, Thomas, 121
Razo, 177
recreation
 biking, 34–36, **91,** 91–94, **94,** 157
 hiking, 89–91, **91, 92,** 187–89
 meditation, 98–99
 thermal baths, 99–106
 yoga, 95–98
regions, 22–23, **23**. *See also individual regions*
Reina Sofía Museum, 162
RENFE (Red Nacional de los
 Ferrocarriles Españoles), 29–31
rentals, 16, 42
restaurants, 74–86

Revista Integral, 25
Ribadeo, 175
Ribadesella, 174
Ronda, 179

S

Sacred Riverbank, 178
sacred sites, 20, 186–93
saffron, 70, 138
Salamanca, 148, 175–76
salt, 173
San Sebastián (Donostia), 58–59, 169–70
Santander, 171
Santa Pola Nature Reserve, 197
Santiago de Compostela
  bicycling, 36
  markets, 67
  routes, **187,** 187–89
  World Heritage Site, 148
Santillana del Mar, 172
Santimamiñe caves, 150, 169
San Vicente de la Barquera, 171
sausage, 70
scooters, 36
secallona, 70
secondhand stores, 133
Segovia, 148, 149
Semana Santa, 26
Senderos Locales (SL) trails, 89
Servas, 17
Sevici, 35, 185
Sevilla
  bicycling, 35
  health food stores, 61–62
  highlights, 184–86
  markets, 134
  massage, 111
  meditation, 99
  restaurants, 84–85
  thermal baths, 101–2
  yoga, 98
shoes, 126–27, 129, 130
shopping, xix–xx, 17–18, 126–37
  books, 135–37
  carts, 50
  ceramics, 128–29
  cosmetics, 130–31
  cotton products, 127–28
  fair trade, 48, 131–33
  leather goods, 129, 130
  local products, 68–74, 128–30
  markets, 63–68, 133–35
  paint, 128
  personal care products, 130–31
  sales, 127

shoes, 126–27, 129, 130
  souvenirs, 129, 130
  thrift, 133
  words and phrases, 69
sidra, 171
Sierra Nevada National Park, 197
Sigmund, Elisabeth, 108
Sil, Río, 178
Skype, 14
Slow Food movement, 17, 47, 48
smoking, 75
soap, 131
soccer, 154, 155
solar energy, 10, 145, 146–47, **147**
Somiedo Nature Reserve, 199
souvenirs, 129, 130
Spanish Civil War, 164
Spanish language
  pronunciation, xiv
  Web site navigation, xiv
  words and phrases, xiii, 69, 86, 89, 201–2
spas, 8, 123–26
Steiner, Rudolf, 107–8, 142, 153
stone structures, ancient, 189
Stop Global Warming Virtual March, 4
sublets, 16
Suñol, Josep, 154
supermarkets, 48–49, 50
surfing, 178
Sustainable Travel International, 3–4
swords, 163
synagogues, 149, 156, 183–84

T

Tablas de Daimiel National Park, 197
Tarragona, 159
telephones, 13–14, 27–28
Terra Foundation, 23
thrift stores, 133
Thyssen-Bornemisza Museum, 162
time, 19, 21
Tito Bustillo Cave, 151
toilet paper, 25
Toledo, 148–49, 163
Tona, 104
Tour de France, 93, 156, 157
tourist offices, 25
Tower of la Calahorra, 183
trains. *See* rail travel
transportation
  air travel, 28–29
  bike rentals, 34–36
  buses, 13, 29, 33–34
  car rentals, 11–12, 28
  distances, 11

transportation, *continued*
  Metro, 34
  rail travel, 12–13, 29–33, 172–73
  walking, 12
traveling naturally
  essence of, 7
  mind-set of, 7–8
  packing for, 9–10
  resources for, 202
truffles, 68–70
Turia River, 160

U
Úbeda, 186
Ujué, 193
Ullastret, 159
UNESCO World Heritage Sites, 20, 147–50, **148**
Urdaibai Reserve, 150, 168–69, 198
Urkiola forest, 169

V
Valdelavilla, 200
Valencia
  acupuncture, 118
  airport, 29
  bicycling, 35
  eco-guides to, 53–54, 160
  health food stores, 53
  highlights, 159–62
  Las Fallas de Valencia, 26
  markets, 67–68, 135, 160
  massage, 111–12
  meditation, 99
  restaurants, 78–79
  thermal baths, 105
  traditional Chinese medicine, 118
  yoga, 96
vegetarians, 16, 17, 48
Verde, Río, 179
Vía de la Plata, 188, 189

Vias Verdes, 90, **91,** 92–93
Vic, 159
vineyards, 140–43, 176
Vipassana meditation, 98
Vitoria, 67, 134, 169
Vitoria, Francisco de, 169
VoIP (Voice over Internet Protocol), 14
Volunteers for International
  Partnership, 19
Volunteers for Peace (VFP), 18
volunteer tourism, xx, 18–20, 200

W
walking, 12. *See also* hiking
water
  bottled, 145
  contaminants, xviii
Way of St. James, **187,** 187–89
Web sites, xiii–xiv, 23. *See also individual organizations and activities*
Wegman, Ita, 108
wifi spots, 14
wildlife, 199
wind energy, 145–46, **146,** 150
wine, 70–71, 140–43, 176
wool, 138
World Heritage Sites, 20, 147–50, **148**
World War II, 22
WWOOF (World Wide Opportunities on Organic Farms), 19, 200

X
Xallas falls, 177, 189

Y
yoga, 95–98

Z
Zarautz, 169
Zumaia, 169

about the author

Dorian Yates has worked for consumer advocacy organizations as an environmental activist and congressional lobbyist; as an advisor on environmental, health, and social justice issues; and as a consultant on nontoxic products, indoor air quality, and  organic farming issues. A researcher and consultant for the books *The Green Pages* and *Ecopreneuring,* she lives in Vermont, United States.